HIS SERENITY THE TASHI LAMA

༄༅། །ས་སྟེང་ཤུ་རྒྱལ་བསྟན་ཡོངས་ཀྱི་བདག་པོ་པཎ་ཆེན་ཨེར་ཏེ་ནིའི་
འདྲ་པར།།

GIVEN TO THE AUTHOR BY THE TASHI LAMA (HIS SEAL IS ATTACHED), FOR A FRONTISPIECE FOR THIS BOOK. THE INSCRIPTION MEANS : "PORTRAIT OF PANCHHEN ERTENE, *i.e.* THE POSSESSOR OF BUDDHA'S RELIGION IN THIS WORLD."

TWENTY YEARS
IN TIBET

Intimate & Personal Experiences of the
Closed Land among all Classes of its
People from the Highest to the Lowest

TWENTY YEARS IN TIBET

Intimate & Personal Experiences of the Closed Land among all Classes of its People from the Highest to the Lowest

David Macdonald
Author of "The Land of the Lama"

With a Foreword by
The Earl of Lytton
G.C.S.I., G.C.I.E.
Sometime
Viceroy of India

PILGRIMS PUBLISHING
◆ Varanasi ◆

TWENTY YEARS IN TIBET
David Macdonald

Published by:
PILGRIMS PUBLISHING

An imprint of:
PILGRIMS BOOK HOUSE
(Distributors in India)
B 27/98 A-8, Nawabganj Road
Durga Kund, Varanasi-221010, India
Tel: 91-542-2314060, 2312456
E-mail: pilgrims@satyam.net.in
Website: www.pilgrimsbooks.com

PILGRIMS BOOK HOUSE (New Delhi)
9 Netaji Subhash Marg, 2nd Floor
Near Neeru Hotel, Daryaganj
New Delhi 110002
Tel: 91-11-23285081 Fax: 91-11-23285722
E-mail: pilgrim@del2.vsnl.net.in

Distributed in Nepal by:
PILGRIMS BOOK HOUSE
P O Box 3872, Thamel,
Kathmandu, Nepal
Tel: 977-1-4700942
Off: 977-1-4700919
Fax: 977-1-4700943
E-mail: pilgrims@wlink.com.np

Cover design by Asha Mishra

ISBN: 81-7769-293-3

Printed in India at Pilgrim Press Pvt. Ltd. Lalpur Varanasi

PREFACE TO THE NEW EDITION

In the first part of the twentieth century far away in Tibet, a lofty land north of the Himalayas, a power struggle continued for dominance of this hidden Shangri-la. But this place was no paradise. It was a harsh land with medieval traditions, where most lived a hard life of toil in rugged conditions. It was not a land though, without compassion, humour, tolerance and people of lively dispositions.

The 13th Dalai Lama was one of the few of the great lamas to live out a full life, and during his tenure some wise and far-reaching improvements occurred. For a time the Chinese imperial designs were thwarted and Tibet remained free of their interference. Relations with the British in India were markedly cordial and this continued for some years after the demise of the Dalai Lama. Throughout most of this time, relations were keenly improved by the charmingly disposed Trade Agent based in both Yatung and Gyangtse. He was David Macdonald, a unique person. His thorough knowledge of Tibet and its language enabled him to interact with all the great players in Tibet of the time.

The Chinese are in retreat, convulsed by political turmoil in the east. Tibet is left to embrace a period of calm, of quiet contemplation and prayer. The great Lamaseries are free, unmolested by outside pressures. But there is still intrigue; the ministers of the Dalai Lama and Panchen Lama vie for power, disturbing the tranquillity, causing minor ripples below the surface. These seemingly minor differences have a long and lasting impact. The Panchen Lama feels insecure and leaves Tibet for China, and in so doing possibly inadvertently sows the seeds of future turmoil on a grand scale.

The story is fascinating, for it delves into many topics. We flow along the great river of Tibetan history, mix with the key figures and follow the yearly life cycles of a culture little understood outside its barren mountainous lands. The traditions of this unique country breathe through the pages, illuminating our interest and enthralling us with fascinating stories.

Bob Gibbons
Siân Pritchard-Jones
Kathmandu, 2004

FOREWORD

by

The Right Hon. The EARL OF LYTTON,

G.C.S.I., G.C.I.E.

MR MACDONALD'S intimate knowledge of the Tibetan language and of Tibetan ways and customs enabled him to render valuable service to the Government of India in that part of the world, and his personal reminiscences of that little-known land will be read with interest both by the few who have been there and by many who will never have that privilege.

The period covered by Mr Macdonald's story was one of unusual activity and special interest on the North-East Frontier of India. It includes Colonel Younghusband's mission to Lhasa in 1904, the flight of the Dalai Lama in 1910, his return to Lhasa in 1912, and many other incidents of lesser importance.

All these historical events are told with great simplicity in this volume, and acquire an added interest from the personal part which the author played in them.

In Mr Macdonald's reference to my own visit to

Tibet, when he accompanied me to Pharijong in 1923 and acted as my guide and interpreter, he scarcely does justice to an incident of rather special interest.

We arrived at Phari one evening in early November, and as we rode towards the little town after sunset I noticed with envy the tempting slopes of the hills which showed up in the moonlight to our left. It was a clear night without a cloud in the sky, and the stars shone brightly through the frosty air. If only these rolling hills were covered with snow, I thought, what lovely ski-ing slopes they would make! Four miles beyond the town, and somewhat to the right, rose the incomparable snow peak of Chomolhari to a height of 22,000 feet—the loveliest mountain I have ever seen.

We had planned to spend the next day at Phari, and as I had brought a pair of skis with me I decided to explore the lower slopes of this lovely mountain. I asked Mr Macdonald to find me a guide from the bazaar who would show me the shortest way to the foot of the mountain. He himself had expressed considerable misgivings when I first announced this intention, and these were increased when he returned from talking with the bazaar folk. Evidently my proposal was regarded as a desecration of sacred precincts. " If the Lord Sahib goes on the mountain," they said, " the goddess will veil her face." I am afraid I received these protests very irreverently. " I am used to goddesses who veil their faces," I said; "in Darjeeling my goddess veils her face every day. I have no objection to ski-ing behind the veil. Get me a guide, and we will start at 8 A.M. to-morrow." During the night an extraordinary thing happened—the only thing which could possibly have prevented me from carrying out my plan. It had snowed, but only in one direction. When I woke and looked out of my window, sure enough the goddess had disappeared behind her veil. There was no sign of the great mountain, and the low intervening hills in that direction were as I had seen them the night before —quite bare. But in the opposite direction the Khambu slopes which I had admired the previous evening were now covered with what appeared to be a sufficient coating of fresh-fallen snow, and all the intervening plain up to Pharijong itself was covered with snow. Accordingly, at breakfast, I announced that I would not trouble the goddess, but would take my skis to the Khambu slopes, which were about seven miles off. As we rode across the intervening plain the sun came out and the snow began to melt. When we reached the foot of the hills we found that the fresh snow was much less than had appeared from a distance and was melting rapidly. Though we climbed to the crest in search of some sheltered slope, ski-ing was impossible. As I looked back towards Chomolhari—now nearly twelve miles away and quite out of reach—the veil began to descend; and when we got back to Phari in the afternoon the goddess was once more smiling in a cloudless sky, and all trace of the night's snowfall had disappeared. Who will dispute that Tibet is a land of mystery!

LYTTON.

PREFACE

MY father was a Scot, my mother of a Sikkimese family of good standing. The Sikkimese are closely allied to the Tibetans, and thus the circumstances of my birth have given me a peculiar sympathy, affection and understanding for the Tibetan people and their country. Many years spent among them enables me to present an intimate picture of my life there.

An outline of my early life and training is necessary to show how I became fitted to handle the varied responsibilities entrusted to me by the Government of India. Reading this outline offers an interesting contrast to the usual schooling and early training of those fortunate enough to take some part in the shaping of our Empire and the carrying out of its policy.

In a thatch-roofed building, perched on a steep Darjeeling hillside, facing the ever-glorious wonder of the Himalayan snow-peaks—and in company with other urchins—I received my first introduction to the arts of reading and writing in the language and script, and later in the tenets, of Sikkimese, and in the form of Buddhism, known as Lamaism, which is practised in the Eastern Himalayas. Not till I was nine years old did I receive any tuition in English. My first teacher was a Lepcha pundit, and from him I learned the rudiments of Lepcha, Sikkimese, Nepali and Hindi. After three years of schooling I entered what is now the Darjeeling High School, and remained there until I was nineteen, studying English and Tibetan.

When I was this age an opportunity presented itself of my going either to Calcutta or to England, for further studies, but intense affection for my native hills, and the offer of immediate remunerative employment in Darjeeling, kept me in India. Nevertheless, I was deeply grateful to the then Deputy Commissioner of Darjeeling, and to the late General Mainwaring, the compiler of the first *Lepcha Grammar* and *Dictionary*, for their interest in me, for they were the moving spirits in the proposal to send me to England.

To the friendship and interest of Colonel L. A. Waddell, C.B., C.I.E., I.M.S., I am indebted for the recognition of my proficiency in the Tibetan language. For some years I assisted this officer in the preparation of his works on the then little known religion of Tibet and Sikkim, Lamaism, and in some portions of his contributions to the *Sikkim Gazetteer* and the *Linguistic Survey of India*. That these works are still standard books of reference in their own subjects is a just tribute to the care and time he devoted to their compilation.

On the advice of Colonel Waddell, who established the first Animal Vaccine Depot for Bengal, at Darjeeling, I joined the Vaccination Department under the Government of Bengal. When not on tour in the Darjeeling District I passed most of my time at the Depot Headquarters at Ghoom, a village four miles from Darjeeling. My duties entailed my making regular tours of the villages in the Darjeeling District, and the twelve years I spent in this work gave me a comprehensive insight into the manners and customs, and everyday lives, of the peasantry of this part of the Himalayas. In 1904 Colonel Waddell took me as his assistant in collecting for the Government of India the largest and most complete collection of Tibetan sacred and lay books ever brought to India or Europe. This was during the Younghusband Mission to Lhasa. These books now enrich the collections of the British and Indian museum libraries.

It was on account of my work in this connection that

I was selected for the appointment of British Trade Agent in Tibet in 1905, a post which I continued to hold until my retirement in 1925.

I continued my study of the languages of the north-eastern Indian frontier, until by 1903 I was a master of Tibetan, Bengali, Bhutanese, Sikkimese, Lepcha, Hindi and Nepali. Naturally sympathetic toward the Christian missionary movement in the hills in which I was born, and profoundly impressed by the good work the missionaries were doing, I took great pleasure in assisting them whenever opportunity offered. In the course of five years at Ghoom I completed, with the help of the Revs. A. W. Heyde and J. F. Frederickson, a revision of the Tibetan translation of the New Testament.

I was married at Ghoom in 1893, and since that time my wife has been my constant companion, both in India and in Tibet. To her encouragement and help is due, in no small measure, whatever success I have made in life.

Lastly, among those to whom I am deeply indebted for assistance in the preparation and publication of this book, I feel I must mention the names of the Rev. Dr R. Kilgour and Mr F. Stanley Service, of the well-known firm of publishers. The former gentleman very kindly read over the MS. and helped with valuable suggestions; without the assistance of the latter the book would never have been published.

DAVID MACDONALD.

Kalimpong, North Bengal.

CONTENTS

LIST OF ILLUSTRATIONS

15

TWENTY YEARS IN TIBET

CHAPTER ONE

*Political Mission to Tibet—Annie Taylor—Yatung—Chumbi Valley
—Dangerous Travelling—Capture of the Jong—
Monastery of Samding*

MY first direct contact with Tibet came in 1904, and for this opportunity of visiting the land in which I was so keenly interested I was again indebted mainly to Lieutenant-Colonel Waddell, I.M.S.

In 1903 the Government of India decided to send a Political Mission to Tibet to settle, once and for all, questions relating to international trade and boundaries, which matters were becoming more and more acute, owing to the Chinese and Tibetan disregard of the provisions of the 1890 Sikkim-Tibet Convention, which had resulted from the Sikkim-Tibet Expedition of 1888. Lieutenant-Colonel Waddell was selected to accompany the 1903-1904 expedition as the principal medical officer in charge of the Mission, and its military escort. As an authority on Tibetan art, religion and literature he was also, by the Government of India, commissioned to make, as far as might be possible, a study of these subjects in Tibet itself, and to obtain a representative collection of such *objets d'art*, books and manuscripts as would prove of interest to Western scholars. Aware of my interest in everything Tibetan, and also of my exceptional proficiency in the language of that country,

Colonel Waddell suggested to Colonel (now Sir) Francis Younghusband, the Political Officer in charge of the Mission, that I should be appointed as his (Colonel Waddell's) assistant in literary research work, my services also being available for interpretation, should necessity arise. The first I heard of these proposals was in May 1904, when I was informed of the appointment by the then Deputy Commissioner of Darjeeling. That officer strongly advised me to accept the offer, which I did, not without, however, a few qualms as to the wisdom of the course I was taking. It must be remembered that at that time Tibet was still an unknown land, and most fearsome tales had filtered across the frontiers into the bazaars as to what might be expected in the way of cruelty should one be so unfortunate as to fall into Tibetan hands as a prisoner. A certain amount of fighting had already taken place in Tibet, and evidence of the ferocity of the Tibetans was then present in Darjeeling in the person of Mr Edmund Candler, the famous war correspondent of *The Daily Mail,* who was attached to the Mission. This gentleman had lost an arm at the engagement of Chumig Shengo, near Guru. I had a talk with him, and found that, as soon as the doctors would allow him to get up, he intended to return to Tibet. I fancy that this determination on his part played a great part in my decision to go to Tibet, for I told myself that, timid as I was, if a wounded man could go there, I, who was whole, should certainly do so. Curiosity to delve into the unknown also played a part in my decision.

Having arranged for my family while I was away, I reported for duty in Darjeeling. There I found that

Mr Magniac, private secretary to the British Commissioner for Frontier Affairs, and Mr Harrison, then Postmaster-General of Bengal, were about to leave for Tibet. These two officers, learning that I was also to proceed to Gyantse to join Colonel Waddell, obtained permission for me to travel with them. After an uneventful journey we arrived in the Chumbi Valley, where a depot of the expedition was located at a village called Shasima, which has since been renamed Yatung. The trek through Sikkim and across the passes has been too often described to warrant further description here, and for those who desire more detailed accounts of this part of the Himalayas I would recommend the recent books dealing with the various Mount Everest expeditions, which contain full itineraries.

On arrival in Yatung we found that General Macdonald, the military commander of the escort to the Mission, was there awaiting the arrival of a column of reinforcements from India. He and his staff were busy making arrangements for its reception. The greatest difficulty the military authorities had to contend with was that of transport. A mule from India arrived in Gyantse with about four pounds' weight of useful load, having eaten the remainder on the way. This was the case until arrangements were made to obtain animal rations on payment from the local Tibetans. On the road between the Sikkim-Tibet frontier and Yatung was the Chinese Customs post of Old Yatung, and here I met for the first time that remarkable woman Miss Annie Taylor. She had been a member of the then defunct Tibet Pioneer Christian Mission, and was carrying on, on her own, living within the Tibet frontier. She and a Miss Bella Ferguson, as far as I know, were the only Christian missionaries who within the past century conducted mission work actually within the boundaries of Tibet.

Annie Taylor was a zealot, absolutely sincere in her profession of Christianity. She had established herself at Old Yatung as a trader-missionary, and had selected that place for her activities because there was usually a British officer employed there by the Chinese Customs authorities. On my return to Yatung later in the year I found her installed in the Trade Mart as a nurse, a capacity in which she undoubtedly did more good than she accomplished as a missionary. I heard that she eventually returned to England, where she died.

Years before the 1904 Mission, Annie Taylor had made an attempt to reach Lhasa from the Chinese side, but she was detected at Nagchuka, a town about a week's journey from the Tibetan capital. She was sent back the way she had come by the Chinese.

Besides General Macdonald, the military commander, Major Iggulden, his Chief of Staff, and Mr Walsh, C.S.I., I.C.S., the Assistant Commissioner for Tibet Frontier Affairs, were also in Yatung, preparing for the expected reinforcements, and arranging details of further operations in the interior. These latter had been rendered necessary by the fact that it had been found impossible to get into touch with any properly accredited representatives of either the Chinese or Tibetan governments at Gyantse, and Colonel Younghusband had decided that there was nothing to be done but to push right into Lhasa.

I was very pleased to find that an old friend of mine, Mr S. W. Laden La, of the Bengal Police, was resident in Yatung as an assistant to Mr Walsh, then in political charge of the Chumbi Valley, and I was saved considerable inconvenience and discomfort by his kind offer to put me up in his tent. This gentleman, Mr Laden La, C.B.E., is now a Sirdar Bahadur, and an Honorary Aide-de-Camp to the Governor of Bengal, having in the course of his career risen from a Sub-Inspector of Police to an Additional Superintendent of Police, by sheer merit.

We remained in Yatung for exactly one month, waiting for the column from India. I was anxious to join Colonel Waddell in Gyantse without any delay, and I therefore applied for permission to proceed at once, without waiting for the troops to arrive. I had heard that the road was fairly safe, and I reckoned on my ability to pass as a Tibetan to extricate myself from any difficulties that might arise. Permission was, however, refused, on the grounds that travel was unsafe, and no troops could be spared for escort duties at that time.

During this enforced halt at Yatung I got to know the Chumbi Valley very well indeed, little thinking, however, that it was to be my home later for over fifteen years. My duties as an interpreter were not very onerous, as everyone was busy with purely military preparations. I spent many a day, with Mr Magniac and Mr Harrison, shooting and fishing in the neighbourhood, and was present when the former succeeded in bagging a fine specimen of the shao, the rare great Himalayan stag.

Prior to the departure of the newly arrived column

from Yatung, Colonel Younghusband himself arrived
from Gyantse with a small escort, to consult with General
Macdonald. That permission for me to proceed to
Gyantse alone had been wisely withheld was evident
from the fact that this party had had a skirmish with
the Tibetans at Kangma, a staging-village some twenty-
eight miles from Gyantse. The attackers had been driven
off without any casualties to the Colonel's escort.

We eventually left Yatung on 15th June 1904, for
Gyantse, and reached Pharijong, twenty-eight miles
farther north, after two days' marching over execrable
roads, the world's worst. The roughness of the road,
however, was more than compensated for by the
grandeur of the scenery through which we passed.
Never have I seen a gorge to equal that of the Amo
river above Yatung for wildness and magnificence.
Captain O'Connor, the secretary and official interpreter
to the Mission, had unfortunately been wounded, so
that I was appointed to act in his stead as interpreter,
while his secretarial duties were taken over for the
time being by Mr Magniac. I was thus brought into
direct personal touch with Colonel Younghusband, the
leader of the Mission. From Pharijong we marched on
along the foot of the mighty Chomolhari range, passing
the scene of the engagement at Chumig Shengo,
where Mr Candler was wounded. The bodies of some
of the Tibetan dead were still lying about, quite well
preserved, except where they had been mutilated by
wolves.

Until approaching Gyantse the column met with
no resistance, but at Saugong, fourteen miles from
that city, information was brought in that the Tibetans

were gathered in force at the monastery of Nenying, which commanded the road seven miles from the city. Why the Tibetans had selected this place in preference to the Red Idol Gorge in which to make a stand is inexplicable. In the latter spot a few men could have held up the column almost indefinitely. Possibly they felt that with the monastery at their backs, and the prayers and incantations of the lamas to support them, they could put up a better resistance at Nenying.

On approaching the place, General Macdonald decided that, since it commanded the lines of communication, the Tibetans would have to be ejected. Accordingly, the monastery was shelled, and a detachment of troops was left to complete the evacuation of the place, while the main body pushed on to Gyantse, which was reached without further resistance. As Colonel Younghusband rode across the bridge spanning the Nyang river, to reach the British Post, closely attended by Mr Magniac and myself, the Mission very nearly lost its leader. A salvo of round-shot from the jingals in the Tibetan fort, which dominated this bridge, missed us by a matter of inches only. Before it could be repeated, however, we had reached the cover of the Post, which was near the bridgehead.

The British Headquarters in Gyantse were then located in a large Tibetan house about a quarter of a mile, as the crow flies, from the Jong, or Tibetan fort, which completely dominated the place, being situated on a spur some seven hundred feet above the surrounding plain. Not for one single day, until the Jong was captured, did the Tibetan gunners cease to drop round-shot into and round our camp. Fortunately for the Mission personnel these men were not the best of marksmen.

To facilitate the capture • of the Jong, General Macdonald assaulted and took the large monastery of Tsechen, three miles north of Gyantse. This monastery was the base of operations for a large body of Tibetan levies, which continually threatened the flank of any attack on the Jong. Once Tsechen had fallen, the way lay open for the capture of the Jong.

After the villages at its foot had been cleared it was taken by storm, on 6th July 1904. I witnessed the operations from the Mission Post, and was surprised at the stubborn resistance put up by the badly armed, and still more badly led, Tibetan militia. After the fall of the Jong all active opposition in Gyantse ended, and the Mission was free to move on to Lhasa. (*Note.*— For full details of the Tibet Expedition the reader is referred to Waddell's *Lhasa and its Mysteries* and Younghusband's *India and Tibet*.)

The last organized resistance to our progress was met with at the Karo Pass, two marches out from Gyantse, on the Lhasa road. In this engagement, fought at eighteen thousand feet above sea-level, the Tibetans were again routed, despite their use of charms, provided by their priests, which were supposed to render their wearers immune from harm from bullets. This action at the Karo La left the way to Lhasa open, the Tibetans offering no further opposition. On 24th July 1904 the Mission and its escort arrived at the Chaksam Ferry, on the Tsangpo, or Brahmaputra. This river was crossed without any opposition on the part of the Tibetans, the only casualty being Major

SHIGATSE JONG

THE STRONGHOLD, FORMERLY OF THE TASHI LAMA, SITUATED IN THE PROVINCE OF TSANG AS A GUARD AGAINST NEPALESE AGGRESSION. THE BAZAAR, OR MARKET PLACE, MAY BE SEEN IN THE FOREGROUND.

Bretherton, of the Supply and Transport Corps, who was accidentally drowned.

At the Chaksam Ferry are still to be seen the remains of a large suspension bridge across the river, these relics being in the form of great iron chains, formerly used to carry the footway. It has not been in use for very many years, owing to the river having cut in behind the massive piers to which the chains are anchored. One of these is now some distance from the bank, in the water. This suspension bridge was erected early in the fifteenth century, by King Tang-Tong, who has since been canonised, and is worshipped in the small monastery near the bridge itself.

At Nagartse, to the south of the Tsangpo, Colonel Waddell and myself rode out to inspect the famous monastery of Samding. On our way there we met a couple of sepoys fairly bulging with looted gilt images. We ordered them to return these at once to the lamas, and saw that they did so, or at least that they replaced them in the monastery, which was utterly deserted. After looking round the place, we returned to camp.

In this monastery is domiciled the only female incarnation in Tibet — Dorje Phagmo, or the "Thunderbolt Sow." She is the only woman in the country who is permitted by the strict sumptuary laws to travel in a palanquin. We were very sorry to miss her, but at a later visit I was privileged to make her acquaintance.

The sepoys we had caught looting were later tried by court martial, as very strict orders against this kind of thing had been issued, since it was desired above everything to create a good impression on the Tibetans.

They were sentenced to a term of imprisonment, and sent back to India.

During the whole of the expedition, so far as I was personally able to observe, there was very little in the way of looting, which speaks very well for the discipline of the troops and followers, especially when it is understood that in every monastery and large house along the route of march were valuable images and bullion, to say nothing of priceless silks, brocades and porcelain.

CHAPTER TWO

THE morning of 3rd August 1904 broke in rain, but as the column moved out of camp the rain ceased, and the sun shone out brilliantly. We had been told that the Potala, the fortress-palace of the priest-kings of Tibet, was to be seen from a ridge some ten miles from the city of Lhasa. As we approached this vantage-point all who were not tied to their places in the ranks broke into a race as to who should be the first living European to set eyes on the Forbidden City of the Lamas. Excitement rose to a high pitch.

Our information proved correct, for miles away, gleaming in the morning sun, were to be seen the golden roofs of the pavilions which crowned the Potala. We gazed on them with feelings not unmixed with awe : we were the first Westerners to tear aside the veil of centuries. I myself was enthralled at the prospect of visiting the shrines of Lhasa, of roaming in its bazaars, and of mixing with its people.

The day we approached the Tibetan capital was an anxious time for General Macdonald, for we had heard that there were twenty thousand fighting monks in the city who had sworn that we should enter it only over their dead bodies. This threat, fortunately, failed to materialise, and, though sullen, the lamas made no attempt to arrest our progress. The Mission headquarters were at first located on the Kyang-thang Naga, a plain to the west of the city, but later they were removed to the large country house of Lhalu, a mansion belonging to the Lhasa family of the same name. To the camp on the Kyang-thang Naga came the Chinese Ambans, then resident in Lhasa, to pay their official call. These officers considered themselves, and indeed at that time were, the real rulers of Tibet, and much of the procrastination and the failure to send properly accredited representatives to treat with the Mission at an earlier date was due to their influence. Their escort was composed of mediæval warriors, armed with halberds, swords and spears, clad in red jackets, embroidered with Chinese conventional signs in black *appliqué* work.

The Ambans arrived in palanquins, and proved to be elderly men of grave demeanour. Their visit was purely ceremonial, China disclaiming any right of interference between the Tibetans and the British. Apart from stating that they would do all in their power to persuade the Tibetans to settle matters satisfactorily to all concerned, the Ambans discussed no business whatever. Their visit was brief, and after presenting the principal members of the Mission with red silk ceremonial scarves they withdrew.

We had again been warned by the Nepalese Resident in Lhasa that the attitude of the thousands of monks

THE POTALA, THE MOST IMPOSING EDIFICE IN CENTRAL ASIA

BUILT ON A ROCK, ON A PLAIN OUTSIDE LHASSA. IT INCLUDES A MONASTERY WITH 300 MONKS, A COLLEGE OF STATECRAFT, THE TREASURY, A STATE PRISON, THE PRIVATE QUARTERS OF HIS HOLINESS AND THE THRONE ROOM.

attached to the three great monasteries near the capital was uncertain, and for this reason no one was allowed to visit the city unofficially until all negotiations had been satisfactorily concluded. I may mention here that during the whole of the Mission's stay in Tibet the Nepalese proved most helpful, and did their utmost to smooth the way for the Political Officer in charge.

Colonel Younghusband, accompanied by his staff, and a strong military escort, entered Lhasa City for the first time on the morning of 4th August 1904, to return the official call of the Chinese Ambans. Passing through the Pargo Kani, the western gate of the city, our cavalcade proceeded through the suburb of Sho, leaving on our right the sombre mass of the Potala. No signs of life were to be seen about this building, though we knew that our progress was being watched by thousands of unseen eyes of lamas who had taken up their quarters in their ruler's palace. The village of Sho was then, and still remains, a rather dirty, depressing place, with pools of stagnant water standing about, and with numerous pigs wallowing in the mire of the roadway. The Potala itself was impressive. Certainly the most imposing edifice in Tibet—and possibly in all Central Asia—the Potala by reason of its associations captured and held the imagination of everyone. One wondered what was going on behind the blind walls, and imagined the lamas invoking all the aid of their magic to overwhelm the intruders who had destroyed the inviolability of their chief sacred place.

Colonel Younghusband was received by the Ambans with all the respect due to an Envoy of the highest

rank, and after the exchange of compliments and the
presentation of return gifts we retired from the city.
It was then found that the Dalai Lama had fled from
the Potala, and though this was disappointing to the
members of the Mission, who had hoped to set eyes
on the incarnate high priest of Tibet, negotiations
probably went through more rapidly than if he had
been present. He had left as his regent the venerable
abbot of the Ganden Monastery, the Ti Rimpoche, a
saintly old man who did all in his power to make the
wheels of diplomacy run smoothly. He took a great
fancy to me, as I was the only member of the Mission
staff who could talk to him in the high honorific
language of Tibet.

I myself, with others, consider that the Dalai Lama,
in fleeing from his capital, took the only course open
to him. Had he remained, and been forced to take
part in the political discussions, he could only have
been humiliated in the eyes of his people, and his
sacred person would surely have been exposed to
indignities in the form of publicity. After all, he is a
literal god on earth to his subjects, and had he been
dragged into the fierce light of political controversy
he would certainly have lost a great deal of the hold
he exercises on the minds of his spiritual as well as his
temporal subjects. His very aloofness from mundane
things and from the mass of his people is a great
part of the attraction his personality exercises over his
followers.

After the Treaty negotiations were over, and only
formalities remained to be completed, permission was
granted for us to visit the city without escort.   In

company with Colonel Waddell I was able to enter and examine many places and articles to which access would otherwise have been impossible at that time, for the Colonel went as the guest of the Tibetan Government, which, once the Treaty had been settled, showed a very friendly attitude towards us, a somewhat surprising courtesy considering that we had invaded their country.

Personally, I was rather disappointed in Lhasa City itself, but this disappointment was more than compensated for by the never-ending wonder of the Potala. At this time we were unable to make more than a cursory examination of this palace, but I was fortunate in being able to go over the whole of it in detail on the occasion of my visit to Lhasa in 1921.

Houses in the Tibetan capital are almost invariably built of rough-hewn stone, set in stamped mud, and are commonly three, or even four, storeys in height, with flat roofs. They are more or less huddled together in some places, and while some of the streets are broad, and fairly clean, others are little better than open drains. The glamour of the unknown had endowed the city of the lamas with a fictitious charm, and it was a great pity that most of this was dispelled in the light of closer acquaintance. The Potala, as I have said, however, recalled all the mystery and fascination that had held our minds through the long march from the Indian frontier.

Most of the nobles and princes of the Church, as well as the majority of the better-class people, had fled from Lhasa at our approach, and only those officials who were directly concerned in the negotiations, and

the poorer people, remained in the city. Dreadful
tales of our ferocity and cruelty had been in circulation
during our march from India, but after we had been
in Lhasa a few days most of the people realised that
these were unfounded, and returned to their homes in
the capital.

If, however, the better-class people were at first con-
spicuous by their absence, their places were more than
filled by the hordes of beggars that collected from all
points of the compass as soon as it became known that
we distributed alms daily, and that unconsidered trifles
in the way of camp leavings were to be had for the
trouble of picking them up. These beggars were a
nuisance, and though they appeared in the main to
be sturdy rogues, quite capable of performing useful
labour in the fields, we were told that in Tibet begging is an hereditary profession, and is authorised by
religion. The beggars went about in families. In
Lhasa they usually congregated round the city gates,
and solicited alms from all who passed by. If they
were the fortunate recipients of a silver coin they raised
a shout of "Hla Gyal Lo!" (or "God is Victorious"),
while for a copper coin they returned no audible
thanks whatever. In the event of their receiving no
largess at all they heaped the most foul abuse and
curses on the head of the close-fisted traveller, and
their language was fearful and wonderful.

Some of these beggar families wander very far afield,
being met with as far south as Benares and Gaya, in
India. They wander along the pilgrim routes, earning
a little by fiddle-playing and dancing, and making
something by pilfering. Father usually provides the

fiddle-music, mother sings, while the children, all those who are old enough to walk, dance a kind of double shuffle, with hand actions. They visit India during the winter, which is very severe in Tibet, and make their way back to their own country in the spring. Until one has seen a really poor Tibetan beggar one does not realise the meaning of the phrase "rags and tatters."

In company with Colonel Waddell I also visited the Chokang, or cathedral, of Lhasa, but as I was able to spend more time in going over this building during later visits to the Tibetan capital it will be described later in this book. I may mention here, however, that a very interesting relic of the old Capuchin Mission in Lhasa, a large bell, on which are inscribed the words : "Te Deum Laudamus," is to be seen in the porch of the Chokang. We were unable to trace any remains of the Catholic chapel which is said to have been built by the Fathers, but the Tibetans stated that, though there certainly had been such a building, the more or less modern monastery of Muru had been erected on its site. Colonel Waddell was particularly attracted by some very good specimens of mediæval armour which were stored in the upper storeys of the Chokang, but the lamas could not be induced to part with any, at any price. The workmanship of certain pieces of chain body-armour was very fine, so fine that I do not think it can have been Tibetan work.

The Lhasa bazaars were interesting. It was extra-ordinary what one found on the stalls. There were to be seen in the streets, mingling with the native Tibetans, representatives of many other Eastern races. Chinese,

c

Mongolians, Buriats from the Russian marches, Bhutanese, Nepalese and Ladakhis, and among all these the British Tommy and the Indian sepoy wandered from shop to shop. The Tommies were a never-ending source of interest to the Tibetans. Women preponderated everywhere, and on inquiry I found that this had always been the case in Lhasa, their numbers being surpassed by those of men only on the occasions of the great religious festivals, when the lamas from the neighbouring monasteries flocked into the city in their thousands.

Almost the entire petty trade of Lhasa is in the hands of women traders, and this is true of the whole country. The assortment of goods displayed for sale on the stalls was very varied, ranging from purely native products, in the form of serges, blankets, provisions and boots, to imported piece-goods, soaps, candles, cartridges, matches, turquoise matrix in large and small lumps, coral beads of various sizes, rings, Indian-made boots and second-hand clothing. Empty bottles were in great demand, and fetched good prices in a country that can produce nothing but the crudest earthenware utensils.

I was fortunate in being permitted to visit the great monasteries of Sera and Drepung, near Lhasa. These institutions are cities in themselves, with thousands of lamas resident in each. It was the abbot of a sister establishment who signed the Treaty on behalf of the Dalai Lama, the Ganden Ti Rimpoche, as Regent of Tibet. This fact gives some idea of the influence wielded by these great monasteries, their abbots, on certain occasions, taking precedence even of the chief

KHANG-HSI PERIOD VASES

TIBET IS TO-DAY THE WORLD'S GREATEST STOREHOUSE OF EXQUISITE CHINESE PORCELAIN.
VARIOUS CHINESE EMPERORS MADE GIFTS TO SUCCEEDING LAMAS AND THEY ARE IN THE
TIBETAN MONASTERIES.

ministers of the country. The monasteries generally were kept in a much cleaner condition than Lhasa town itself, though even this is not saying much. It is terrible to think what would happen to the inmates of their colleges if the average temperature of the country were suddenly to rise a bare ten degrees, or even if the air were to be heavily moisture-laden.

At the monastery of Drepung I was able to examine the system on which the place was administered. It was divided into four colleges, each under the control of an abbot. The priests lived in messes, discipline being maintained by a special officer assisted by a posse of lama police. Many of the lamas, especially those who have no private means, become what are called " fighting lamas," and these train themselves regularly in the use of arms, their services being utilised as escorts to high Church dignitaries and priest-traders. When we first arrived in Lhasa it was for some time feared that these warrior-priests would cause trouble, but happily there was nothing of the kind, due to the good control of their abbots. Their leaders evidently saw the folly of breaking the truce that had tacitly existed once the Mission had reached the capital, and the lamas, though sullen, did not demonstrate against our force. One of the minor officials of Drepung remarked to me that the British had no right whatever to invade his country, and that by so doing we had violated the sanctity of the sacred city of Lhasa. The Tibetans at first regarded the British as a nation utterly devoid of finer feelings, and entirely without religion of any kind, an attitude that became considerably modified as time went on. One old official, years later, when discussing British and Tibetan relations, said to me : "When the British first came to Tibet we hated the sight of them, but when we came to know the Indian rupee we loved them." If I remember correctly, a song was composed with this sentiment as its theme.

An unfortunate incident, in which a lama was concerned, marred the tranquillity of our camp soon after our arrival in Lhasa, just when we thought that all trouble was past. A fanatical priest made a futile attempt to assassinate General Macdonald, in the course of which he badly wounded two I.M.S. officers with a sword. He was apprehended, and tried by court martial, being sentenced to be hanged. Before he was executed I asked him why he had done such a foolish thing, and he replied that he must have been possessed by a devil, or have suddenly become mad. In actual truth, I afterwards discovered, he was a fighting monk of Sera, and his attempt was made in the nature of a feeler to find out what would happen to the perpetrators of such wanton attacks. The Sera Monastery was fined five thousand rupees over this matter, which sum was paid, partly in cash, but mostly in kind, in the form of barley and other grains. This stern example of punishment put a stop to outbursts of this nature.

About this time I spent a most interesting day visiting Chakpori, the medical college of the lamas, in company with Colonel Waddell and other medical officers attached to the expedition. The lama physicians and students were quite friendly, and seemed glad of the opportunity of airing their knowledge before foreigners. Diagnosis and treatment were of the weirdest descriptions. All the queer ingredients of mediæval European medicines were present, with some even more repulsive ones from Tibet and China. Disease was diagnosed by observing the beats of seven pulses in the body, each of which was alleged to communicate with an important organ.

The doctors were all priests, and combined their practice of the healing art with that of religion. One of the lamas told me in all seriousness that the heart of a man was on the left side, while that of a woman was on the right side of the body. Asked how he had arrived at this conclusion, he stated that it had been observed during dissection. In cases of suspected infectious disease the lama physician will instruct his patient to tie one end of a long cord to his wrist and throw him the other end, alleging that he can feel the pulse through several yards of string. The lamas even go so far as to assert that they can tell the state of health of a consultant's relative, even though he be miles away, by the feel of the former's pulses. Tibetan doctors possess very little in the way of instruments, and surgery seems to be very seldom practised. Beyond a lancet, a cupping horn for blood-letting, and a branding-iron for cauterisation, I saw no instruments.

For cold in the bowels a patient is given a draught of water in which a holy image has been washed. For hoarseness a concoction of powdered roots is administered. In cases of poisoning due to eating bad meat, bad eggs, and from poisoning due to copper pots, pills of various kinds are given, made from the excreta of wolves, mud, rust, and other ingredients. Bathing in hot springs is recommended for all complaints. Rheumatism, pain in the joints, and so forth, are treated by branding the affected part with a red-hot iron, and affixing charms. Sometimes a particularly holy lama will spit on the part, and this is considered very effective. Smallpox cases are not permitted to eat any salt, cheese or meat, nor may they drink whey, of which every Tibetan is very fond. Barley beer is allowed in moderation. For headaches and neuralgia the lamas provide small plasters which are affixed to the parts where the pain lies, usually the temples. In the preparation of these plasters one of the chief ingredients is aconite.

At Chakpori are preserved wonderful images of Tara, made of turquoise, of Tse-Pa-Me, the God of Long Life, fashioned from coral, and of Chenresi, of carved shell. Prominent on its altars are the Eight Buddhas of Healing, while hung on the temple walls are various charts showing the parts of the human body. These diagrams are used when delivering lectures to the students. The latter are recruited from the various monasteries all over the country, and when their course of instruction is over—it usually takes about eight years—they return to their own institutions, and there practise their arts for the benefit of their monastery. No layman ever becomes a really popular physician. The principal item in all treatment seems to be the reciting of appropriate prayers and the performance of religious ceremonies. It is the learning of these prayers by heart that occupies so much time in the course of study.

The Treaty was formally signed at a Durbar held on 7th September 1904, the Ti Rimpoche of Ganden Monastery signing for the absent Dalai Lama, the

Abbots of Sera and Drepung on behalf of the Church, the Chief Ministers on behalf of the Kashak, or Council of State, while the Tsongdu, or National Assembly, also affixed its seal. Colonel Younghusband signed for the Government of India. This ceremony was, of course, attended by everybody of any importance then in Lhasa, and after the various signatures and seals had been made and appended the Tibetan Government invited all the British to witness a performance of the Tibetan drama entitled *Kheu Padma Obar*. It is of interest to note that I was the only member of the expedition personnel to spend a night away from the camp. This I was compelled to do owing to the hospitality of one of my Darjeeling Tibetan friends whom I met again in Lhasa. He insisted on entertaining me, and when the party broke up it was too late for me to return to the camp without disturbing the guards. My host made me stay in his house, guaranteeing my safety while I was beneath his roof. Two of the Tibetan interpreters attached to the Mission were manhandled by Tibetan soldiery while they were in Lhasa City unescorted, so that this guarantee was really necessary.

The Mission and its escort finally left Lhasa on 21st September 1904, arriving at Pharijong, *via* Gyantse, on 17th October, in a blinding snowstorm. Captain O'Connor was left in Gyantse as the first British Trade Agent of the new Treaty Trade Mart established in that place. He took up his quarters in the house that had been occupied by the Mission during its upward march to Lhasa, and retained a company of Indian troops as his personal escort. A short distance out from Lhasa a pleasing ceremony, typical of Tibetan courtesy, was performed. The Chief Ministers had ridden out of the city a little before us, and had tea and refreshments ready for the officers of the Mission. Tents had been pitched, and a pleasant half-hour was thus spent. This ceremony is always performed to speed the parting guest in Tibet. Silk ceremonial scarves were presented to every British officer of importance.

Leaving Pharijong we marched, descending all the time, to Gautsa, where we saw forest again, after six months. So much did we miss trees that everyone was delighted at the first sight of pine forest. In Yatung I found that Mr (now Sir Charles) Bell, I.C.S., had been installed as the Assistant Political Officer in charge of the Chumbi Valley and the Yatung Trade Mart. I had met Mr Bell before, in Darjeeling, where I had assisted him in the preparation of his *Manual of Colloquial Tibetan* and in the compilation of his small *Tibetan Dictionary*. This officer was my immediate superior during most of the time I afterwards spent in Tibet. I owe much to his kindness during my service in that country.

We finally arrived back in Siliguri, the base of operations, on 25th October 1904. One result of the Younghusband Mission was that a survey was carried out of the Amo Valley. The Amo river, after passing through the Chumbi Valley, and Bhutan, becomes the Torsa, finally flowing through the rich plains of the Bengal Dooars tea-districts, to meet the Brahmaputra. Estimates were prepared for the making of a road from Madarihat, on the Bengal Dooars Railway, to Yatung. This road would have avoided all passes, and been of an easy gradient all the way. It was, however, found that the volume of possible traffic was too small to give any return on the money that would have to be invested, and the project was abandoned. I hear that nowadays the question of the construction of this road is again being considered, and should it ever be made it will afford the easiest outlet from the southern Tibetan Plateau, and would cheapen the cost of everything imported into and exported from Tibet. The lamas have always opposed this scheme, as they fear that increased facilities for intercourse between their own people and the outside world will eventually result in the decline of their own influence. This is no doubt true, but it is impossible for the priesthood to hold up for ever the march of progress in Tibet, and the opening of the country would benefit the masses of the people, who now have to support so great a number of unproductive priests.

CHAPTER THREE

MY duties with Colonel Waddell were now over, so without any delay I was able to return to Ghoom, where I was reunited to my family, who had naturally been anxious during my absence. I resumed charge of the Vaccine Depot in that place, but I was not to remain there for very long.

My missionary friends had asked me to observe the conditions in which the Tibetans lived, and their religious practices. This I had done, as far as I was able, and I was in a position to give them a fairly comprehensive account of the Tibetans, lay and lama, and also of what Lamaism stood for in Tibet, and of its tremendous power in that country. I told the missionaries that while the time was certainly ripe for missionary effort in Tibet it would be hard, uphill work.

In January 1905 I was detailed for special duty to Calcutta, where I was placed in charge of the work of classifying and cataloguing the collection of books, manuscripts and curios which Colonel Waddell and myself had gathered in Tibet. These objects amounted to over four hundred mule-loads, and comprised many rare and valuable manuscripts of Lamaist sacred works, images, religious paraphernalia of all descriptions, armour, weapons, paintings and porcelain. A large collection of the last was dispatched to the late Lord Kitchener, who was a keen collector. I heard that, unfortunately, many pieces of this consignment arrived at their destination damaged beyond repair.

All these valuable *objets d'art* had been stored at the Indian Museum, and I carried on my work in that building. Many of the things were afterwards divided among the British Museum, the Indian Museum, the Bodleian Library, and the India Office Library. While I was at work cataloguing, Lord Curzon and Lord Lamington visited the museum several times, the former, then Viceroy of India, himself selecting certain articles for presentation to the Victoria Memorial Hall in Calcutta.

During my stay in Calcutta I was asked by Sir Stuart Fraser, then Foreign Secretary to the Government of India, if I would accept a post, should a vacancy occur, in the Foreign and Political Department. I naturally jumped at this offer, and was shortly afterwards informed that my name had been registered for such employment.

When my work at the Indian Museum was finished —it took me about four months—I returned to Ghoom once more, for the last time on duty, and almost immediately I received an appointment as a Sub-Deputy Magistrate and Collector, being posted to Darjeeling. I obtained this appointment through the kindness of Sir Andrew Fraser, then Lieutenant-Governor of Bengal, and his Chief Secretary, Sir Robert Carlyle.

For promotion in the Bengal Civil Service, of which I thus became a member, it was necessary for me to pass departmental examinations in law, revenue administration, accounts, and so forth. Finding little difficulty in doing this, I concentrated on languages. I have passed the higher standard tests in Hindustani, Bengali, Nepali, Bhutanese, Sikkimese and Lepcha, but although I was appointed to the Board for selection of papers for candidates for the examination in Tibetan by Government in 1906, strangely enough I passed no examination in that language until 1923, when I was permitted to sit only for the Higher Proficiency test. I may mention here that on this occasion I was able to correct my examiners, even though these were Tibetans. I also have a working knowledge of Mandarin Chinese.

In 1907 I again received promotion, and was deputed to Dharbhanga, in Bengal, on Famine Relief work, remaining there for almost a year. While not particularly severe, there was a considerable amount of local distress due to the failure of crops owing to floods. Mild though it was, however, I do not ever wish to see another famine, for human distress always affects me to an intense degree. The usual relief works—in the form of excavations for reservoirs, making of roads and the establishment of food-kitchens—were organised by Government. My work consisted in supervising the work of circle officers in direct charge of groups of labourers. Being totally unaccustomed to the plains of India, the hot-weather season affected my health. I was fortunate, however, in escaping malaria, which claimed most of my colleagues as its victims.

A good report on my work in Dharbhanga was

rendered by Mr W. Egerton, I.C.S., the Collector in charge of Famine Relief, who wrote: "Among the Assistant Charge Superintendents Mr David Macdonald has done the best work." He himself was indefatigable, and was ably assisted by Mr Lindsay, I.C.S., now the Indian Trade Commissioner in London. On my return to Darjeeling, promotion gave me control of the Western Khas Mahal of that district. "Khas Mahal" means Government Estates. I was now a Deputy Magistrate and Collector. Soon after I took over charge of the whole of the Khas Mahal in the Darjeeling District, in which post I was offered a permanency. At this time, however, Mr Bell, I.C.S., then Political Officer in Sikkim, in charge of Tibetan Affairs, offered me the post of British Trade Agent at Yatung, which I accepted.

Mr Bell had spoken to the then Foreign Secretary, Sir Harcourt Butler, about my peculiar qualifications for this post, and together they obtained the Viceroy's sanction to my appointment. At that time I considered I had a good chance of eventually getting into the Foreign and Political Department, and it was this prospect which led me to accept the post of Trade Agent in preference to the permanent appointment in the Khas Mahal at Kalimpong, in 1908. The appointment was definitely settled in May 1909, and in June of that year, accompanied by my wife and young family, I proceeded once more to Yatung, travelling *via* Gantok, the capital of the little Himalayan state of Sikkim, a protectorate under the Government of India, and headquarters of the Political Officer for Sikkim and Tibet.

My elder children were left at school in Darjeeling, joining me for their Christmas holidays in December. On my arrival in Gantok I found that Mr Bell, the Political Officer, was away in Gyantse on his annual visit to Tibet, but I remained in that place for about a month, obtaining some idea of the duties of my new office from his staff. I eventually arrived in Yatung, and took over charge of the Trade Agency on 8th July 1909, from Captain Kennedy, I.M.S., who returned from Gyantse with Mr Bell. Up to that time the former officer had held dual charge of both Yatung and Gyantse Agencies.

While in Gantok I made the acquaintance of the late Maharaja of Sikkim, His Highness Sir Thutob Namgyal, and his Maharani. I also met this ruler's two sons, the younger of whom, His Highness Sir Tashi Namgyal, K.C.I.E., is the present Maharaja, his elder brother, a most enlightened young man, educated in Europe, having died shortly after he had ascended the throne.

On my arrival in the Chumbi Valley I found the Chinese complete masters of Tibet, and their representatives in the valley were in full control of the administration. For several days after taking charge of the Trade Agency I was engaged in receiving and returning the calls of the Chinese and Tibetan officials stationed in the neighbourhood, and in interviewing the chief lamas of the monasteries in the vicinity, the headmen of the villages, and the local landowners and traders.

The Chinese and the Tibetans are sticklers for official etiquette, and this calling and returning calls took a considerable time. Among the Chinese, the custom when calling was for the officer concerned to send a messenger ahead to my house, with a large red visiting card, on which his master's name and titles were inscribed in black lettering. The official himself always came with an escort of several soldiers in red jackets, armed with halberds, battle-axes and huge swords. Presents were invariably offered, consisting often of dried Chinese fruits, biscuits, sweetmeats, and other delicacies. It was a peculiarity of the Chinese in Tibet that for ceremonial escort purposes they always employed these mediæval men-at-arms, though their actual soldiers were armed and garbed in a more or less modern fashion. The Tibetans called on me after all the Chinese had done so. They were not permitted to take precedence of their suzerains in this, or indeed in any matter. The Chinese looked on the Tibetans as an inferior race, and openly alluded to them as barbarians. The Tibetan custom also demands that a messenger be sent ahead of the caller, but the latter presents a white ceremonial scarf to the person on whom he is calling, with his own hands.

This scarf, being white, is supposed to be symbolical of the caller's purity of motive, and is accompanied by a selection of gifts, which may consist of trays of eggs, bags of barley flour, butter sewn into yakhide bags, with the hair on the inside, small carpets, and a carcass or two of raw dried mutton, which last are placed in a sitting attitude before the person to whom they are being presented. When first I received the trays of eggs I considered myself very fortunate, and my wife was delighted with them. When they came

to be used, however, it was a different story. As often
as not they would be bad, and in some cases the shells
contained absolutely nothing, the entire contents having
evaporated in the dry air of the plateau. Refreshments,
in the form of tea and wine, biscuits, dried fruits and
sweets, must be offered to the caller. Politeness demands that the latter shall not partake of these until
pressed several times to do so by his host.

Each call was a lengthy proceeding, the Tibetans
especially drawing out their visits for hours on occasion, as they expected to receive assistance from the
British against the exactions of the Chinese, and were
therefore prepared to do the British Representative
every possible honour. In Tibet, the longer a caller
remains the greater honour he does his host, especially
if he is of high rank. When a visitor took his departure
he was presented in turn with a white ceremonial
scarf.

In returning these calls the procedure was reversed.
The gifts I presented were usually imported goods
that were not easily obtainable in Tibet, such as
kerosene oil, English biscuits, wheaten flour, European
wines and liqueurs, sugar and soap, which were highly
appreciated by the Tibetans. In Tibet one must never
call empty-handed, at the very least a scarf must be
presented. All these presents cost money, and in order
that their representative shall not be out of pocket in
the matter, and to enable him to make suitable gifts,
the Government of India permit an entertainment
allowance. So much entertaining has to be done in
Tibet, however, that I personally always found that I
had to meet a portion of its cost from my own private

means. Prestige means a great deal in that country, and no course other than spending my own money was open to me. The Chinese especially gave the most lavish entertainments, and I could not allow my Government to " lose face " by failing to reciprocate in like style. Moreover, money thus spent was well spent, for I found that it was often easier to settle an important case, or to obtain information, after a good dinner than in the ordinary course of inquiry conducted officially.

After I had been in the Chumbi Valley for a few weeks the wives of the Tibetan Chinese officers began to call on my wife, and this was of the greatest help in cementing the friendship that was even thus early growing between myself and their husbands.

At the head of the Chinese administration in the Chumbi Valley was the Chinese Frontier Officer, Ma Shih Tou. He was assisted by an army officer, General Chou Ping Yuan, in command of the Chinese garrisons in that part of the country. A Commissioner of Customs, then Chung Yuk Tong, was stationed at Phema, some four miles below Yatung, at the junction of the two roads from India, one *via* the Jelap Pass, the other *via* the Nathu. This last officer had a good command of the English language, and I had many interesting talks with him, discussing both public and private affairs. This officer was ably assisted by Wangchuk Tsering, a Tibetan, who eventually succeeded him, but who, when the Chinese were forced out of Tibet, was later compelled to retire to Darjeeling, where he is now a landed proprietor. A detachment of fifty Chinese soldiers, under the command of a captain, watched over

D

the Indo-Tibetan trade route at Old Yatung, seven
miles within the Tibetan frontier, north of the Jelap
Pass. I also was provided with an escort of twenty-
five sepoys of the Indian army and a section of
Gurkha police. The latter were sent back to Gantok
in 1911, as the employment of Gurkhas for service
in Tibet was found to be unsuitable, owing to racial
prejudices between the two peoples. The sepoys were
supplied from the detachment at Gyantse, which was
under the command of an officer of the Indian army.

As British Trade Agent at Yatung, my jurisdiction
extended along the trade route from the Sikkim frontier,
at the Jelap and Nathu passes, to the Tang Pass,
beyond Pharijong, which commanded the head of the
Chumbi Valley. In addition to its military importance,
Pharijong is also the chief trade mart of southern
central Tibet. Were it possible to live in any comfort
in this place the British Trade Agency would have been
placed there. During and just after the Younghusband
Mission to Lhasa there was a Post at Pharijong,
but the sepoys of the garrison were so decimated by
pneumonia and kindred diseases, and the place was
so bleak and inhospitable, that it was abandoned.
Nowadays only a Post and Telegraph Master and his
assistant are permanently stationed in Pharijong, their
offices and quarters being located within the dak-
bungalow compound, away from the Tibetan town.
Pharijong is under the jurisdiction of two jongpens, or
magistrates, and these officials are responsible for the
collection of revenue, which is considerable, and the
administration of justice. Crops never ripen in Phari,
which is fifteen thousand feet above sea-level, the

summer being too short, and the climate too severe.
They are grown solely for the straw they provide for
the thousands of pack-animals that visit the place,
most of which are used in the wool trade. All grains
for food for man and beast have to be imported either
from the Chumbi Valley, Bhutan, or from near Gyantse.
Pharijong is important as it commands both the Indian
and Bhutan routes from the plateau.

Yatung, where the British Trade Agency is situated,
divides the Chumbi Valley into two parts, known as
Upper and Lower Tromo, the former including the
mart of Pharijong. The valley is drained by the Amo
Chu, which continues on through Bhutan, eventually
debouching on to the north Bengal plain, where
it is known as the Torsa. It finally runs into the
Brahmaputra. The Tromowas are a prosperous people,
especially those of the lower valley, where crops such
as barley, wheat, buckwheat, potatoes—which were
introduced by my wife—green vegetables, and so forth,
thrive. The inhabitants of the upper valley have their
wealth in immense herds of yak, which may be seen
grazing on the slopes of the valley sides below
Pharijong. Both divisions have a monopoly of the
wool-carrying trade within their own limits, and as this
route is the only outlet to the markets for several
hundred miles along the southern Tibetan frontier they
derive considerable wealth from this source. The
Chumbi Valley is one of the last strongholds of the old
Pre-Lamaist Bon worship, a form of Animism, and its
monasteries may be seen here. In these everything
is done in the opposite way from that of orthodox
Lamaism.

It is customary for the Buddhist as he chants his prayers to make his prayer-wheel move from right to left, in the direction the hands of a clock travel. This is in strict accordance with the orthodox view, whereas the Bonpo turns his prayer-wheel in the opposite direction. And while passing a mendong—a sacred wall on which is inscribed prayers—the Buddhist always passes in such a way that his right hand is nearest it, whereas the Bonpo passes alongside with his left hand next to it.

Up to the time of their expulsion from Tibet the Chinese controlled the Chumbi Valley, everything having to be sanctioned by them before the local Tibetan officials could engage in any project. They had garrisons placed at intervals along the valley, and the ruins of their barracks are still to be seen. The Tibetans have never occupied these buildings, and they are crumbling to ruin through lack of proper care and maintenance. The Chinese used to keep very careful statistics of all imports and exports that passed through Yatung, though they levied no duties there. Taxes on Tibetan exports were realised in Pharijong, while after the Younghusband Mission, up to the present time, no import duties have been levied on Tibetan goods imported into India. Up till 1904 it was practically impossible for any foreigner to get past all the Chinese guard-houses in the Chumbi Valley without a pass, and it was thus that the Chinese were able to enforce the policy of the isolation of Tibet as far as that frontier was concerned.

According to the Treaty of 1904 a Tibetan Trade Agent was appointed to each of the Treaty Trade Marts to work in conjunction with the British Trade Agent. In Yatung, after the departure of the Chinese, this official was at the head of the Tibetan administration of the valley. Executive duties were performed by the various village headmen, who were elected by their fellow-villagers. The Tibetan Trade Agent had an escort of thirty soldiers under the command of a rupon, or colonel, but I found that these men were, as a rule, used more as private servants than as soldiers. The Tibetan Trade Agent was assisted by the two Phari jongpens, whose office, incidentally, is considered one of the most lucrative in the whole of Tibet. A very junior officer, styled a traksho, was stationed at Khambu Jong, which commanded a branch of the Chumbi Valley, the Khambu route being the only possible way from the plateau into Yatung, other than the Phari-Gautsa route. The Tibetan Trade Agent had his headquarters at Pibithang, a village about three miles below the British Trade Agency. He had built his porch out across the only road, so that no trade could pass except through his compound. He used to levy quite unauthorised fees from all traders, usually in the form of presents in kind.

My duties in Yatung consisted of administering the Trade Mart, caring for the interests of British subjects trading in Tibet, and watching and forwarding reports on the political situation to the Government of India. As long as the Chinese were in Tibet the position was not easy. Each party, either Chinese or Tibetan, invariably disclaimed responsibility in any important matter, and it was most difficult to get decisions from them. I found that the best course was to invite each party in turn to a lunch at my house, and to get them to agree to my proposals. Occasionally quarrels broke out between the two parties, and I was constantly being called in to mediate—in other words, to save the Tibetans from degradation and punishment, for the latter always went to the wall when there was a dispute.

The territory allotted for the Trade Marts was inviolable, and British subjects residing thereon enjoyed extra-territorial rights. In all cases where a British subject was involved he had the right of trial before the British Trade Agent, the Tibetan Trade Agent, or his representative, sitting on the bench to watch over the interests of Tibetan subjects when such were parties to a case. Tibetan subjects who were resident in the British Trade Marts were handed over when necessary to the Tibetan authorities for punishment, as laid down in the provisions of the Treaty.

The climate of most of the Chumbi Valley is ideal, not unlike that of England, but with nothing like so much rain. The winters, of course, were colder. Yatung itself is a tiny place. Beyond the Agency House, the Post and Telegraph Office, the sepoy lines, and quarters for the Commissariat and Agency personnel, there is only the small bazaar.

By the end of 1909 I had succeeded in getting things running more or less smoothly in the valley. I had fostered friendships with both Chinese and Tibetan officials, who even at that time, so soon after my having taken over the Agency, began to refer purely personal matters to me for arbitration and advice. That I was thus able to gain their confidence was of the greatest assistance in my work, and, as events proved,

A TYPICAL TIBETAN VILLAGE IN THE CHUMBI VALLEY

enabled me to preserve order in the Chumbi Valley during the troubled times of 1910-1912, when the rest of central Tibet was in a ferment.

I had full magisterial authority, and was empowered to inflict even the death penalty. There was, moreover, no appeal from my judgments, save by reference to the Government of India direct. In cases where British and Tibetan nationals were jointly tried I was able to prevent a lot of the corruption that was practised in the native courts, whose decisions could always be purchased. One of my difficulties was in connection with Nepalese subjects involved in disputes in the Trade Mart courts. The Nepalese enjoyed extra-territorial rights in Tibet, and were entitled to have a magistrate of their own Government on the bench when a case in which they were involved was heard. There was, however, no Nepalese magistrate nearer than Gyantse, one hundred and thirty miles away, and it was in most instances not convenient—and in the case of poor litigants utterly impossible—for them to proceed to that place from Yatung for their cases to be tried. Nor would the Nepalese officer come down from Gyantse. It was finally decided that such cases should be tried by a panchayat, or committee, consisting of representatives of those nations whose nationals were concerned. The Nepalese agent agreed to enforce the decisions of such panchayats, provided they were held under my supervision.

Finding that this system worked well, the local Tibetans also began to bring purely private disputes to me for settlement and arbitration, and abided by my decisions—which were, of course, entirely unofficial.

By doing this many Tibetans were protected against the bribery of their own officials, and were at the same time assured of justice.

The Government of India had established a Trade Registration Post at Pibithang for the purpose of ascertaining the actual volume of trade passing up and down the Chumbi Valley, with a view to fixing, at some later date, when the business would justify it, import and export duties on goods entering and going from India. Such duties have not up to the present been established, and the Pibithang Registration Post was abolished in 1924, trade from that time being registered at Pedong, within Indian limits.

My quarters in Yatung consisted of the original three-roomed bungalow, with loopholed walls, which had been erected at the time of the Younghusband Mission in 1904, for the accommodation of the Assistant Political Officer then stationed in the valley. I soon found that this house was far too small for my growing family, and I had to add another four rooms, and a large, wide, glassed-in verandah. Even with this increased accommodation, when all my children were home for their holidays, we were cramped for space. I was not entirely alone in Yatung, for there were two British military telegraphists in charge of the Post and Telegraph Office, and in the early days of my stay a British Head Clerk of the Agency. There was also an itinerant Inspecting Telegraph Master, responsible for the maintenance in good condition of the telegraph line between the Indo-Sikkim frontier and Pharijong. The Chinese especially made great use of the telegraph while they were in Tibet ; in fact, the cost of the lengthy

messages they used to send almost daily to their
Government in Pekin nearly paid for the upkeep of
the Yatung section.   These Chinese telegrams were
mostly in code.   There was also telephonic communication between the various stages on the road all the
way from the Indian frontier to Gyantse, so that the
Trade Agents were never out of touch with their
headquarters for more than a few hours at a time.

In those days all travellers in Tibet were official, for
to other persons the country was still closed.   These
had to pass through Yatung on their way up and down
the line, and their visits served to break the monotony
of the daily round, and to introduce fresh topics of
conversation into our limited circle.   Travellers halted
in the dak-bungalow, where excellent accommodation
was available.   In fact, all along the route between
India and Gyantse first-class staging-houses, roughly
a day's march apart, have been erected by the Government of India, for the convenience of officers and others
travelling in Sikkim and Tibet.   I made it a rule always
to invite visitors to Yatung to my bungalow for at
least one meal, and in this way I had the pleasure of
meeting many interesting people.

The common people among the Tibetans were extraordinarily friendly, and were always ready to help me
and my family in every possible way.   My wife—by
distributing clothing and medicines, advising their
womenfolk, looking after them when they were sick,
and by finding work for them and for their children—
especially endeared herself to the hearts of the Chumbi
Valley peasantry.   The Tibetan is a likeable fellow,
always cheery, with a song on his lips, and will do

anything. He has no caste prejudices like the Hindu, in whose country a separate servant must be kept to do each individual task about the house. The Tibetan will turn his hand to everything, and with a little teaching will do good work.

Lamas from the local monasteries made a practice of calling on me at fixed intervals, and were always ready to entertain me and my family in return at their monasteries. In the Chumbi Valley one finds both sects of the Established Church, the Gelukpa and the Kagyupa, as well as the small communities of the followers of the Bon faith already alluded to.

English vegetables, introduced by my wife, did extraordinarily well, and nowhere else have I seen them grow to such a size while still retaining their flavour. We had to collect enough vegetables in the autumn, before the frosts set in, to carry us through the winter, as the expense of importing them from India was prohibitive.

I could not have wished for a more delightful spot in which to be stationed. My wife and I never missed the excitements and amusements of town life, for we were, and still are, lovers of the wild. We had all the company we desired in the visitors who came to Tibet, in the officials who were stationed in that country, and in our own children. The Tromowa, as the Chumbi Valley people are called, have undoubtedly a strain of Bhutanese and Sikkimese blood in their veins. They are different in appearance and manners from the Tibetans of the plateau, and have a much higher standard of living. Their houses are large and substantial, and they can afford, thanks to the fertility of

1. A NGAKPA LAMA OF SIKKIM

MEMBER OF A MYSTIC ORDER, WHO CLAIMS THE POWER OF BEING ABLE TO DISPEL ALL EVIL
SPIRITS. AS OCCASION DEMANDS A THIGH-BONE IS SOUNDED, OR A CANTATION IS DRONED TO THE
BEAT OF A DRUM.

2. GENERAL MIRU GYEPO, TIBETAN TRADE AGENT AT YATUNG

A FORMER COLLEAGUE OF THE AUTHOR.

their soil and their monopoly of the carrying trade, to import more of the luxuries and conveniences of life than their poorer upland brethren.

Formerly, the royal family of Sikkim used to spend the rainy season in the Chumbi Valley, to escape the very trying rains of Sikkim. None of the pests that make life unbearable in the latter country are found in Tibet. As late as 1912 the Sikkim ruler held estates in the Chumbi Valley, but in that year these were definitely resumed by the Tibetan Government, as for many years the Rajas had never come near them. At my intercession, however, these lands have since been granted as a fief to Raja Tsotra Namgyal of Tering, near Gyantse, a scion of the Sikkim royal house, now domiciled in Tibet. The Terings are the descendants of the late Maharaja of Sikkim, Sir Thutob Namgyal, and are, as a matter of fact, the senior branch of the family. All their interests, however, now lie in Tibet, from whence, as landed proprietors, they will never return to settle permanently in Sikkim.

CHAPTER FOUR

EVENTS of great political importance for Tibet
were brewing towards the end of 1909. In
December of that year the Dalai Lama, who, it
will be remembered, had fled to Mongolia and China
at the time of the 1904 expedition, returned to Tibet,
and took up his residence in the Potala. He had,
after wandering in Mongolia and China, been staying
in Pekin for some time as the guest of the Chinese
Emperor, and from what His Holiness told me afterwards he considered that he had been fortunate in
getting away from that city with his life. The Chinese
feared his growing influence with his own people, lest
he should utilise this as a lever for throwing off the
Chinese yoke.

It must be remembered that the present Dalai Lama
is the first during the past century of the pope-kings
of Tibet to reach and pass his majority. Very many of
his predecessors failed to reach governing age, probably
owing to the machinations of the Chinese, working
through the Tibetan regents, who had no desire to
hand over their powers to a young ruling prince.
Even after he had reached Lhasa, and was among his
own people, the Dalai Lama still did not feel safe,
and when he heard through spies that a force of two
thousand Chinese troops had been dispatched from

Pekin immediately after his own departure from that city, and that they were hard on his heels, he made all preparations for immediate flight should such a course become necessary. These troops had been sent to Tibet ostensibly to reinforce the Chinese garrisons in that country, and to police the Trade Marts. Their real objective was, however, undoubtedly the capture, and possibly the assassination, of the Dalai Lama, and the strengthening of the Chinese hold over Tibet. The advance party of these troops arrived in Lhasa at the end of January 1909, marking their entry into the city by firing on the crowd of Tibetan onlookers gathered to witness their arrival.

Whether, as the Chinese alleged later, the Tibetans interfered with their progress, or whether the trouble was deliberately brought about by the Chinese themselves, cannot now be definitely ascertained. Each party blamed the other. Among others a certain Tibetan official was wounded. The crowd ran for cover, offering no resistance, while the Chinese marched on to the yamen of their Ambans. These officers, as soon as they heard of the incident, made it the excuse for the immediate arrest of the Tibetan chief ministers, and sent troops to seize their persons. These latter, however, somehow found out what was afoot, and gathered at the Potala to consult with their ruler. A hasty council decided that the Dalai Lama, with his ministers, should take immediate flight to India. That the Tibetans were not entirely unprepared for the turn events were taking is to be seen from the translations of their letters contained in the Government Blue-book dealing with Sino-Tibetan affairs.

India was selected as the place of refuge, as it was the only country to which there was any hope of getting through. Moreover, the Prime Minister, the Lonchen Shata, had already visited Darjeeling in connection with the 1890 Treaty negotiations, and therefore knew something of the country. There was also the fact that a treaty existed between Tibet and the Government of India.

Hastily packing what treasure they could carry on their persons, the Dalai Lama and his ministers, with a very small following, rode out of the Potala at midnight on 12th February 1910. They had to make their move at once, before the arrival in Lhasa of the main body of the new Chinese troops, which could have invested the Potala. Travelling day and night, *via* Ralung and Kangma, thus avoiding the Chinese garrison at Gyantse, the refugees arrived safely at the Chatsa Monastery, some three miles north of Pharijong. By this time the Dalai Lama's following had increased to a hundred or so, many of them being armed. As soon as His Holiness had arrived at Chatsa, the Phari Jongpen telephoned to me at Yatung asking permission for that prelate to occupy the British dak-bungalow in Pharijong, and requesting me to ride up with my escort to protect him from the Chinese. In the meantime the Government of India had issued orders that all British officials in Tibet were to maintain an attitude of strict neutrality between the Chinese and Tibetans, and I was therefore unable to comply with the latter part of the Jongpen's request. I did, however, obtain permission from the Government for His Holiness to use the dak-bungalow. That it should become a sanctuary was forbidden.

Telegrams now came in from Gyantse informing me
that the Chinese Trade Agent in that city, Ma Chi Fu,
was in close pursuit of the Dalai Lama, having been
informed of his flight by special runner from Nagartse,
through which place the fugitives had passed at night.
The Chinese could have missed the Grand Lama at
Kangma only by a matter of hours. Owing probably
to the fact that he had taken refuge in the British
dak-bungalow in Pharijong, which they did not dare
to attack, and partly owing to the smallness of their
numbers, the Chinese in Phari did not attempt to
arrest His Holiness, but contented themselves with
watching his movements, while awaiting the arrival of
their troops from Gyantse and Lhasa. Meanwhile the
Chinese general from Choten Karpo, a village above
Yatung, proceeded to Pharijong with about sixty
soldiers. Though he certainly got to that town, for
some unknown reason he did not remain there.

By this time Tibetan levies, about three hundred
strong, had gathered at Phari, and more were arriving
every hour. The Dalai Lama, however, did not feel
safe in that place, and decided to push on to Yatung,
and there place himself under my protection. Of the
two possible routes between Pharijong and Yatung,
the Grand Lama, by divination, selected that which led
down the Chumbi Valley through Gautsa, and, despite
an exceptionally heavy snowfall during the night, left
the former place at dawn on 20th February 1910, with
a strong escort.

Those Chinese troops who had gone up from Choten
Karpo, and returned from Pharijong, under the
command of a general, joined forces with another body

dispatched from Old Yatung by the Chinese Frontier
Officer, and at Ta Karpo, a Chinese Post Office fourteen
miles below Pharijong, were awaiting the arrival of the
Dalai Lama and his party. They had received instructions to arrest the Dalai Lama and his ministers, and
to try to persuade them to return to Lhasa peacefully.
In the event of failure in the latter, their orders were
to slay the ministers, and take the Dalai Lama back to
his capital in strict custody. The ruins of Ta Karpo
Post Office are still to be seen above Gautsa.

At Dotak, between Pharijong and Ta Karpo, the
Dalai Lama was met by a further body of Tibetan
levies under the leadership of the Pishi Depon, the
Tibetan Trade Agent at Yatung. This official, in a
state of panic, had come to me the day before. He had
gathered all the men he could, and intended proceeding to his ruler's assistance as soon as possible, as the
Grand Lama had still to force his way past the Chinese
at Ta Karpo and Choten Karpo, which places could
not be avoided. The Pishi Depon was rather nervous
at the prospect of fighting, for he was not a warrior.
I myself am of the opinion that the great advantage
in numbers that the Pishi Depon's detachment gave to
the Tibetans prevented the Chinese attacking them,
thus saving much bloodshed, and the possible altera-
tion of Tibetan history. I also consider that had the
Chinese attacked in earnest the majority of the Tibetan
levies would have fled, leaving the Dalai Lama to his
fate.

Some hours before the Pishi Depon set out from
Yatung, Ma Shih Chao, the Chinese Frontier Officer,
accompanied by the Chinese general, had taken the

road for Pharijong. The former does not seem to have met His Holiness. The latter went right through at night to Pharijong, and endeavoured to persuade the Tibetan ministers to wait in that place. They, however, wisely would not listen to him, being fully aware that he was merely trying to gain time, and that a large body of Chinese troops was hot on their trail.

On the way down from Pharijong the Dalai Lama's escort came on the Pishi Depon's detachment round a corner in the road, and very nearly opened fire on them, mistaking them for Chinese, whom they knew were on the road. Their error was, fortunately, discovered before any damage was done, and the combined forces moved on to Yatung, their numbers preventing any interference from the Chinese. It was five o'clock in the afternoon, and quite dark, when the Dalai Lama reached Yatung. He came straight to the Agency House, and asked for British protection. I was thus the first living European to set eyes on the God-King of Tibet in his own country. He offered me a very large silk scarf, called nangdzo, and shook my hand. Even though tired out, worried, and uncertain whether he would be alive on the morrow, this ruler did not permit these things to interfere with his natural courtesy and politeness.

I had received instructions from the Government that if the Grand Lama claimed sanctuary in the Agency it was to be given to him, and I was therefore able to welcome him and to grant his request for protection while under my roof. For His Holiness's reception I had prepared my own bedroom, and I showed him into this, and offered him refreshments. Without the

E

slightest hesitation he accepted from my hand a cup
of milk, probably the first food he had ever taken
without it first being tasted by another for fear of
poison. He looked very tired after his journey from
Lhasa, which he had done in record time, but otherwise he looked quite well, though obviously very
worried. His six ministers were accommodated in
my sitting-room, as I had no spare bedroom available,
so limited was space in the small Agency House. The
Tibetan escort billeted itself in the Agency Bazaar
near by.

As a precaution against possible trouble I placed
a guard of my own sepoys round the Agency, a fact
which, I noted, gave intense satisfaction to His Holiness
and the ministers, who that night, I fancy, had the
first undisturbed sleep for many days. The situation,
however, remained quiet. During his stay with me the
Dalai Lama had all his meals at my own table, partaking
of all the English dishes served, exhibiting absolutely
no prejudices about food. He was eager, in view of
his visit to India, to learn what he could of European
manners, and took careful note of how to use our
crockery, cutlery, napery, and so forth. Immediately
on his arrival, the local Tibetans flocked to the Agency
in large numbers, to touch his horse, saddle, and any
article with which he had come into personal contact.
Such things were considered sacred owing to this
contact, and I had the greatest difficulty in preventing
devout worshippers from stealing everything in my
house. He solemnly blessed me, and all the members
of my family who were then with me, with both hands,
laying them on our heads, a privilege which gained me

considerable prestige among the Tibetans, for none but those of the highest rank among laymen are ever blessed thus.

I shared a bedroom with His Holiness, for he would not hear of my giving up my room entirely to himself. The close personal contact thus maintained with their ruler during his stay in the Chumbi Valley had a great deal to do with my influence in after years over all Tibetans with whom I had anything to do. That night the Lama was at first nervous, but I was able to reassure him as to his safety, and showed him the sentries pacing round the house. Before turning in, I visited the ministers in the next room, and found them all sitting up awake holding revolvers, acting as a bodyguard. Persuaded that their vigilance was unnecessary, they, too, lay down for a much-needed rest.

One reason that influenced me in giving protection to the Dalai Lama and his ministers was that I had received private information that the Chinese fully intended to slay the latter and to arrest the former. I was also told that there would be few questions asked by the Chinese Government if the Grand Lama himself happened to be killed as well. This, of course, was tantamount to his death-warrant should he fall into Chinese hands. Later, a price of ten thousand rupees was placed on the head of the Tibetan Prime Minister, the Lonchen Shata, but fortunately it was never claimed.

CHAPTER FIVE

*Arguments & Persuasions by the Chinese—Meeting of the Dalai Lama
& Chinese—Resumed Flight of the Dalai Lama—Arrival at
Gnatong—The Dalai Lama's Statement—Chensa Namgang*

THE next morning I received a letter from
Chung Yuk Tong, the Chinese Commissioner
of Customs, asking permission for Chinese
officers to occupy the dak-bungalow in Yatung. This
permission I readily granted. During the forenoon the
Chinese wrote asking if I would interview them, and
I agreed to do so, guaranteeing them safe conduct to
and from the Agency House. They were afraid of
the Tibetans at this time, as practically all their troops
were elsewhere, while the valley was full of Tibetan
levies. The officers, on ponies, had come ahead of
their soldiers.

When the Chinese arrived at the Agency they immediately asked me to arrange a conference between
themselves and the Tibetan ministers, and requested
permission to interview the Dalai Lama. The ministers
did confer with them, but only after a great deal of
argument and persuasion did the former allow any of
the Chinese to see His Holiness, and then only on the
strict understanding that I should be present, and that
they would ask no questions. The object of the Chinese
in asking for this audience was to assure themselves
that the Dalai Lama was really in Yatung, and not
merely a substitute playing his part.

They did their utmost to persuade the ministers not

68

to leave Tibet, but the latter were willing to remain only on condition that all the Chinese troops who had been dispatched from Lhasa and Gyantse in pursuit of His Holiness should be ordered back to their headquarters, and that the reinforcements which had arrived in the capital from China should be sent back to Pekin forthwith. As was to be expected, the conference ended in a deadlock, but the Chinese had gained a little time, and their troops were so much the nearer Yatung, which after all was the real object in asking for the conference.

Then came the matter of them seeing the Dalai Lama, who at first flatly refused to have anything to do with them. Only on my promising personally to search every one of the Chinese for concealed weapons, and to conduct them myself, one by one, into his presence, did he consent to receive them. Accordingly, having gone over each Chinaman very carefully, for my own satisfaction as much as for the Dalai Lama's, for I did not want a regrettable incident to occur in my house, while His Holiness was more or less under my protection, I led them one at a time into the Presence. Each of them offered the Dalai Lama a silk ceremonial scarf, receiving a bare nod of acknowledgment in return. The prelate uttered no word during the whole of the proceedings.

After they had left the Lama, the Chinese did their best to induce me to persuade him and his ministers to remain in Tibet. I, of course, refused to attempt to influence either party, Chinese or Tibetans. The Chinese officers then retired to the dak-bungalow, there to await the arrival of their troops from

Pharijong. Before leaving the Agency they assured the Tibetan ministers that they would telegraph the conditions on which the former were willing to remain in Tibet to the Chinese Government, asking them to await a reply from Pekin, which would arrive in a day or two. The Chinese never telegraphed anything of this nature, their only object in making the statement being to gain time for their soldiers to arrive.

On the afternoon of 21st February 1910 I read and translated a telegram addressed to the Dalai Lama by the Pharijong headmen to the effect that the main body of Chinese troops was then crossing the Tang Pass, eight miles from Pharijong. This meant that, by doing a forced march, they would be in Yatung by the evening of the next day.

It now became imperative, if the Grand Lama and his ministers wished to escape from Tibet, for them to cross the frontier into Sikkim without further delay. In that country, which was a protectorate under the Government of India, the armed forces of China dared not follow them. The Tibetan ministers begged me to accompany His Holiness on this last stage of his flight, and to take my military escort with me, but this, of course, in pursuance of the instructions regarding neutrality I had received from the Government of India, I was unable to do.

Meanwhile, from Pharijong, the Tibetan officials in that place had telegraphed to the Dalai Lama asking if it was his wish that they should attack the Chinese. I strongly advised him to forbid this, as it would only result in the badly armed Tibetan levies being wiped out by the more numerous and greatly superior armed

Chinese. Moreover, no useful purpose would be served, owing to his decision to fly from Tibet. His Holiness sent orders in accordance with my advice.

Early next morning I informed the Dalai Lama that information had just been received that the Chinese troops were about to leave Pharijong. He was still in bed when I gave him this news, and he hurriedly arose, dressed, and prepared to take the road. His ministers also lost no time in getting ready, and within an hour the whole party, muffled to the eyes, to escape the recognition of which member was the Dalai Lama, left the Agency for the Jelap Pass. They were escorted by the Tibetan militia, and succeeded in reaching the frontier safely. They had a very rough journey across the pass, for it was snowing hard when they left Yatung, and continued so the whole day. Once they reached the frontier the militia returned, leaving the Lama and his six ministers to travel on alone.

The party arrived at Gnatong, the first village in Sikkim, after nightfall, in a snowstorm. I had telephoned to the two British military telegraphists who were posted there to keep a look-out for His Holiness, and to report his arrival. I quote the actual words of one of these typical pre-war British Tommies, in describing the arrival of the Grand Lama of Tibet in Gnatong.

" Me an' Tubby," reported this military telegraphist, "was sittin' in front of the office fire abart eight pip emma, when we 'ears someone knockin' at the door.

" ' 'Oo's thet? ' I shouts, an' gets no arnswer.

" Arter a bit we 'ears another knock on the door, an'

I gets up an' opens it. I sees seven Tibs standin' there. ' An' 'oo the 'ell er you? ' I asks.

" ' I'm the Dally Larmer ! ' one of 'em says.

" 'Ho ! Yus ! ' I arnswers, ' yer the Dally Larmer, are yer? I've 'eard abart you ! Come in an' 'ave er cup er tea ! '

" An' 'e comes in an' sits darn in front er the fire an' 'as a nice 'ot cup er tea. The other coves stands up rarnd the walls, an' wouldn't sit darn ! The ole bloke made us bring our rifles in an' keep 'em in a corner, while 'e dossed darn in front er the fire ! We gave 'im what grub we 'ad, but it wern't much. 'E left early next mornin' ! "

And so the priest-king of Tibet, a fugitive from his country, was watched over by two British Tommies, who took his arrival as a matter of course in the duties of the day. How he and they managed to understand each other passes my comprehension, but it takes a lot to defeat the British soldier.

Before leaving Yatung, the Dalai Lama handed me a statement regarding his flight, which I at once translated and forwarded to the Foreign Office in Simla. It ran as follows : " The Chinese have been greatly oppressing the Tibetan people in Lhasa. Chinese mounted infantry arrived there and fired on the people, killing and wounding them. I was obliged, with my six ministers, to make good my escape. My intention is now to go to India for the purpose of consulting the British Government. Since my departure from Lhasa I have been greatly harassed on the road by Chinese troops. A force of two hundred Chinese infantry was behind me at the Chaksam Ferry, and I

1. AUTHOR IN LÁMA'S DRESS

2. GENERAL PISHI

FORMERLY TIBETAN TRADE AGENT AT YATUNG, NOW POSTMASTER-GENERAL OF TIBET.

left a small party there to hold them back. A fight took place there, in the course of which two Tibetans and seventy Chinese were killed. I have left a Regent and acting ministers at Lhasa, but I and the ministers who are with me have brought our seals with us. I have been receiving every courtesy from the British Government, for which I am grateful. I now look to you for protection, and I trust that the relations between the British Government and Tibet will be those of a father towards his child. Wishing to be guided by you, I hope to give full information on my arrival in India."

The Viceroy, in telegraphing this message to the Secretary of State for India, remarked: "The Trade Agent's attitude has been scrupulously correct"—*vide* Blue-book, East India, Tibet, Telegram No. 311 (1910).

When departing from Yatung, His Holiness and his ministers thanked me warmly for my help and advice, and insisted that they would be my lifelong friends, which promise those of them who remain alive have kept. In the afternoon of the day on which the Dalai Lama left the Chumbi Valley, the Chinese Trade Agent from Gyantse, with a small escort of troopers, arrived in Yatung, having pushed on ahead of the main body of Chinese troops. As soon as he found that His Holiness had made good his escape this official completely ignored my existence.

Two days later I received a letter by hand from the Phari Jongpen, stating that the bearer of the note was a devoted adherent of the Dalai Lama, named Chensa Namgang. The Chensa wanted to join his ruler across the frontier, and I was asked to help him to do this.

Namgang had been left in command of the party detailed to fight the delaying action at the Chaksam Ferry, and had certainly put up a splendid resistance, holding the Chinese up for several hours with only a handful of troops. It was by this action that the Dalai Lama had been able to get well ahead of his pursuers. After the fight was over, the Chensa ordered his men to disperse and hide themselves in the neighbouring villages, while he rode day and night to overtake his ruler. The Chinese were keeping a close watch for him, as it was known that he would make for India. However, disguised as a muleteer, he managed to elude their sentries.

Since that time the Chensa, now risen to be one of the chief ministers of Tibet, has been my firm friend. He has always exhibited strong pro-British sympathies, and has been the sponsor of many reforms, and the introducer of many Western ideas into Tibet. These sympathies have, however, recently cost him his position as Commander-in-Chief of the Tibetan Forces, though he still remains a chief minister.

The Chensa had been sent on to Pharijong by Captain (now Lieutenant-Colonel) Weir, then the British Trade Agent at Gyantse. It may be mentioned here that Lieutenant-Colonel and Mrs Weir paid a visit to Lhasa in 1930, and were well received by the Dalai Lama.

CHAPTER SIX

CAPTAIN WEIR, the British Trade Agent at Gyantse, was in March 1911 appointed Acting Political Officer, and posted to Gantok, in Sikkim, while I was given charge of both the Yatung and Gyantse Trade Agencies for a period of three months.

Events directly affecting Tibet were now happening in China. It must be noted here that, from the time he left his country, the Dalai Lama had been constantly working through emissaries with the object of freeing Tibet from Chinese domination. An interesting fact concerning the revolution in China is that the Tibetans firmly believe that the Emperor was overthrown because of his action in driving the god-king of Tibet from his country. The Dalai Lama had, it is true, left a Regent and acting ministers to carry on the government in his name, but these were soon rendered powerless by the Chinese Ambans, who completely dominated the country. The latter were able to overawe the Lhasa populace by their troops, of which at this time there must have been a considerable number in the capital.

In November 1911 came the overthrow of the Monarchy and the establishment of the Republic in China. The immediate effects of this, as far as Tibet was concerned, were that the Chinese garrison and officials in

75

that country were left without orders or pay. Chaos reigned in their motherland, and the trouble quickly spread to the Chinese in Tibet. Dissensions broke out among the officials, some declaring for the Monarchy, others upholding the Republic. The Tibetans were quick to take advantage of this state of affairs.

Trouble first broke out between the two nationalities in the Chumbi Valley, where, fortunately, I happened to be at the time. One bitterly cold morning in November a Chinese non-commissioned officer arrived at my house in a most agitated condition, and besought me to protect him from his fellow-soldiers. From what I could gather, he was a monarchist, and his comrades, who were republican, were pursuing him. It appeared from his statement that, in accordance with their political beliefs, the rank and file of the Choten Karpo garrison had mutinied, had seized the persons of their monarchist officers, and looted their belongings. They had tied their commander to a stake, with the avowed intention of torturing him to death. The troops also demanded their arrears of pay, which, of course, the officers were unable to give. I was powerless to assist him in any way, having strict orders not to interfere. The Government of India, rightly, were very strict in the matter of their representatives in Tibet mixing in any way with the affairs of that country except when they directly affected the safety or treatment of British subjects or policy. The Chinese non-commissioned officer left the Agency, and I never saw him again. I assume that he made his way out of Tibet through Sikkim, to India.

Two days later the commanding officer of the

Choten Karpo garrison managed to escape, and he also fled to me for protection. He did not wish to desert his post, but since he could do no good by remaining in Tibet he decided to make his way to China, *via* India. I heard later that he had somehow managed to reach China.

It was not long before the Chinese garrison of Choten Karpo, short of food and money, began to loot the neighbouring Tibetan villages, intimidating their remaining officers into acquiescence. When this looting began, as was usual whenever there was any trouble, the Tibetans came straight to me. The headmen of the affected villages asked me if they should kill the Chinese, but I advised them to do this only in defence of their lives. No one could tell at that time which way the wind of power would blow, and the Tibetans would have been extremely ill-advised to attack the small garrison of Choten Karpo, a proceeding that might have brought down on them the wrath of the Chinese in the Lower Chumbi Valley. It was better to lose a few goods and provisions than for the whole valley to be embroiled in a cut-throat conflict. After all, China was still master of Tibet.

The headmen returned to their villages saying that they would do their best to prevent bloodshed, but I heard next day that there had been fighting in which both sides had suffered casualties, several Chinese also having been taken captive. These latter unfortunates had, I was informed, been suspended from beams by their thumbs only, with their toes just touching the ground, as a reprisal for their looting of the Tibetans' houses.

On hearing this, I suggested to the Tibetans that, instead of torturing their prisoners, it might be wiser to keep them confined. I warned them that, if this kind of thing went on, the Chinese in Lhasa and Gyantse would certainly revenge themselves on inoffensive Tibetans in those places. The prisoners later escaped, with, I think, the connivance of their captors, who did not wish to go to the expense of feeding them for an indefinite period, and who, after my warning, were afraid to kill them. These Chinese soldiers afterwards came to me and asked my assistance, and I was able to send most of them to India, where many of them settled down, especially in Darjeeling and Kalimpong.

A week later the Chinese at Old Yatung, the frontier post, decided that there was nothing to be gained by remaining in Tibet without pay, and in the midst of a hostile people. They sold their rifles, ammunition and equipment to the local Tibetans, and marched over the Jelap Pass to India. It is worthy of note that in no case where the Chinese disposed of their arms to the Tibetans did the latter ever use the weapons against the sellers. Feeling against the Chinese was steadily growing all over Tibet, and it needed but a spark to set burning the fire of massacre and reprisal wherever the Chinese were to be found. Most of the Chinese had taken Tibetan women to wife and, through the latter, information of all that was afoot was not long in reaching them. At the same time, it must also be remembered that there was within Tibet itself a party of Tibetans who did not wish to see the Chinese driven from the country, as it meant the loss of lucrative positions held by them under the Chinese administration. These persons were regarded with disfavour by the Tibetan Government, and naturally desired the Chinese to retain their power in Tibet.

Chung Yuk Tong, the Chinese Customs Commissioner, the very man who formerly had adopted a very aloof and superior attitude towards everything British, after my refusal to persuade the Dalai Lama to remain in Tibet, was now compelled to seek refuge with me at the Trade Agency. His fellow-countrymen, knowing that he had large sums of Chinese Government money in his possession, desired this to finance their escape into India. They surrounded his house, with the intention of murdering him and making off with all they could loot. Fortunately for himself, he received word from a friend of what was afoot, and just managed to get out of his yamen before it was surrounded. He succeeded in reaching the British Trade Agency, where he remained for a fortnight, managing at length to cross the frontier in disguise. He lost everything he possessed.

He was accompanied by the Chinese postmaster from Lhasa, and several junior officers from the Gyantse garrison, who arrived in Yatung about this time. With this party was a friend of mine, the Chinese schoolmaster from Gyantse, a very likeable young man, typical of the Young China that was responsible for the revolution. This unfortunate youth, however, was suspected of being a ringleader of the republicans in Tibet by the Chinese Trade Agent at Gyantse, who hired a Chinese assassin to murder him at Yatung. He was shot in the back, his murderer making good his

escape to India. Very ill-advisedly the assassin returned to the Chumbi Valley to receive the blood-money
promised for the work, which had been remitted by
money-order from Gyantse, through the British Post
Office. He had not been in the valley a day before
the friends of the late schoolmaster found and killed
him in revenge. Both murdered and murderer lie side
by side in the Chinese cemetery at Pibithang, three
miles below Yatung.

Trouble then began in Pharijong, and the Jongpen
of that place, which fell in the sphere of the Yatung
Agency, wired asking me to go there and prevent
bloodshed. I had to refuse, as such action on my part
was forbidden by Government. I did, however, speak
privately on the telephone and advise the Jongpen not
to interfere with the Chinese except in self-defence. I
also told him to try to persuade them to come down
to Yatung.

My advice was followed, and the Chinese garrison
of Pharijong, armed to the teeth, shortly afterwards
arrived in the Chumbi Valley. The situation that then
arose was not without its humour. The Tibetan Trade
Agent at Yatung, the Pishi Depon, and the commander
of the Chinese were each frightened of the other, and
came at different times to the Agency House to request
protection each against the other. Eventually, I
managed to get them together, and soon had them
talking. Finally, they arrived at the point where the
Chinese wanted to sell the Depon thirty rifles and some
ammunition, but further disagreement occurred over
the price. I thereupon told them both that I washed
my hands of the whole affair, and that they could go

and fight matters out. I sent them to the Agency Bazaar, where, after a lot of haggling, as I knew would be the case, a price of fifty Indian rupees per rifle was agreed on, the ammunition being thrown in free. As soon as the purchase money was paid the Chinese handed over the rifles, and moved out of Tibet to India.

CHAPTER SEVEN

The Tibetan as a Fighting Man—Appeals from Both Sides—The Problem solved—Agreement between China & Tibet—A Breach of Faith—Flight of the Tashi Lama

MR C. A. BELL, I.C.S., returned to Gantok in June 1911, and resumed charge as Political Officer in Sikkim. Captain Weir resumed charge of his substantive appointment as British Trade Agent, Gyantse, but was there for only a few months, during which time affairs remained quiet. He then proceeded on long leave. He was nearly three years in Tibet, and was liked and respected by the Tibetans. As soon as he had gone down to India the general unrest among the Chinese spread to Gyantse. I again held dual charge of the Gyantse and Yatung Agencies. On receiving information that trouble was brewing I went with all haste to the former place, in the hope of settling matters between the Chinese and Tibetans peaceably. Prior to my arrival the Gyantse Tibetans had sent a body of troops to prevent the Chinese garrison of Shigatse from joining up with that of Gyantse. This move was the signal for the opening of hostilities. Conditions in Gyantse were different from those in the Chumbi Valley, for in the former place there was a permanent detachment of regular Tibetan troops, and numerous levies were available for action against the Chinese.

One would not class the average Tibetan soldier as

a good fighting man, for he is untrained, badly armed and badly led, but once started on a project he will see it through to the end, even though he may die. The Tibetans are persuaded to this last course by the fact that their Government, having issued certain orders, will take absolutely no excuse for them not being carried out. Failure means severe punishment.

On inquiry, it appeared that a body of Tibetan troops had set out to ambush a party of Chinese coming to Gyantse from Shigatse, and for this purpose had hidden themselves in a house at Yayegang, near the famous hermitage of Nyangto Kyiphu, some twelve miles from the former place. From this vantage-post they fired on the passing Chinese, who at once returned their fire. The Chinese then attacked the house, and killed several Tibetans, among them the second-in-command of the party. Finding, however, that they would have some difficulty in forcing an entrance, the Chinese were about to set fire to the building, when the Tibetans threw down a white scarf, intimating that they surrendered. They were disarmed, tied pigtail to pigtail, and marched into Gyantse. There, after an inquiry by the Chinese, thirty-six of them were shot, and their commander beheaded. I arrived just as this had happened, too late to prevent it.

A body of Chinese troops from Lhasa, roughly one hundred in number, shortly afterwards arrived to reinforce the Gyantse garrison, and fighting between the Chinese and Tibetans became general. The first act of the Chinese was to capture the Tibetan jong, and to establish themselves therein. On no occasion during the whole of the Sino-Tibetan troubles was any attack made, or even threatened, against the British Trade Agencies, by either party. The Chinese soon found that their position in the jong was untenable, by reason of the Tibetans cutting off their water-supply. They were thus forced to evacuate this strong position and take shelter in a much more exposed place, the paper factory at the foot of the hill on which the jong is situated, and which is entirely commanded by the latter.

Officers of both sides came regularly to call on me at the Agency, and, despite my constantly reiterated declaration of strict neutrality, were always trying to persuade me to assist their respective sides. From a humanitarian standpoint I did what I could to minimise the casualties and the cruelties, but there was only one conclusion possible in the matter from the very start —the extermination of the Chinese, who had no hope of support from their own country. That the Chinese could still strike fear into the Tibetans was evidenced by the fact that they sent an ultimatum to the Abbot of the Palkhor Chhöde Monastery, in Gyantse, that, unless the Tibetan troops who had been given shelter in that institution were turned out, the monastery would be burned to the ground. These soldiers were at once sent away by the lamas. The day the Chinese evacuated the jong I rode out alone to see what was happening. Fortunately for myself I was wearing a white sola topee, and this fact saved me from death, or at least from being wounded, for unwittingly I got between the Chinese and Tibetans, who were firing at each other. As soon as they saw my hat, the only one of its kind in the place, both parties ceased fire until I was out of the danger zone.

Tibetan troops in considerable numbers now began to arrive from the country north of Gyantse, gathered by Chensa Namgang, of Chaksam Ferry fame. With these soldiers the Tibetans were able to surround the paper factory. One afternoon an English-speaking Chinese, named Su-Ez, made his way to the British Trade Agency. " Old man ! " he said. " Save us ! "

He was almost abject in his prayers for protection, and begged to remain in the Agency. I gathered that the Chinese were in a very bad way at this time, with no food, and almost no water, but I could not afford him asylum in our Post. In a similar way I had to refuse sanctuary to a Tibetan officer, Jongpen Shakjang, a fifth-rank official, who asked me to protect him. Both Chinese and Tibetans requested me to conduct negotiations between them, but this I was officially not able to do. Both parties feared some kind of treachery should they come to an agreement that was not made under my supervision, and they used to come to the Agency to discuss terms, using me as a medium.

One day both the Chinese and Tibetan delegates arrived at the Post together, and, having greeted each other with the utmost punctiliousness, announced their desire to come to a definite understanding. The position seemed to be that while the Chinese had good modern rifles and plenty of ammunition they had no food. On the other side, to force their opponents out of the paper factory the Tibetans would have to cross a wide field of fire, and would certainly suffer many casualties in doing so. The proposal now was that the Chinese should deposit their weapons with me, and that as soon as the Tibetans had deposited ten thousand rupees, as payment for these, I should hand the rifles over to the Tibetans, and the cash to the Chinese, who undertook to leave Tibet without giving further trouble. On their part, the Tibetans promised to provide the Chinese with free transport and rations as far as the frontier at the Jelap Pass.

Deciding that something ought to be done to stop the useless slaughter that was going on, I assisted unofficially at the negotiations. The actual transaction took place the next day at the Gyantse dak-bungalow, which was situated midway between the headquarters of the opposing parties. My colleague, the Nepalese representative, Lieutenant Lal Bahadur, was also present. This officer was afterwards promoted to the charge of the Nepalese Agency in Lhasa. For some reason the Tibetans were at first annoyed at his presence, but, as events proved, it was fortunate that he was there. When the argument over the price to be paid for the rifles grew heated, and it seemed that negotiations would fall through, he broke into the conversation in halting Tibetan, which language he was then learning, and his clumsiness in phraseology raised a roar of laughter, which relieved the tension of the situation.

The problem was eventually solved by the Tibetans paying over, on the spot, nine thousand two hundred and fifty Chinese rupees, and receiving in exchange one hundred and forty-four rifles, plus a large quantity of ammunition. The demand for free transport and rations was also agreed upon. At that time the Chinese rupee was worth only three-quarters of the value of the Indian coin of the same denomination.

Four copies of an Agreement were drawn up, and

signed by the Chinese and Tibetan leaders, and by the Nepalese representative and myself as private witnesses. I give below a translation of this document, as it is of some interest. The Agreement was written both in Chinese and Tibetan, the latter text having been translated here.

AGREEMENT BETWEEN THE CHINESE AND TIBETANS

The modern drilled Chinese troops have committed excesses on Tibetan subjects at various times. Firstly, they attacked the escort of His Holiness the Dalai Lama, and when they were about to be defeated offered proposals for peace through Mr Macdonald, the British representative, and also through the Nepalese representative, requesting mediation between themselves and the Tibetans.

As they pressed the matter, the Tibetan civil and military officers could not refuse their requests, especially in view of the advice tendered by the British and Nepalese agents, although the behaviour of the Chinese troops was such that they deserved to be driven out of the country by force of arms.

Article 1.—The Chinese undertake not to commit further excesses, and promise to act in a friendly manner. They will not create any disturbance, nor ill-treat any Tibetan subjects. They promise to return to China through India, and none of them shall remain in Tibet.

Article 2.—The Tibetan authorities undertake that all wounded Chinese soldiers shall, as soon as they are well enough to travel, be provided with riding and baggage animals, and escorted to the Sikkim-Tibet frontier, whence they shall return to China. They further undertake not to molest or persecute in any way the Tibetan wives of the Chinese, should these women desire to remain in Tibet.

Article 3.—As the Chinese are penniless, and without food, they have sold one hundred and forty-four rifles to the Tibetan officers, in consideration of a cash payment of nine thousand two hundred and fifty Chinese rupees, which have been paid to them by the Tibetan authorities. The Chinese will not be permitted to raise any questions on this matter afterwards.

Article 4.—The Chinese troops undertake not to remain in Pharijong or in the Chumbi Valley on any pretext whatever. They shall not say that they have been ordered to do so by their officers, nor make any other excuses.

Both parties, Chinese and Tibetans, have settled all questions, and this treaty will be drawn up in quadruplicate. If the Chinese fulfil these conditions they shall be provided with free riding and baggage animals, and responsible officers will be detailed to escort them to the frontier.

———

This document was signed and sealed by the following officers :

For the Chinese.—Major PHAN and Major AI FE SI, the officer commanding the Chinese troops.

For the Tibetans.—The TELING DEPON, the civil officer, So NOR, and the monk officials, YESHE NGAKWANG, LOBSANG and TAMDRING WANGYAL.

David Macdonald, British Trade Agent at Gyantse, and Lieutenant Lal Bahadur, Nepalese representative,

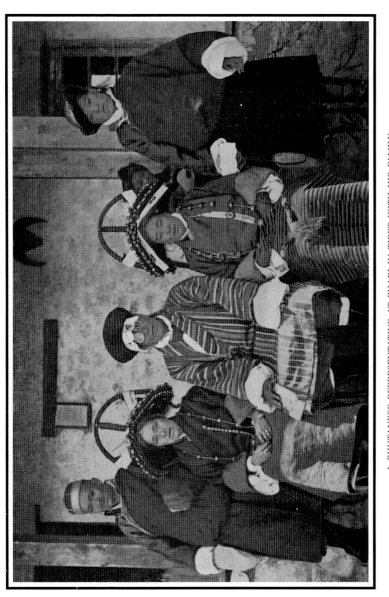

A BHUTANESE REPRESENTATIVE AT PHARI IN TIBET WITH HIS FAMILY.

signed as witnesses. The Agreement was dated 3rd
April 1912. Two of the monk officials who signed
this document were afterwards promoted by the Dalai
Lama, who thus showed his approval of the methods
employed to get the Chinese out of Gyantse. Yeshe
Ngakwang was made a full general, while Lobsang
was promoted to the fourth rank as a Khenchung, and
posted to Chiamdo, in Eastern Tibet, a most important
frontier station. My colleague, the Tibetan Trade
Agent, was not, I am afraid, a very courageous man,
for during the troubles with the Chinese in Gyantse
he hid himself in the Ganden Rito hermitage, just
outside the city. He was shortly afterwards superseded
by Khenchung Lobsang Jungne, a monk official, who
was my colleague for very many years, and who still
holds the post of Tibetan Trade Agent at Gyantse. He
is a cultured man, and has travelled widely in China
and Mongolia with the Dalai Lama, with whom he was
a great favourite. He has retained his ruler's confidence
through all the storms that have swept across the
political stage in Lhasa.

Once they had received the money for their arms
the Chinese left Gyantse, and reached India without
any serious trouble. As they marched out of the city
the populace gathered in large numbers, and, amid
scenes of great rejoicing, threw dust after them, thus
delicately implying that they were no more than devils.
But there were some who were sorry to see them go.

At Pharijong the Jongpen held up the unarmed
Chinese, and wired to the Tibetan ministers then in
Darjeeling asking if he should massacre them or let
them go. The ministers drafted a reply to the effect

that if the Chinese were weak they should all be killed, but that if they were strong they should be allowed to depart in peace. This was a deliberate breach of faith, and the authorities in Darjeeling did not allow this reply to be telegraphed. On hearing of the matter I also took action, and had a heart-to-heart talk with the Tibetan commander at Gyantse, who eventually ordered the Phari Jongpen, by telephone, not to harm the Chinese in any circumstances, as a treaty had been made with them. This incident is a striking example of the peculiar mentality of the Tibetans, who consider that if they themselves are not personally concerned in an affair they are not bound to accept or adhere to arrangements and undertakings entered into on their behalf by others. For the repatriation and reception of the Chinese refugees from Tibet arrangements were made by the Government of India. Many of them settled down at Kalimpong, where they followed the trades of boot-making, wood-working and cooking, in preference to returning to their own country.

After the conference in Gyantse both Chinese and Tibetans sent word to their compatriots in Shigatse to cease hostilities, as peace had been made. Despite these instructions, however, the Chensa Namgang, who had returned to Tibet, attacked the Chinese in the Shigatse fort, but was beaten off with heavy loss.

After this futile effort a treaty similar to that made in Gyantse was effected between the Chinese and Tibetans in Shigatse, the former selling their arms and ammunition in order to obtain funds for their journey to China. They went down to India by the same route as their Gyantse confrères.

During the fighting in Shigatse and its environs some stray bullets had struck the walls of the Tashilhunpo Monastery, where the Tashi Lama was in residence. This prelate, alarmed for his safety, promptly fled towards Khamba Jong, a town on the northern Sikkim-Tibet frontier. I was in Gyantse at the time, and a courier arrived with a letter addressed to me from His Serenity asking me to meet him at Kala, a staging-post on the Gyantse-Pharijong road, on a matter of life and death. As things were quiet in Gyantse I was able to proceed at once to Kala, but on arrival there I was told that the Tashi Lama was at a monastery a day's journey away. He requested me to meet him there. I got to this monastery only to find that the Lama had again gone on, and, despite my making forced marches, I did not succeed in catching him up before he reached Khamba Jong. This was in March 1912. I had met the Tashi Lama before this, when he was returning from Lhasa to Shigatse, *via* Gyantse, after his visit to the capital on the occasion of the flight of the Dalai Lama in 1910.

His Serenity was very glad to see me, and so were his ministers, whom I knew fairly well. I had, too, been in more or less regular correspondence with the Tashi Lama, who apologised for not waiting for me in Kala as arranged, but he gave no reasons for breaking this appointment. He asked me what course he should pursue in these troublous times, and I strongly advised him to return to Tashilhunpo and to remain there quietly, watching events. After considering for a while he decided to do so, especially as I pointed out to him that to absent himself from Shigatse at this time would only lead to his being suspected of pro-Chinese sympathies. His enemies would be certain to connect the departure of the Chinese and the Lama's flight. His Serenity invited me to lunch with him. The meal was simple, consisting of tukpa, or spaghetti, cooked in soup, roasted mutton, and butter-tea. He himself drank out of a gold-lined wooden cup. Before I left Khamba Jong — I stayed only one day — the Tashi Lama presented me with a fine riding-mule. I returned post-haste to Gyantse, travelling direct, and not by the circuitous route *via* Kala by which I had come.

Mr B. J. Gould, I.C.S., arrived in March 1912, to take over the duties of British Trade Agent at Gyantse, and I returned to Yatung to my substantive appointment there. The situation in Tibet, with the exception of the capital, was now quiet. As I came into Yatung the last of the Chinese from that part of the country were being evacuated over the frontier. After a brief halt in Yatung I went on to Darjeeling, where I again met the Dalai Lama and his ministers. They asked me all about the situation in Tibet, and inquired what were the prospects for their return. I was able to make only non-committal replies. I returned to Yatung at the end of May 1912.

CHAPTER EIGHT

The Dalai Lama at the Agency House—Routine of the Dalai Lama—
Lamas at variance—The Dalai Lama's Tutor—Missions &
Propaganda—A Conference—Proposals to depose the
Dalai Lama—Tashi Lama's Entry into Gyantse
—Tashi Lama's Explanation

IN June 1912 the Dalai Lama's advisers considered
that the time was ripe for His Holiness to return to
Tibet. I received information that he was arriving
in the Chumbi Valley, and rode out with my escort
some six miles to receive him. His ministers had
written from Kalimpong that the Lama had expressed
the wish to stay with me while he was in Yatung, and
wanted the same rooms that he had used during his
flight, over two years before. I reported this request
to the Government of India, and was instructed to
conform to the Dalai Lama's wishes in this matter.

To make room for him and his party in the Agency
House I had to shift my family across to the dak-
bungalow, as accommodation was required for about
twelve people. The Dalai Lama's visit was, of course,
a great honour for the people of the Chumbi Valley,
among whom he remained for nearly a week. Every
day of his stay crowds of Tibetans presented themselves
with gifts of all kinds, and solicited his blessing. One
day was specially set aside for blessing the actual
inhabitants of the valley, and as the house was small,
and the crowd great, His Holiness came outside and
touched each one's head with a red silk tassel attached

to a short wooden rod. The people were formed up into a queue, and passed before him one at a time by the officials of the Lama's suite. As each supplicant bowed before him he laid a scarf, containing a gift of money tied into one corner, at the prelate's feet. In this way considerable sums were collected, for everybody contributed as much as he or she could afford, for it was not every day that the Grand Lama of Tibet came to the Chumbi Valley country. Judging by the reverence displayed by the crowds, and by the numbers that flocked into Yatung to see him, the Dalai Lama was very greatly respected by his people, who regard him as an actual god on earth.

One morning the Dalai Lama asked me to accompany him to Phema, a village four and a half miles below Yatung, as he had been invited by a prominent trader to bless his family and his house. The ministers told me that such a proceeding was very unusual, as it was not the custom for His Holiness to visit any but the greatest houses in the land, and even those very seldom, but that an exception was being made in the present case. After having received the Lama's blessing the trader presented him with a bag containing certainly not less than three thousand Indian rupees, a very acceptable *douceur* after a morning's ride.

When staying in my house the Dalai Lama's daily routine was as follows. He rose at about five in the morning, and spent an hour or so in private prayer. After this his chaplain prepared *torma*, or rice offerings to the gods, which were used in certain ceremonies, and then thrown away. There was great competition among

my Tibetan servants to secure these leavings, as they
are considered very holy. The mere possession of
them was considered to bring good fortune. During
the celebration of this private worship I could hear the
tinkle of His Holiness's bell and the rattle of his skull-
drum, as he invoked the spirits. After breakfast, taken
with me in European fashion, the Dalai Lama attended
to correspondence and issued orders on reports prepared
by his ministers.

During the morning he also spent an hour or so
blessing the people. In the afternoon he would chat
to me about politics and religion. He told me, one day,
that what had impressed him as much as anything
during his wanderings in exile was the fact that
wherever there were British people there was a church,
and from this observation he concluded that they were a
people who devoted much of their time to the pursuit
of religion, and that therefore they and the Tibetans,
who were a like-minded race, should always be in
harmony. It is a fact that, as far as outward observation
of religious matters and practices goes, the Tibetans
are a deeply religious people. Their whole lives are
bound up in their faith. One of the main grievances
they harboured against the Chinese was the latter's
disregard of religion and their contemptuous treatment
of sacred objects in Tibet.

Towards the end of his stay with me His Holiness
received a letter from the Government of India, which
assured him that if he faithfully observed the provisions of the 1904 treaty, and those of the Trade
Regulations of 1908, the autonomy of Tibet would be
respected in every way. This letter appeared to give

him much pleasure, and set at rest any doubts he might have had regarding British aggression.

I knew that there was very little love lost between the two Grand Lamas of Lhasa and Tashilhunpo, so that I was not surprised when one of the latter's fourth-rank officers came to me in Yatung bearing a request from his master that I should intercede with the Dalai Lama on his behalf, as he feared that the existing ill-will might develop into open enmity. I spoke to His Holiness on this matter, and he assured me that, though considerable ill-feeling did exist between his ministers and those of the Tashi Lama, personal enmity towards his brother prelate found no place within his own heart. I therefore approached the ministers in the affair, and received the assurance from the Lonchen Shata, then Prime Minister, that no personal harm should befall the Tashi Lama, at any rate at the meeting which had been arranged between the two Lamaist dignitaries at Ralung, two days' march north of Gyantse on the high road to Lhasa.

The Lonchen Shokang, another powerful adviser of the Dalai Lama, did, however, ask me why, if the Tashi Lama and his ministers had done nothing against the Dalai Lama's interests, they were evincing such concern. To tell the truth I also was wondering at this. The Lonchen Shokang added that as I had broached the subject, and had interceded on behalf of the Tashi Lama and his ministers, he would remember this and, as far as he personally was concerned, would deal with them in as friendly a manner as possible. I was therefore able to assure the Tashi Lama's envoy of his master's personal safety, at any rate for the immediate future. He returned to Shigatse with my message, and with him I sent gifts to His Serenity, who was due to start any day for the conference at Ralung.

Before he left Yatung, the Dalai Lama presented me with a large gold medal, together with a silk ceremonial scarf, as a token of gratitude toward the British Government. He thanked me most warmly for all I had done for him and his ministers. After the small ceremony of presenting this medal was over the Lonchen Shata took me aside, and told me that he felt a strange affinity towards me, which he attributed to a link in our former existences !

When His Holiness finally left the valley I escorted him as far as the Tang Pass, eight miles beyond Pharijong, where my jurisdiction ended. The Dalai Lama again halted at the Chatsa Monastery, near Phari, where he had rested during his flight.

The next morning, while I was watching the ceremony of blessing the people, a stoutly built man in Tibetan dress, with an extraordinarily large head, stepped out of the crowd, and, having offered me a ceremonial scarf, told me that he was Dorjieff, the former tutor of the Dalai Lama, and the Russian Agent in Tibet. Dorjieff was a Buriat, his tribe living on the Russo-Mongolian frontier, and was a very astute individual indeed. It was considered at one time that he was responsible for His Holiness's flight from Lhasa when the Younghusband Mission entered that city in 1904. I invited Dorjieff to visit me at the Pharijong dak-bungalow, where I was staying. He accepted, and came to lunch. After the meal he told me parts of his life-story.

He seemed very anxious to convince me that he was

G

in no way anti-British. I asked him if it was true that he had incited the Tibetans to fight against us in 1904, but he vehemently denied this, laying all the blame on the Chinese. Dorjieff told me that he left his tribe when still a boy, and came to Lhasa, where, as a monk, he studied in the Drepung Monastery for nearly fifteen years. From there he was appointed as a tutor to the then youthful Dalai Lama. He stated that he now wished to return to his own country, and asked if I would permit him to travel *via* India. This, of course, was beyond my powers, but I suggested that he should apply to the Government of India through me. This he never did, and had he done so I doubt very much if permission would have been granted.

This man seemed to be, even at that time, high in the favour of the Dalai Lama, and lived with the ministers as one of themselves. Despite his protestations, however, Dorjieff was certainly responsible for a lot of the trouble leading up to the 1904 mission, acting on behalf of Russia, which country he hoped to place in the position of "Protector of Tibet." Russia at that time was certainly regarding Tibet with covetous eyes, as influence there would have meant an open road to India. After the Younghusband Mission, however, Russia's prestige in Tibet declined. The Tibetans reproached her for not having been able to assist against the British, and from that time until 1925 Russian influence was almost negligible. The fact that during his exile in India, when a refugee from the Chinese, the Government of India had treated him with every courtesy, and had paid the entire expenses of his stay in Darjeeling, made a great impression on the Dalai

Lama, who avoided any dealings with Russia for many years, dismissing the agent Dorjieff, and not accepting anyone else in his place.

In 1926, however, a Russian Mission, consisting of twenty-three delegates, in the guise of pilgrims, arrived in Lhasa, and were received with some honour, a military guard being furnished for their reception. They made large presents to the Dalai Lama and high Tibetan officials, and also to the great monasteries. Many of the delegates were Lamaists, and were well received by the lamas. Most of them were Buriats, of the same tribe as Dorjieff. The mission remained three months in Lhasa. Since that time several other parties of Russian subjects have visited Tibet, and at the time of writing a Mongolian Mission is in Lhasa. Evidence of the lessening friendliness between the Tibetans and the British is present in the fact of these Russian subjects being received officially by the Dalai Lama's Government.

With regard to Dorjieff, it was eventually arranged that the Tibetan Government should request him to leave their country, and after some time he was compelled to do so. Before leaving he made very large presents to the great monasteries, the real seats of power in Tibet, funds for this being supplied by his Russian masters. He travelled to Russia *via* the Chang Tang, and through Mongolia. I heard recently that he is still alive, and high in the councils of the Bolsheviki.

Mr B. J. Gould, then British Trade Agent at Gyantse, met the Dalai Lama at the Tang La, to escort him to the limits of that agency. My duties with His Holiness over, I returned to Yatung. Before finally parting from me, he asked me to write to him as often as possible, and this I have done ever since. He has never failed to reply to each of my letters, even though I have now left Tibet.

On arrival at Kangma, two stages from Gyantse, where a direct track branches from the main trade route to Lhasa, the Dalai Lama talked to the Tashi Lama on the telephone. The latter was then in Gyantse. The two pontiffs, however, did not arrive at any settlement of their differences. His Holiness did not visit Gyantse, but took the direct road from Kangma to Ralung.

I had communicated with Mr Bell, the Political Officer in Sikkim, regarding the Tashi Lama's request for assistance in his dealings with the Dalai Lama, and he had agreed with me on the course I had taken in speaking to the Lhasa prelate on the matter. This undoubtedly helped to smooth affairs. By this time both the Grand Lamas had telegraphed to the Government of India asking that I should be sent to Ralung to attend the conference, and to act as a mediator between them. However, much as I would have liked to have been there, I felt that since Ralung was within the sphere of the Gyantse Agency it would be more fitting if the British Trade Agent from that place attended the meeting. It had been ascertained by this time that two dismissed officials of the Tashi Lama were responsible for a great deal of the trouble between the Grand Lamas.

These men have since died, but not before they caused considerable further trouble in Tibet. One of them, a Jongpen by rank, became a depon, or general, under the Lhasa Government, while the other was appointed a dronyer chhempo, or high chamberlain, in the Potala. In this position he wielded considerable influence, and having the ear of the Dalai Lama was continually intriguing to bring about the complete downfall of his former master.

What transpired at the meeting between the two Grand Lamas at Ralung was never fully ascertained, but the Tashi Lama returned to Shigatse in safety. That matters had not been settled was apparent from a letter I received from the Lonchen Shokang shortly after his return to Lhasa. It was only when I read this that I realised the extent of the hatred some of the Dalai Lama's ministers bore towards the Tashi Lama. Among other accusations, the following chief charges were brought against him and his ministers :

1. That the Tashi Lama had gone to Lhasa at the invitation of the Chinese, during the absence of the Dalai Lama, and had seated himself on a throne in the place usually occupied by that of the latter. (This, of course, was tantamount to a charge of usurpation. In this connection it must be noted that the Chinese had officially deposed the Dalai Lama from the rulership of Tibet in 1910, after his flight to India, and had asked the Tashi Lama to take his place. The Tashi Lama was wise enough to refuse to do this, but committed a political blunder in going near Lhasa at all during that time. His visit at least gave the impression that he was prepared to consider the Chinese offer.)

2. That certain of the Tashi Lama's ministers were pro-Chinese in their sympathies.

3. That at the time of the Younghusband Mission, in 1904, the Tashi Lama's Government was reluctant in assisting the Central Government at Lhasa.

4. That the Tashi Lama's Government was in arrears of revenue contribution to the extent of several lakhs of rupees, these arrears having accumulated since 1904.

The Lonchen Shokang asked me to arrange for the publication of these charges in the prominent Indian newspapers, which, of course, I refused to do.

When the Dalai Lama escaped from their clutches, in 1910, the first action of the Chinese Ambans in Lhasa was to issue a proclamation deposing him from the pontifical throne, and declaring that he was no true incarnation. The masses of the Tibetan people, however, refused to accept either of these ukases, and, while for the time being outwardly bowing before their Chinese overlords, were at heart devoted to His Holiness. To influence the people, and in an endeavour to place a man at the head of the Tibetan party whom they could control for their own ends, the Ambans pressed the Tashi Lama to come to Lhasa, where they hoped to persuade him to supplant his absent ruler. Though he certainly did visit Lhasa—possibly he had no alternative but to comply with the Chinese request —the Tashi Lama soon saw the folly of remaining there, and returned to his monastery towards the end of 1911, travelling *via* Gyantse, where I was stationed at the time.

Every Chinese and Tibetan official in the city rode out to meet him, but I did not consider that it would be wise for me to do so, for fear of hurting Chinese susceptibilities, as I never went out to meet any of their high officials who were visiting the Trade Marts. I watched the Lama's entry into the town from the roof of a house by the roadside. He was escorted by one hundred Chinese and one hundred and fifty Tibetan soldiers, all mounted. The Lama himself was borne in a palanquin, a privilege reserved for the two Grand Lamas, one female incarnation, and the Chinese Ambans. He was accommodated in a special guest-house in the Palkhor Choide Monastery, where I, with the other British officials stationed in Gyantse, called on him the same afternoon.

After we had exchanged ceremonial scarves, and shaken hands, he made me sit next to him, the others being given seats near by. We talked on various matters for an hour or so, after which his lunch was announced. We then got up to go, but he insisted on my remaining for the meal. I could not very well refuse, nor indeed did I wish to do so, for this gave me an opportunity of talking privately with the Lama. The other British officers bade him farewell, and returned to the Agency, leaving me to follow later. After lunch, a most elaborate affair of over thirty courses, served in the Chinese fashion, we talked for several hours.

The Lama told me it was true that the Chinese wanted him to take the Dalai Lama's place in Lhasa, but that he had flatly refused. He admitted that he had sat in the latter's throne-room during an interview with the Ambans, but explained that this was only because no other seat had been provided. He seemed to think that this incident had been deliberately planned by the Chinese to implicate him in their schemes. The Tashi Lama insisted that he went to Lhasa on this occasion only under compulsion, and that he would sooner die than act contrary to the Dalai Lama's interests. He appeared to be desirous of maintaining friendly relations with both the British and the Chinese, and spoke with evident appreciation of his visit to India, where he had met His Majesty King George, then Prince of Wales, in Calcutta. He remembered His Majesty, and asked after his health, and that of the Royal Family, and it was a pleasure for me to be able to give him all the information he desired. It is noteworthy that each of the last three incarnations of the Tashi Lama have evinced more than ordinary feelings of friendship toward the British, so much so that one wonders if this is not a trait now ingrained in the Tashilhunpo incarnation.

I invited His Serenity to lunch with me at the Fort the next day, which invitation he accepted. During our conversation he refused to permit anybody to enter the room in which we were seated, though Chinese officers attempted several times to break in on our privacy.

Next day, at the Agency, after lunch, we had further conversation. He pressed me to visit him at Shigatse. This I was unable to do, for without special permission from the Government of India it was impossible for any British official to go beyond Gyantse.

We established at that time a friendship which has endured through all the years till the present time, even though His Serenity is now a refugee in China. I still hear from him occasionally, and I hope one day to see him return to his country.

Before the Tashi Lama left Gyantse, the next morning, I went to bid him farewell at the monastery. There he presented me with a golden emblem to commemorate our first meeting. He was escorted on his way by Chinese and Tibetan troops.

The Maharaja of Bhutan—Reception at Paro Jong—The Penlop of
Paro—The Bhutanese as Raiders—Bhutanese Food

I FIRST met the late Maharaja of Bhutan, Sir Ugyen Wangchuk, G.C.I.E., K.C.I.E., in 1904, when he joined the Younghusband Expedition to Lhasa. He rendered most useful services on that occasion by persuading and advising the Tibetan Government, with whom he had considerable influence, to abandon their policy of obstruction, telling them that this could lead only to their undoing. He became very friendly with me, and kept up a correspondence until his death, a few years ago. The late Maharaja of Bhutan was an exceptionally far-sighted ruler, and was responsible for the consolidation of his country, and for putting an end to the continual internecine strife that was ruining it. He concluded treaties with the Government of India. His foreign policy was controlled by the latter, but no interference was ever to be made in the internal administration of Bhutan.

In Sir Ugyen's suite was the late Raja Ugyen Dorje, the Prime Minster of Bhutan, a progressive and enlightened nobleman, who has been succeeded in his office by his son, Raja Sonam Tobgye Dorje, who accompanied the party when I visited Bhutan in company with the Earl of Ronaldshay in 1921. Two medals, one gold and one silver, were presented to me by the late Maharaja of Bhutan in recognition of

105

services that I was able to render him, and these I value very highly.

Information was received in Gantok, in 1911, that the then Paro Penlop, one of the greatest feudal barons of Bhutan, and a very influential man, had received a visit from the Chinese Trade Agent at Gyantse, and had received him with every honour at his castle of Paro. In this connection I was deputed to visit Bhutan. I decided that my best course was to go straight to Ha, the castle of my friend, Raja Ugyen Dorje, and this I did, travelling *via* the Chumbi Valley, over the same route as that taken by Sir Ashley Eden, and later by Mr Claude White, when those officers visited Bhutan. Arrived at Ha Jong, I found that Raja Ugyen was away at Kalimpong, where he had estates, and where he used to spend much of his time. His deputy, however, received me most courteously, and, having provided transport coolies for myself and staff, saw me on my way to Paro, the summer seat of the Paro Penlop.

Notice of my visit had been sent ahead, and as I drew near Paro Jong a guard of honour, commanded by the Druggye Jongpen, and composed of Bhutanese men-at-arms, in polished steel helmets, and armed with broadswords and bows, met and escorted me the last eight miles of the road. A very fine riding-mule, with gorgeous trappings, was sent for my use. Trumpeters marched ahead of the cavalcade, while two dancers danced in front of the procession for the whole of the last five miles to the castle. These are honours paid, in Bhutan, only to officers of the highest rank, and to personal friends of the princes. For my

1. PAULINE AND JOE

TWO OF THE AUTHOR'S CHILDREN ASTRIDE A YAK IN THE CHUMBI VALLEY.

2. A GAILY CAPARISONED TIBETAN MULE

SENT BY THE PARO PENLOP, TO CONVEY THE AUTHOR ACROSS THE BORDER ON THE OCCASION OF
HIS VISIT TO BHUTAN.

accommodation the Penlop had a small wooden house specially built, while my clerks and orderlies were lodged in a basha, or temporary thatched outhouse, near by. On the afternoon of my arrival, after a short rest, I called, as was demanded by courtesy, on my host, and having presented him with a silk ceremonial scarf offered him the gifts I had brought. Next morning he returned my call, and presented me with a most beautifully worked Bhutanese sword, in a silver scabbard, with gay silken trappings, and a very fine dagger to match.

During the feast which followed, in the Chinese fashion, he introduced me to his son and daughter-in-law. The Penlop was an old man of seventy-five, and told me that he did not think he had long to live. He asked me to extend the friendship I bore towards himself to his son, which I was only too pleased to do. This young man and myself have since been friends, and we have corresponded frequently. The Penlop told me that his cordial reception of the Chinese envoy was not due to any desire on his part to negotiate with China, but because refusal to receive him would have been unwise, as he, the Penlop, had interests in Tibet which would certainly have suffered had he incurred the enmity of the Chinese. He was able to convince me that he was sincere in this statement. Had he wished to throw himself into the arms of China he would never have treated a British representative with such great courtesy.

While I was in Bhutan on this occasion I had the run of the Paro Valley, and visited all parts of it. I also spent several days exploring the Pa Jong and its

surroundings, and lunched many times with the
Penlop *en famille.* I found that his son, though a very
good-natured young man, did not, unfortunately, live
long to enjoy his inheritance. As there were no other
male heirs in the Penlop's family the Maharaja of
Bhutan appointed one of his own grandsons as the
next Paro Penlop, and I met this young baron during
my visit to his country in 1921.

Soon after my return from this mission I happened
to be in Pharijong when a certain amount of friction
arose between the son of the old Paro Penlop and the
Tibetan officials of that place. For his father's sake I
was pleased that I was able to settle the matter amicably.
It appeared that the Penlop's son was returning
from a cure at the Khambu Hot Springs, which are in
Tibetan territory, *via* Pharijong, when he happened to
pass, just outside the town, a party of Tibetan officers
amusing themselves with an archery contest. Some
of the arrows fell perilously near the young Bhutanese
noble. Whether the Tibetans deliberately tried to
frighten him, or whether the whole affair was an
accident, I never really found out. Both parties, however, arrived at the dak-bungalow complaining about
each other's conduct. The Penlop's son asserted that
grave discourtesy had been shown him, and demanded
satisfaction and apology, while the Tibetans insisted
that the Bhutanese had been insulting and threatening
them. Probably there was truth in both statements.
The Tibetans refused to apologise, and the Bhutanese
prince vowed vengeance if compensation was not
forthcoming. He had a large armed following, and
matters began to assume a serious aspect. However,

by pointing out to him that after all he was in a foreign country, and therefore could not expect the respect and deference that was his right in his own land, and by persuading the Tibetans to make some sort of an excuse for their behaviour, I managed to settle the affair.

There is at the best of times very little love lost between the Bhutanese and the Tibetans, the latter fearing the former intensely, especially along the frontiers. There is a proverb in the Chumbi Valley which says that if a Bhutanese draws his sword the whole of the valley trembles. This is to a very great extent true even at the present time. The Bhutanese were inveterate raiders, and in former days did an immense amount of damage along the Chumbi Valley-Pharijong trade route, as many ruined and deserted villages and houses testify. At the same time, all the abandoned dwellings that one sees in Tibet are not the results of Bhutanese raids, but, round Gyantse and Lhasa especially, are due to the ravages of smallpox, and the depredations of the Tartar invaders of Tibet, who swarmed over and plundered the land in 1641.

One of the most noticeable things in Bhutan was the extraordinary prevalence of goitre among the people, both rich and poor. Almost every other person seemed to be suffering from this disease. Even in the Chumbi Valley it is not uncommon. The Bhutanese are very addicted to the practice of chewing " pan," which is apparent from the red-stained teeth that one sees everywhere. This stain is caused by the juices of the areca-nut and betel-leaf, combined with lime, of which the pan is made. The variety of areca-nut that is grown in Bhutan is far stronger in flavour than that of India, and will, to those unaccustomed to its use, cause giddiness and sickness. When chatting with a friend, a Bhutanese will offer him his pan-box in the same way that a European will offer his cigarette-case. The Bhutanese people have never taken to smoking to any great extent. Like the Tibetans, they usually prefer tobacco in the form of snuff.

It was during this visit to Bhutan that I first sampled real Bhutanese food. I have never tasted anything so fiery in my life. They are very fond of pork, and eat huge quantities of this flesh, usually in the form of a curry. With it they eat literally whole mouthfuls of very hot chillies, also cooked as a vegetable curry. The Bhutanese are very hospitable, and go out of their way to make a visitor comfortable. At the same time, the tour of a high foreign official in their country causes much hardship to the peasantry, who have to supply free labour for the carriage of tents and luggage from one halting-place to the next. In a sparsely populated country like Bhutan some of the coolies have to journey several days before reaching camp.

CHAPTER TEN

Trouble in Lhasa—Trouble in the Chumbi Valley—Loot—A Deposed
Chinese Resident—Evacuation of Lhasa—A Homecoming—
Christmas

THE Sino-Tibetan trouble in Lhasa, the last stronghold of the Chinese in Tibet, came to a head in September 1912. There was continuous and heavy fighting, in which the Tibetans were as a rule worsted, chiefly owing to treachery in their own ranks. It was found that the Chinese were always informed beforehand of any move that the Tibetans intended making. A careful check was instituted, and a high Tibetan official was found to be sending messages fastened to arrows into the Chinese yamen. He was executed on the spot, and this salutary example put a stop to similar leakage of news.

One of the then chief ministers of Tibet, the Tsarong Shap-pe, the only one to remain behind and carry on his duties when the Dalai Lama and the rest of the ministers fled to India, was also suspected of pro-Chinese activities. The lamas of the Sera Monastery dragged him from the council chamber at the Potala and killed him without any form of trial. Several other high Tibetan officers, including one of the sons of the murdered Tsarong, were also suspected of aiding the Chinese. They were killed by the Sera priests at the same time.

In the end the Chinese were conquered by starvation,

111

for all sources of supply were cut off. Allegations, well founded, of cannibalism in their ranks have been made by the Tibetans, and their evidence tends to prove their statements. Dissension broke out in their ranks, and the Chinese soldiery deposed the Amban Lien Yu. They robbed him of all his possessions, and elected Chien Hsi Pao in his place as their leader. He, however, did not keep his power for long. After a month or so he was himself a refugee, and fled to India through the Chumbi Valley, whence he returned to China. He was shortly afterwards followed by Hai Tsu, the Chinese High Commissioner for Tibet. General Chung eventually took over command.

On 7th September 1912 I received a letter purporting to be signed by Lien Yu, Chief Minister of Tibet, and Chung Yin, Lieutenant-General and Acting Resident at Lhasa, asking me to assist the Chinese garrison of two thousand men who were then on their way to India. These troops eventually arrived in the Chumbi Valley, where they halted to await the arrival of General Chung, who was following them down. After the General had arrived many of the men wanted him to remain on in the valley, and hold it for China. The local Tibetans were naturally very alarmed at this proposal, and came to me for aid and advice. I, of course, had to remain neutral, and could do nothing for them. The Tibetan officials began to collect levies with the object of driving the Chinese out by force, and I foresaw the beginnings of grave troubles in my peaceful valley.

The situation was, however, relieved by telegraphic orders arriving from China, depriving General Chung

of his command, and instructing him to return to that
country at once. I heard later that on his arrival there
he was tried on two charges, and shot. It was alleged
that he had instigated the assassination of Lo, a former
Chinese High Commissioner for Tibet, and also to
have failed in his duty in that he had not been able to
suppress the Tibetan revolt. Once General Chung had
left, the Lhasa troops departed from Chumbi without
giving further trouble. By this time, with the exception
of the eastern marches, Tibet was entirely free of
Chinese garrisons. When the Lhasa troops arrived in
Yatung they were fairly bulging with loot of every
description. Priceless jade and porcelain were to be
bought from them for next to nothing, and, had col-
lectors been on the spot, fortunes might have been
picked up for practically the asking. The Chinese,
though possessing all these valuables, were unable to
transport them out of Tibet. They needed ready cash,
and sold their goods for what they would fetch.

Lien Yu, the deposed Chinese Resident at Lhasa,
was the last of the Chinese to leave Tibet, passing
through Yatung in December 1912. He lunched with
me, and gave me his views on the recent troubles.
He blamed principally the newly raised troops who had
been sent to garrison Tibet. He stated that these
were not properly disciplined, and that their officers
had not the slightest hold over them. They revolted,
looted, and set up Chien Hsi Pao, to whom Lien Yu
alluded as a brigand, and only stopped short of murdering their former Resident. It was pathetic to see this
aristocratic mandarin of the old regime, used to the exer-
cise of the greatest powers, and the late ruler of Tibet,

reduced to his present extremity. He had not a rupee to his name, and possessed only the clothes he wore.

The evacuation of Lhasa by the Chinese enabled the Dalai Lama to proceed as far as Samding Monastery, where he remained until the Chinese had been completely driven out of Tibet. His Holiness finally entered his capital at the end of December 1912, and since that time has been supreme authority in his country. Having entered the Potala, one of his first acts was to disestablish the " royal " monastery of Tengyeling, and to disperse its monks, who were accused of aiding the Chinese. This monastery has since been turned into a Post and Telegraph Office.

Thus a settled form of government was established in Tibet. In March 1913, Mr B. J. Gould left Gyantse, and from that time until April 1916 I held charge of both Gyantse and Yatung Trade Agencies. This double charge involved frequent journeys, one hundred and thirty miles each way, between the two posts, as I did not care to leave either unvisited for more than a few weeks at a time. I did, however, as far as was possible, arrange to spend a couple of months during the winter at Yatung with my family, for at this time of the year my elder children were home from school in Darjeeling for their long vacation. To give myself a change from the almost endless riding I purchased a light American buggy, which I used on the plains above Pharijong. This was the only wheeled vehicle in use at that time in Tibet, and created no little astonishment on its first few trips. As a matter of fact, for years afterwards, people used sometimes to come from miles away just to see this buggy go by. It gave

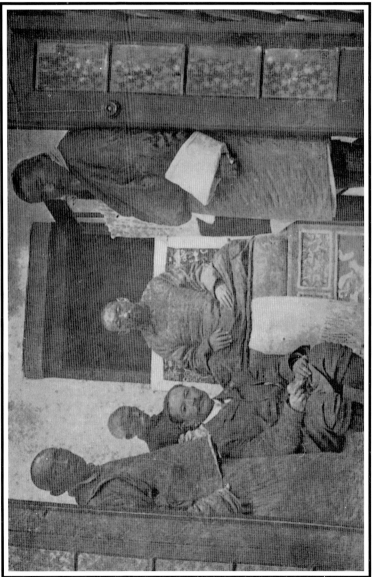

THE DALAI LAMA

TWO COUNCILLORS OF HIS HOLINESS (*left*) AND THE LATE RAJA UGYEN DORJI (*right*), THE AUTHOR IS SEATED IN THE FOREGROUND. TAKEN AT YATUNG IN 1912 ON THE DALAI LAMA'S RETURN FROM INDIA.

me many years of good service, and eased many a mile on the high plateau roads. Only where there was heavy snow was it impossible to use it.

The great event of the year, as far as my family was concerned, was the homecoming of the children. These young people had as difficult and hazardous a journey to and from their school in Darjeeling as any children in the world. Coming home for them meant a ride of hundreds of miles through the heart of the highest mountains in the world, over passes full of snow, and over the most execrable roads imaginable. Their school closed during the winter months, so that they had to travel at the worst time of the year. I used to send mules and ponies for them from Yatung, and when they were on the road they were in sole charge of my eldest daughter, Anne, who assumed entire control of her younger brothers and sisters once they were away from home, shepherding them across some of the most hazardous country in the world. It speaks volumes for her self-reliance and ability that no accident or mishap ever occurred, beyond their baggage being swept down the hillside once or twice. I have known her, when her presence was urgently required in Yatung on account of her mother's sickness, ride from Darjeeling to that place in thirty-six hours, going day and night. Her performance is almost incredible to anyone who knows the road, and has only been equalled by a journey once made by her husband, who rode from Gyantse to Darjeeling in seventy-six hours, with snow falling for a hundred miles of the way. The normal time for this trek is, even doing double marches, twelve days.

At Christmas all the children were at home, and we had great times together. In Yatung we had the Christmas of the picture-books. Outside was glistening snow, and pine-trees, their white branches heavy laden, the air keen and crisp. In the daytime, unless snow was actually falling, the valley was bathed in brilliant sunshine, though it was bitterly cold at night. Inside the house all was cosiness and warmth, huge pine-log fires going all day long in every room. We had fireplaces that *were* fireplaces in Tibet. Each of them would comfortably take two hundredweights of wood.

An illustration of the bitter winter blizzards is given by an experience of my children, when out for a walk one morning after a heavy snowfall. Coming round a corner in the road, not very far from the Agency, they saw what they took to be three Bhutanese coolies carrying large loaded baskets, halted by the roadside to rest, their loads being supported on short sticks stuck in the snow. As the youngsters came closer they thought that these men were grinning at them, and hailed them, but got no reply. This was extraordinary, as in Tibet one always receives an answer when one addresses anybody. On closer inspection it was found that the three coolies had been frozen to death, standing up. Apparently the men had stopped to rest, supported by their loads, and while dozing had frozen to death. Their grins were caused by the retraction of their facial muscles. I went out to inspect the bodies, and ordered their burial, itself no easy task in the frozen ground.

Christmastide was as eagerly looked forward to by all our Tibetan followers as by ourselves, for at this season my wife was a veritable Lady Bountiful to the whole of the Agency following. At the Christmas tree, which we never failed to have, there was a gift for everyone in the Yatung Trade Mart, man, woman and child, with a great feast to follow.

Christmas in Gyantse was a very different affair, though the Christmas spirit was there just the same, and the festival was celebrated by the few Britishers stationed in the fort with just as much zest as we celebrated it in Chumbi. In Gyantse, however, the weather was the reverse of pleasant in the winter. Much colder than Yatung, the Gyantse plain was swept by violent duststorms every day, making it impossible to get out of doors for hours at a time. In Gyantse we had double windows, and at the beginning of November we used carefully to shut and seal these up with strips of stout paper, to keep out the wind and dust. They were not opened again until the end of March. Even in Gyantse there was a Christmas tree, carried a hundred and thirty miles by coolies, for there are no available trees near the place. Every resident in the fort had a gift, and a feast was provided for the entire personnel. Everything had to be brought all the way from India on muleback, the only food locally available being mutton. Even vegetables had to be imported for the greater part of the year. The turkey and the ham, the oranges and the other fruits, had invariably frozen solid. As a special treat, bottled beer was always imported by the Gyantse men for Christmas— it was too expensive to drink at ordinary times, as the cost of carriage from India was high, and there was always a heavy loss due to breakages en route. This

Christmas beer also arrived in solid form, and had to be thawed out in a basin before drinking. I spent only a couple of Christmas-tides in Gyantse during the whole of my time in Tibet, but I know that it was always a great occasion there.

In winter Yatung was not at all an unpleasant place, especially when my children were there. It was nothing like so cold as Gyantse, and there were no duststorms. In front of the Agency House in Yatung I had a grass tennis court, and in winter we used to flood this the last thing in the afternoon, and by the morning there would be an excellent skating rink. In the mornings it was one of the servant's first tasks to chop out the ice that had formed overnight in our wooden water-flume. Our water-supply came down in this from a stream we had tapped about three hundred feet above the house. We had a tennis court in Gyantse also, but it was impossible to play on this in the winter owing to the dust. The wind rose regularly at half-past ten every morning, and continued blowing until dusk. Football, hockey and polo were played regularly by the officers and sepoys of the escort.

In Gyantse one had to dress very warmly to combat the cold, especially at night. Everyone, including sepoys and followers, donned furs and gilgit boots, with the warmest lamb's-wool underclothing. These articles were a ration issue to all personnel. The cold at night was so intense that the sepoys of the quarter guard could do only about three-quarters of an hour's sentry-go at a spell, and even then they had a great brazier filled with glowing coals outside the guard-room, at which they could warm themselves during their tour of duty. The men at one time used to keep a huge, shaggy Tibetan mastiff, and they trained this dog to sit between their legs whenever they halted on their beat. In the Chumbi Valley the winter days were very short, the sun not rising above the eastern hills until after nine each morning, and setting behind the western ridges by half-past two in the afternoon.

CHAPTER ELEVEN

ABOUT this time, 1913-1914, the situation in Tibet was quiet, and normality was restored after the Chinese trouble. I used to spend much time visiting and being visited by the Tibetans in Gyantse and Yatung. Many happy hours were thus passed. I also spent many a day in exploring the country round the two Agencies.

Entertainment on a comparatively large scale is expected of the British Trade Agents in Tibet; they must keep practically "open house." For this purpose Government makes them a special sumptuary allowance. At each Agency a department known as a "Toshakhana," or "gift-house," is maintained, into which all presents received by the Trade Agents in their official capacities are deposited on behalf of Government, which has to pay for the gifts made in return. The accumulated presents are periodically sent down to India, where they are sold, and the proceeds credited to Government. Officials on the spot may, however, at their proper valuation, purchase any such presents should these be desired for their private use, the price realised being placed on the credit side of the Toshakhana account.

To anyone not a lover of the wild, life in Tibet would seem monotonous in the extreme, especially

during the winter. I have known men posted to the
Agencies who did nothing but bemoan their luck in
being stationed in such an out-of-the-way place, and
who passed most of their time devising some scheme
which would obtain them a transfer. Others did all
they could to get an extension of their term of duty.
To myself and my family the life was full of interest,
especially when we were roaming the countryside, in
touch with the real lives of the people, and visiting
interesting places.

Among my many Tibetan friends are numbered
most of the kongdus, or headmen, of the big villages,
especially in the Chumbi Valley. These headmen are
usually chosen from among the well-to-do farmers and
chief tenants of the great landlords, and are of a class
which corresponds to the yeomen of Saxon England.
These headmen are responsible for the collection of
revenue in their own jurisdiction, and for the trying
of petty cases, which are usually settled by a committee
of the village elders, similar to the panchayat of India.
The kongdus occasionally hold meetings at which
matters affecting their districts are discussed, such as
the raising of militia, the provision of free labour and
transport for Government works and officers.

In the Tromo country, as the upper Chumbi Valley
is known to its own inhabitants, these headmen are
elected by the villagers, and hold office for a period
of either two or three years, after which they must
resign, but are eligible for re-election. This system,
with slight variations in the time for which the office
is held, is followed all over Tibet. The kongdu has an
assistant called a latho, who officiates for him when he

happens to be away from his village on business or pleasure. It usually happens in practice that one head-man, invariably the richest and most influential person in the place, is re-elected time after time until his heir takes his place. Probably most of the villagers are in his debt, and therefore do not care to make an enemy of him by electing another candidate.

In the Chumbi Valley five headmen in all are elected at the same time, three for the upper and two for the lower divisions into which this part of the country is partitioned. After the elections are over the newly appointed kongdus sacrifice black yaks to propitiate the gods, and swear on the carcasses to carry out their duties faithfully, and to care for and protect the interests of the people who have elected them.

Incidentally the manner of slaughtering these animal sacrifices is the same as is always followed when kill-ing an animal for food, or for any other purpose, in Tibet. The animal—yak, bull, pig, sheep, or whatever it may be—is securely tied with rope so that it cannot move a limb, after which a butcher thrusts a sword or pointed stake from the shoulder down to the heart. If this does not cause immediate death, or if the sword should miss the heart, the butcher thrusts his hand into the wound and gropes round for the heart, which he squeezes till the beast dies. Only one of the lowest class will do butcher's work, as the taking of life in any form is a heinous sin, according to the lamas, who, however, do not scruple to eat flesh itself. Because they do not actually take life they consider themselves free from spiritual blame, while a butcher's soul is automatically damned for all eternity.

The headman with whom I was best acquainted was the Bakcham kongdu. He lived but a few hundred yards from my house in Yatung, across the Amo river. He had a very large and fertile farm, and my family and I spent many a happy hour picnicking on his estates, which bordered the river-bank. When the wild strawberries were ripe we used to collect hundred-weights of this fine-flavoured fruit for jam-making, for with eleven children one can do with a reserve of this nature.

Always hospitable, he often prepared a light lunch and sent it out to us, and we would call at his house on our way home, where we would be entertained by the singing and dancing of his family of boys and girls. He had one of the most beautifully decorated private chapels I have ever seen in Tibet, where some of the wood-carving is very fine indeed. While I was in the Chumbi Valley his son used to attend the small school, run by my wife, in the Agency Bazaar. Near by, and under his patronage, was an old monastery of the Nyingmapa, or Unreformed Sect of the Lamaist Church, in which was kept a shoe alleged to have been worn by the famous Lamaist saint, Latsun Chhempo, who passed through the Chumbi Valley on his way to establish Lamaism in Sikkim, in 1641.

In this kongdu's house lived a famous Sikkimese hunter, who one day went out after a shao, the great Himalayan stag. He followed one of these beasts for three days over the highest mountains in the neighbourhood, finally managing to shoot it with his old gaspipe prong gun. He was, however, so exhausted by his efforts that he collapsed across the carcass, in which position he was picked up several days later by a search-party.

The Chumbi Valley originally formed part of the Sikkim state, but a Bhutanese army overran it, and was ejected only by the aid of Tibetan troops. Once the Tibetans were in, the Sikkimese found it impossible to drive them out again, and since that time this fertile district has remained a possession of the Lhasa Government. I was able to obtain much material of historical interest from an old lama who used to live in a retreat in the hills near the Yatung Trade Mart.

Among other things he told me that at one time the Sikkim Rajas owned a lot of land in the valley, even after it had been taken over by the Tibetan Administration, and that they had a large residence in which they stayed during the rainy season in Sikkim. When the Tibetans lost their influence in Sikkim in 1888, owing to British pressure, this estate lapsed to the Tibetan Government, who have since, as mentioned earlier, leased it to Raja Tsotra Namgyal of Tering.

A unique ceremony, performed only by the followers of the Bon, or Animist pre-Lamaist faith, at one time universal in Tibet, is to be seen in the Chumbi Valley. Its object is to ensure success in procuring the various medicines and herbs used as ingredients for pills, and so forth, employed in the treatment of various illnesses. Performed in the winter season, the Bon priests dress up in gorgeous allegorical robes, and, wielding their swords aloft, dance and leap in great bounds about the monastery courtyard. After the head priest has performed for some time he works himself into a frenzy, during which he predicts whether the coming year will be fortunate or otherwise. Another priest-dance is performed during the summer months, and is largely attended by the followers of the Bon faith in the Chumbi Valley. Huge trumpets, cymbals, and a little gong, which, when struck with a piece of hard wood, gives a peculiarly sweet sound, are used in the invocation of the spirits. Branches adorned with multicoloured threads are placed on the roofs, to bring good fortune. Every Bon household performs an annual divination ceremony, for which a priest is called in, who visits every nook and corner of the building, striking his little spirit gong, and muttering prayers. After he has completed his round of the place, and having observed the omens, he pronounces the fortunes of the family during the ensuing twelve months.

To purify a house or a village, the Bonpo priest, preceded by an acolyte carrying the stuffed skin of a species of wild cat found in Tibet, and followed by another assistant swinging a censer, sprinkles holy water in various places. For these services the people, of course, have to pay, either in cash or in kind, or both. The Bon priests are entitled to the flesh of all animals and birds killed for sacrifices. Although the Bonpo are not too popular among the followers of the established Church, the members of which regard them as being in league with the Evil One, they have considerable followings in certain parts of the country. The Bon priests are styled "Thripa," or "President," and when they die are succeeded by their nearest male heirs. They are permitted to marry. The chief stronghold of the Bon faith is the monastery of Ra-lag Yung-trung, two days' journey north of Shigatse, where the written scriptures of that religion are said to be preserved. These would be of absorbing interest to students, but I have never been able even to see them, let alone translate any. At Ri-shing, near Gyantse, I met a family who said that they were descended from the founder of the Bon faith, and their claim was admitted by their Lamaist neighbours. The Bonpo worship the goddess Sipa Gyalmo, the " Queen of the World," as their patroness saint.

Divination plays a very great part in the everyday life of the Tibetans, and in every case of sickness, marriage, building of houses, trading ventures—in fact, in every incident of their lives—the Tibetans consult and pay an Astrologer Lama. This individual, by divination in one way or another, will give his opinion as to the good or ill fortune of a proposed undertaking, and will fix an auspicious date for its commencement. Moreover, the lamas themselves believe in this form of fortune-telling, and I have seen a High Lama sit down and throw dice or bones to decide whether he should set out on a journey or not, or to decide which of two alternative routes would be the better.

Various means are used to ascertain the will of the gods. For instance, two slips of paper on which respectively are written good and bad fortune are enclosed in two barley-dough balls, which are then shaken up in a bowl. One ball is then withdrawn. The writing on the paper thus selected is indicative of the will of the deities. At other times, after worshipping the image of King Kesar, a warrior-saint included in the Lamaist Pantheon, the suppliant for heavenly guidance is directed to withdraw from a vase

one of a hundred or so bamboo slips, on which reference marks are made corresponding with the pages of
a book. According to the number on the slip, the
applicant's fortune is read out to him from this volume.
Divination is sometimes performed with the aid of
three ordinary dice, which are shaken and thrown by
the astrologer after suitable prayers and invocations.
Propitious totals are seventeen, fifteen and thirteen,
while those of nine, seven and five denote only average
good fortune, all other totals being unlucky.

Oracles also play on the superstition of the people.
I write here of the wandering oracle-priests who are
to be seen travelling round the countryside, and not
of the well-known oracles, such as Karmashar, in
Lhasa, who seldom leave the monasteries to which they
are attached. The people go to them. The wandering seers simply force their services on those simple
villagers who may be overawed by their threats. They
will pester a household, beating a drum, and reproach
the people living there for not worshipping their controlling spirit more often. They threaten that if this
is not done misfortune, and possibly death, will overtake the family. In the majority of cases this alone is
sufficient to persuade the victim to worship the spirit—
in other words, to make a present to the spirit's medium
on earth. As soon as these parasitical pseudo-oracles
have received something they depart, and will leave
that particular victim in peace till their next visit,
usually a year or so later.

On one of my periodical journeys between Yatung and
Gyantse I was fortunate in meeting the junior abbot
of Sakya Monastery, one of the oldest institutions

in Tibet, and the headquarters of the sect bearing the same name. Though nowadays this sect, the Sakyapa, has lost all its temporal power, and much of its spiritual, its abbots at one time wielded great influence in the State, before the establishment of the Reformed Church, of which the Dalai Lama is the head. I met this young abbot at Kala. In 1921, in Gyantse, I met the senior abbot of the sect, and entertained him at the Agency. He had never seen a European before, and was keenly interested in our manners and customs, and mode of living. He asked innumerable questions about our country, religion and armies. He was not, as highly placed priests usually are in Tibet, of very great erudition, but he appeared to possess a good share of natural ability. His monastery is even to-day one of the most famous in Tibet, being situated some seven days' journey to the south of Shigatse.

The Sakya sect has a peculiar organisation. There are two abbots, senior and junior, each of whom may marry. In addition, there is also what is termed a " president " of the institution, who is usually the son of one of the abbots. This president must remain celibate. The abbots themselves are succeeded by their eldest sons. The senior abbot claims to be the incarnation of Jamyang, the God of Wisdom, but this is not admitted by the Reformed Church, who assert that this deity was incarnate in the persons of the Emperors of China. Nowadays there are only about two hundred monks in residence at Sakya, and a few nuns, called Rabjungma, who have a great reputation for sanctity, and who spend much of their time in solitary meditation in hermitages in the near-by hills. Sakya is noted throughout Tibet for many things. Among its jealously guarded relics is a conch-shell covered with alleged naturally formed figures. It is credited with the power to perform miracles. In a temple dedicated to the fierce deities many witches are said to be kept in chains. The monastery is also the resting-place of the sword of Manjusri, the patron saint of the Nepalese Buddhists. Sakya possesses a very fine library, which contains many works unobtainable elsewhere, in manuscript form. There are altogether about twenty temples, supported by the revenue from some sixty villages, all that remains of a once great principality. Sakya boasts the honour of having the tallest prayer-flag in the whole of Tibet, and worshippers come from all over the countryside to worship there.

To anyone, like myself, fond of a lonely existence, and happy in the study of a country and its people, days spent among the Tibetans in their own homes cannot fail to be full of interest. During the long winter evenings the Tibetans play " Ba," a domino game. I and one or two of the military officers stationed in Tibet from time to time learned this game. It is, in my opinion, far superior to Mah Jong, which is also played a little in Tibet by those who have lived in or visited China. We used to play " Ba " with our Tibetan hosts and guests, and found it an entertaining way of passing an hour or two. Other indoor games were Chinese cards, " Sho," played with dice, and a kind of halma and ludo, the latter being known as the rebirth game. Women join in these pastimes, and occasionally one finds among them expert players.

I

THE city of Gyantse — so called from the
"Victorious Peak" on which its fort is perched
—was, according to the Tibetans, founded only
some three hundred years ago. It was originally known
as She Kar Gyantse, the " Victorious Hill of the White
Crystal Pillar." This pillar was first erected within
the fort itself, but after several years of flood—due to
the Nyang river, on which the town stands, overflowing
its banks—the lamas decided to remove the pillar to
the opposite side of the stream, where it was thought
that its magic influence might keep the waters to their
proper channel. It still remains there, being housed
in a building called Rabgye Surkhang, almost opposite
the now British fort. With it is an image of Buddha,
about three feet high, which the Tibetans declare has
spoken. The famous Palkhor Chhöde Monastery was
built at the same time as the fort, and by the same prince,
Chhogyal Rabten Kunsang. This ruler's private apartment is still shown to pilgrims and others visiting the
monastery. His queen was buried within the monastery
walls, and her tomb is pointed out to the pious who
worship there. Her golden ornaments were fashioned
into two massive altar-lamps, which are still to be seen.

1. "THE LONG JUMP"

A POPULAR EVENT DURING THE ANNUAL ATHLETIC COMPETITION AMONG THE MONKS OF THE PALKHOR CHHODE MONASTERY IN GYANTSE. THE LEAP IS TAKEN FROM A RAISED PLATFORM.

2. A COMPETITOR IN THE GYANTSE MARTIAL GAMES

NOTE THE EQUIPMENT, INCLUDING PRONG GUN, AND BOW.

Palkhor Chhöde has a nominal complement of eighteen hundred lamas, accommodated in eighteen khamtsans, or dormitories. Monks of the three most important sects are in residence, but those of the Gelukpa, or Reformed Church, greatly preponderate in numbers. The other two sects admitted are the Sakyapa and the Nyingmapa, old unreformed orders which have now been superseded by the Gelukpa.

Prince Rabten is also said to have built the huge eleven-storeyed choten in the monastery, the design being taken from the original Bodh Gaya temple in India. The well-known monastery of Kumbum, in Kham, is similarly fashioned. The Palkhor Chhöde possesses a very fine library, having among other priceless manuscripts a copy, in gilt lettering on black paper, of the *Gye Tong Pa*, or *Sermons of the Buddha*. I admired this huge volume, weighing well over two hundred pounds, including its marvellously carved wooden book-covers, and on mentioning this to the Khenchung Kusho, the Tibetan Trade Agent in Gyantse, who was a high lama official, he told me that if I could carry it away unaided I could have it. Needless to say, I tried my best, but being a small man it was beyond my powers. I could not even lift it! Near the main temple is a huge prayer-wheel, ten feet high and eight feet in diameter, containing millions of repetitions of the sacred "Om! Mani Padme Hum!" formula, written on very thin paper. This is revolved by every pilgrim who visits the shrine, each revolution being marked by the striking of a bell, which thus records that the prayers have been wafted to the gods. In a comparatively new building, erected only some seventy years ago, is a very fine image of Tsong Khapa, the Lamaist Reformer, and founder of the sect to which the Dalai Lamas belong. This image is considered very efficacious in cases of rheumatism, and sufferers from this complaint may be seen rubbing their affected parts against its pedestal, which now has a high polish on this account.

It was the abbot of the Gyantse Monastery who sent the seven lamas to Europe, in company with Captain J. B. Noel, F.R.G.S., the official photographer to the Mount Everest expeditions. I have heard it said that these men, who toured Europe in connection with the film entitled *Epic of Everest*, were ordinary Darjeeling rickshaw and dandy coolies. This is not so. They were genuine Tibetan lamas, and had never before been out of their country. In the vicinity of Gyantse are several nunneries and small monasteries, each with some thirty inmates. I found that these small institutions were well worth visiting, and I became quite friendly with their abbots and abbesses. I have spent many a pleasant morning in their company.

In each of the numerous valleys opening out on to the Gyantse plain are many ruined villages and monasteries, evidence that the population had once been much more dense than at the present time. Certain of the deserted villages show prevalence of smallpox epidemics, while others testify to the ruthlessness of Tartar invaders, who penetrated as far south as Gyantse. At Rinang there is a small monastery, now inhabited by only a few monks. It has some exceptionally fine images, among them being one of Phagmo, the pig-headed goddess, which is claimed to have flown to its

IDOL IN THE GORGE NEAR GYANTSE

present position from India. Here also are to be seen the Five Dyani Buddhas, whose images also arrived in the temple in a miraculous manner. Inhabitants of Gyantse make regular pilgrimages to a rock face of the temple, and there do homage to the gods, for they believe that should water issue from this face pestilence will ravish the land.

I had many friends among the landowners in this part of the country, and I and other officers stationed in Gyantse spent many a pleasant week-end entertaining and being entertained by these Tibetan gentlemen. Our favourite host was a Sikkimese nobleman, domiciled in Tibet, named Lhasse Kusho. He has now been succeeded by his nephew, Raja Tsotra Namgyal of Tering. This family had fled from Sikkim many years before, and has elected to remain permanently in Tibet, where it has large estates at Tering, near Gyantse, and Dobtra, not far from Khamba Jong. Its members form the senior branch of the ruling family of Sikkim, Raja Tsotra Namgyal being the eldest half-brother of the present Maharaja.

Tering was noted all over Central Tibet for its hospitality, and we frequently took advantage of this, as we knew that the family were genuinely pleased to have our company. When spending a few days with them we played badminton—which we taught the ladies of the family—engaged in archery contests and other outdoor games, while the evenings were spent in singing, dancing, and playing " Ba " and " Sho." The eldest son of the Raja, Kumar Jigmed, was sent to school in Darjeeling, and he spent the greater part of his annual holidays with us at my place in Kalimpong.

He has now married the only Tibetan girl who has been educated on Western lines, the daughter of a former chief minister of Tibet. The Raja's half-brother is an incarnate lama, and has his own monastery near the family mansion at Tering. This lama, one of the best-educated and kindly natured priests whom I have ever met, has recently been appointed to hold charge of all the monasteries in Sikkim, and has taken up his residence at Pemayangtse, the chief lamaserai in that country. I have always honoured his friendship. In his own private monastery is a " self-created " image of black stone, which is an object of veneration to the whole countryside.

One of the great days in Gyantse is the eighteenth of the fourth Tibetan month, when an immense religious banner, of silk *appliqué* work, depicting the Buddha, is displayed for a few hours on a specially built wall in the monastery. Of the side-pieces a panel about forty feet long and ten feet wide is missing, and the Tibetans say that it was stolen during the 1904 mission. I made inquiries about this matter, but could find no foundation for their assertion. Possibly it was taken by the Chinese.

In Gyantse City is an old Chinese temple, with large figures of King Kesar and his ministers. Despite the Chinese having left the country, this temple is still cared for by one old priest, who for a small consideration will tell the fortunes of visitors. One is instructed first to offer up a prayer, and then to select a slip of bamboo from among a hundred or so kept in a long vase. Having referred to the hieroglyphics on the bamboo, the old man looks up a corresponding page

THE ANNUAL DANCE AT THE PALKHOR CHHODE MONASTERY

THE MONKS WEAR ANIMAL MASKS AND BEAUTIFULLY EMBROIDERED SILK DRESSES. THE DANCE
IS CONDUCTED TO THE BEAT OF DRUMS AND SOUNDING OF LONG BRASS TRUMPETS AND CYMBALS.

in a book, and pronounces the fortune. I was told that I would live to be eighty-five, would have thirteen children, and would be successful in any lawsuit in which I might be involved! I have had the thirteen children!

Serchok, the residence of my old friend, Diwan Bahadur Phala Se, honoured with his title by the Government of India for long and good service with the Political Officer in Sikkim, was another favourite rendezvous for all of us in Gyantse. The Diwan Bahadur gave periodical entertainments, and would take no refusal of his invitations to British officials who happened to be in the place. He recently spent a year in Britain as the guest of Sir Charles Bell, his former chief, assisting that gentleman in the preparation of his books on Tibet.

From the Tibetan point of view, the greatest event of the year is the Losar, or New Year festival. This is kept up all over the country, in the tents of the nomads as well as in the mansions of the wealthy. The feast usually falls at the end of February, and everyone makes it the occasion of a general holiday, donning their finest apparel, and spending as much as they can afford on the entertainment of themselves, their friends and relatives. The celebrations are naturally on the largest scale in Lhasa, but in Gyantse and Yatung also the celebration is full of interest. Everyone has time to spare, as work in the fields is impossible owing to the earth being frostbound.

On New Year's morning people of every rank keep open house for anyone who cares to enter. Cakes, fruit and plentiful supplies of chang, the native barley-beer, are offered as refreshment. The lesser officials, dressed in their best clothes, pay their respects to their superiors. Even the servants come round with scarves of butter-muslin and small bowls of tsampa, or barley-flour, from which one has to take a pinch and scatter it skywards as an offering to the gods. Sometimes people taste a little, and then wipe their fingers on their left shoulder for luck. With the tsampa is offered chang, of which one is expected to taste a few drops. When offering their bowls of flour and beer the Tibetans wish their friends "Tashi Dele Phunsum Tsho," or "Prosperity and Perfect Happiness." The correct reply is "Tendu dewa thob-par sho," "May happiness be always present." In the bowls of the beggars and poor people it is customary to place a small coin.

During the afternoon each house has its family party, and feasting and merrymaking continue till a very late hour. The New Year festival lasts for two days.

At this time of the year, after receiving visitors in the morning, we used to ride round the city and look in on the parties of our Tibetan friends, where we joined in the dancing and games. We were always heartily welcomed; indeed, it was difficult to get away at a reasonable hour.

In Yatung the people believe that unless it snows on New Year's Day the crops will not flourish during the ensuing year, and it is a strange fact that every year while I was in the Chumbi Valley it did snow at that time, and during the whole of my time in Tibet the crops in that place never failed.

For the Losar, the professional Tibetan dancing-

parties prepare huge grotesque paper figures of mytho-
logical beasts and birds. These are illuminated and
used in the dances at night. Every year the Chinese
were in Tibet they made an immense paper dragon,
a hundred feet or so in length. With smoke belching
from its nostrils and mouth, and with large glowing
eyes, it would be carried round the town by men
concealed in its middle. At night a truly terrifying
spectacle. Attached to each dancing-party was the
inevitable humorist, who got himself up as a monstrous
bird and went from place to place laying illuminated
eggs the size of a football.

Diwan Bahadur Phala Se was a scion of a very old
family that had once been high in the councils of State.
His house, as already mentioned, was in Gyantse, and
he used to accompany Sir Charles Bell and myself,
when the former officer was in Gyantse, on excursions
in the neighbourhood. Phala Se was for many years
the confidential secretary to the Political Officer in
Sikkim, and I doubt if a more reliable man could have
been obtained to give advice on Tibetan political affairs.
One day he took me to see his old family mansion,
a very large place some ten miles below Gyantse, on
the Nyang river. On the way he told me the story of
how his family came to lose their power and estates.

Kyabgon Sengchen Rimpoche was a very famous
and holy lama attached to the Phala family. This
venerable priest resided at Dongtse, where the family
property was situated. To him, in 1882, there came
one Sarat Chandra Das, a Bengalee, who was suspected
by the Tibetans of being an emissary of the Government of India. At that time the Tibetans strictly

prohibited any foreigners except the Chinese from travelling in their country, and had proclaimed that any of their nationals who were found assisting any such persons should be severely punished. Sarat Chandra Das had obtained letters of introduction recommending him to the care of the Kyabgon Sengchen Rimpoche, who received him with all hospitality.

Sarat became the Lama's pupil, and studied Buddhism under his tuition, in return teaching his master Sanskrit. Sarat Chandras Das lodged in the Phala mansion close by for three months, during which he so endeared himself to the Phala Depon, then the head of the family, that he was able to persuade the Depon's wife to take him among her servants to Lhasa. He reached that city safely, and after a brief stay managed to get away undetected, and returned to India. Somehow or other the news of the Indian explorer's sojourn in Tibet came to the ears of the Tibetan Government, who proceeded to punish in the most severe manner all their subjects who had sheltered or aided him, so that in future no one would venture to assist other foreigners who might attempt to travel in Tibet. Kyabgon Sengchen Rimpoche was drowned, and the Phala Depon, a fourth-rank official, and his wife were imprisoned, flogged and tortured until they died. All the family estates were confiscated and all the property was appropriated by the Tibetan Government. The execution of the Sengchen Rimpoche created a profound impression among his countrymen, who revered him as a saint. The Phala family did not again raise its head until my friend the Diwan Bahadur began to retrieve its fortunes.

On arrival at the Phala mansion, which had been sealed by the Tibetan Government, and which, except for a couple of caretakers, has remained empty ever since, we were shown over it by those men. It is a typical Tibetan house of the better class, four storeys in height. We saw the room occupied by the Kyabgon Sengchen Rimpoche, who very obviously was a lover of animals, for on the wall of this apartment was the picture of a little dog, underneath which was written: "This is my dog," and the Lama's name.

Years before I had met Shabdrung Lama, one of the chief actors in this drama. He was formerly a personal attendant of the Lama, and an old trusted family retainer. This man had been arrested at the same time as his master, and had been placed in a prison at Shigatse, where he had undergone the most fearful tortures. He had been mercilessly flogged, starved, and had had bamboo splinters driven into the quicks of his nails. He survived, however, and managed to escape, making his way to Darjeeling, where he obtained a post as a teacher in the Bhutia Boarding-School.

He never forgave the treatment meted out to his master and himself, and was always planning revenge. He was engaged as a secretary and interpreter by Captain O'Connor at the time of the Younghusband Mission to Tibet, and once he was in that country he never omitted to impress on every Tibetan official with whom he came into contact that the expedition was the result of his working against the Tibetan Government, and that it had come to exact vengeance for the murder of his master. Many of the Tibetans believed him, especially those who had regarded the execution of that holy man as a heinous crime. Shabdrung Lama gave excellent service, and was rewarded with the title of Rai Saheb by the Government of India. I met Sarat Chandra Das many times in Darjeeling, and still have with me some of the manuscripts he gave me. He was an exceptionally proficient Tibetan scholar, and after his return from Tibet devoted the rest of his life to research work in Tibetan literature. His greatest work is his *English-Tibetan Dictionary*, which still remains a standard reference-book.

On another occasion Sir Charles Bell and I went with Kusho Phala Se to the hermitage of Nyangto Kyiphu, thirteen miles from Gyantse along the Shigatse road.

According to the strict laws of the lama orders every priest is supposed at some time during his life to retire into complete seclusion for purposes of meditation. The period should be three years, three months and three days, and should be performed in order to acquire an ascetic mode of life. This rule, however, is seldom carried out to the letter, most priests contenting themselves with retiring into meditation, every other year or so, in their own quarters, for periods of a few weeks at a time. Few of them will submit to the prolonged hardships that a lengthy spell of solitary introspection involves. Great spiritual merit attaches to the souls of those who retire from the world for years at a time, while rebirth in a higher plane, or even the attainment of Nirvana itself, is assured the devotee who remains in hermitage for the whole of his adult life.

The Nyangto Kyiphu Hermitage, or "Cave of Happiness of the Upper Nyang River," is maintained by the Kargyupa sect of the old Church. About fifty cells are to be seen, many of which are occupied by the ordinary hermits, who immure themselves only for the three-year period. Certain of the huts have, however, been occupied by the same inmates for anything up to fifty years. During my visit to this place I was filled with a feeling of sadness at the tragedy of lives thus cut off from humanity. It is amazing what these people will endure for their faith.

Founded about two centuries ago by the Indian hermit saint, Saraha, Nyangto Kyiphu has never since that time been without its quota of devotees. These, once they have taken their vows, are shut away from the world and from their fellow-men in small, filthy cells, without light or heat, or creature comforts of any kind. At the time of my visit there were about thirty tokden, as these hermits are styled, actually in the cells. A brief account of the procedure followed when installing one of these monks in his hut may not be without interest. Attached to the institution is a monastery, whose lamas are responsible for the feeding arrangements for the hermits.

On a devotee deciding to undergo a term of self-immurement he presents himself before the abbot of the monastery, who, incidentally, is an incarnate lama, and this prelate determines the terms and extent of the penance. First of all, religious preparation must be made, and only after this has been satisfactorily completed is the candidate permitted to enter one of the regular hermit huts, and then only for a preliminary period of three months and three days. At the expiry of this he comes out into the light again, and re-enters the monastery for further preparation by the reciting and learning by heart of passages from the Lamaist Scriptures. This first short period of solitary confinement is frequently sufficient to cause the candidate to abandon the idea of further confinement, but those who desire to pursue their vows to the full in due course enter on the second stage of their penance, which lasts for three years, three months and three days. During this second period many of the hermits become mentally afflicted, while others become fanatics.

At the expiry of the three-year term the hermit comes out of his cell once more, and by still further religious study prepares himself for the next term, which in many cases lasts until death. I saw a few lamas who were engaged in this last spell of study, and not one of them seemed normal, one of them being nearly blind. It struck me that such persons had very little say in their future arrangements, which is very satisfactory to the monastery officials, for should the supply of hermits fail they would suffer considerable financial loss from the drop in revenue from pilgrims, who at present visit this holy place in considerable numbers.

When the hermit enters his cell for the third time he usually looks his last on the sun, and speaks his last words to his fellow-men. Once he is closed in he must not utter a word, nor show his face to anyone from the outside world, not even to his lama attendants who bring him food. I saw the cell of a hermit who had been incarcerated therein for the almost incredible period of fifty-three years. Beyond his thin, skeleton-like hand he would show nothing of himself to anybody.

The last entry of the devotee into his cell is celebrated by an impressive religious ceremony, the entire staff of the monastery escorting him in procession to his living tomb. Once he has crossed the threshold of this the doorway is walled up, not even the smallest chink by which light might enter being left between the stones. The only articles he may take with him into his cell are one or two images, a bowl for tea, a cup, a rosary, and a wooden framework, the use of which will be seen later. His food is brought once daily by a lama attendant, who places it on a shelf outside the cell, in the wall of which is left a small aperture, closed by a shutter, through which the food, drink and utensils may be passed in. Some hermits when putting their hand out for the food drape it in cloth, so that not even that small part of their bodies may come into contact with the light.

During the first few years of this confinement the hermit is given only just sufficient food and drink to keep him alive, but later the ration is increased. Having eaten his food, and drunk his butter-tea, the hermit replaces the utensils on the shelf, and again closes the trap. On inquiry as to what happened if a hermit fell ill I was told that should the food remain untouched for three days his death is presumed, and the cell is broken open. I was also informed that a hermit who has once taken vows of lifelong retirement could in no circumstances break them, nor could he ever obtain his freedom, but I doubt if this rule is invariably observed.

When the hermit lama feels the approach of death he somehow crawls to the wooden frame which was carried into his cell years before. With its support, seated in Buddha fashion, with crossed legs, and hands folded in lap, he awaits his dissolution. To prevent his body from slipping from this position after death he ropes himself to the framework with his girdle. After breaking down the stone door, the attendant lamas examine the body, but on no account must it be touched. The corpse remains thus for a week or so, until it is found to have inclined to the right. Once this has happened it is ceremoniously removed, and disposed of either by burning, or by being cut up and fed to the vultures. Wonderful phenomena are said to have been observed at some of these cremations. I was told that sometimes a self-created image was found inside the deceased's skull, and several of these were treasured in the monastery. Those I saw seemed merely to be some kind of bony excrescence that had escaped the flames.

It is alleged that on other occasions a considerable number of tiny white rings of a very hard substance have been found among the ashes of the funeral pyre, and these are said to have the power of multiplying themselves by magic. The ashes of dead hermits, indeed of any holy lama of note, are always carefully collected and mixed with clay. The mixture is then fashioned in moulds into small conical figures, and placed on the shelves of chotens, or preserved in the monastery. Some are presented to pilgrims, who regard them as talismans.

The cells in which the hermits imprison themselves

are small, about twelve feet square, with low roofs. A drain runs through them, and this is the only means of sanitation. The condition of these places after years of continuous occupation can therefore be imagined. No fireplace is provided, nor is any artificial means of heating ever introduced. I was told that the longest period for which any hermit had been incarcerated at a stretch was fifty-nine years, an incredible time. Deprivation of the sunlight alone is a serious hardship in a cold country like Tibet. I came away from Nyangto Kyiphu depressed.

K

CHAPTER THIRTEEN

*British Trade Agency Headquarters—A Trade Agency—Game—Fishing
—An Outside Clinic—Medicine—Voluntary Military Service*

UP to 1912 the headquarters of the British Trade
Agency in Gyantse were located in a large
Tibetan mansion called the "Changlo," which
had been used as the British Post during the Younghusband Mission. In 1912 it was decided to build a
small fort, after the North-West Frontier pattern, in
which the entire Agency personnel could be adequately
accommodated. There was at first great difficulty in
obtaining a suitable piece of land for the purpose,
as the Tibetans demanded an unreasonable rental. At
length a site was agreed upon, for which an annual
payment of twenty-seven thousand rupees was asked.
After considerable haranguing with the Tibetans I
managed to get this rent reduced to nine hundred
rupees a year. The lease was signed by British, Tibetan
and Chinese representatives, and holds good to this
day.

The new fort was built, almost all the wood used in
its construction having to be carried to Gyantse from
the Chumbi Valley. This made the construction very
expensive, and so great was the value of a beam or a
plank at Gyantse that we had to maintain a very strict
guard over the woodstack, or the loss from theft would
have been very heavy. The fort was two-storeyed,
divided into compounds for the various quarters and

departments. Ample accommodation was provided for over three hundred persons permanently resident.

In charge of the Trade Agency was, of course, the British Trade Agent, with an escort of Indian troops commanded by one or two British officers. A warrant officer of the Supply and Transport Corps of the Indian Army was in charge of the commissariat department, while two British military telegraphists were responsible for post and telegraph arrangements. The Trade Agent's head clerk was also an ex-military man. Up to the outbreak of the Great War we had a British officer of the Indian Medical Service in charge of the hospital at Gyantse, but in 1914 we lost this officer, as well as the subaltern of infantry. They were not replaced until 1922. For many years we were therefore a small community of six persons. Under these conditions social restrictions, due to disparity in rank, were to a certain extent relaxed, and we were like one big family.

Differences of opinion arose among us, as is inevitable when a few men are billeted together from one year's end to another in a small place, with practically no society other than their own. But all the years I was in Tibet no serious quarrel ever occurred among the British personnel. In a few cases, however, the narrowness of the life drove men almost to the verge of insanity. One must possess the right temperament to live in such remote places. To some the life was an ideal one, and they endeavoured to prolong their tour of duty in Tibet. Little things served to amuse some of the people there. For instance, one of the officers commanding the escort extracted great amusement from dropping detonators down his neighbours' chimneys at night, nor did his "joke" fail in its appeal until his comrades retaliated by pouring buckets of water down his. Another had a mania for night alarms, in winter as much as in summer, when everybody in the fort, man, woman and child, had to turn out to alarm-stations in the bitter cold. Even the menials had to parade with buckets of water ready to put out fires. It must be admitted that there was a rum issue for all those who wanted it when the practice was over, but, even so, the alarms were not popular. We eventually scotched this enthusiastic soldier by getting a medical order published that it was dangerous for the troops' health to parade on cold winter nights.

There is plenty of game in Tibet, and the keen sportsman may obtain some very fine trophies of the animals that roam the plateau. For visitors, shooting and fishing is strictly prohibited, but during my time of office in the country, and still, as far as I am aware, officials stationed there are permitted to shoot and fish, provided they do not kill anything in the immediate vicinity of a monastery or nunnery. Very few of the Tibetan officials themselves hunt, for the lamas discourage the taking of life in any form, but there is a small class of hunters who make their living by trapping and shooting fur-bearing animals and musk-deer. Every year thousands of furs are sent out of Tibet, despite the Government having issued orders prohibiting the killing of game. Few Tibetans, however, are averse from sharing the spoils of the chase once the quarry has been killed. The officials with whom I have come into contact have repeatedly told me that there was no objection to the few British officers stationed in their country shooting, but that they did not wish Tibet to become the venue of hunters in large numbers, as is the case in Kashmir. There is a law forbidding any shooting and fishing whatever in the vicinity of the sacred city of Lhasa, but this regulation is constantly being violated by the Nepalese, which fact has undoubtedly something to do with the growing ill-feeling between Tibet and Nepal.

Game found in Central Tibet includes ovis ammon, burrhel, Tibetan gazelle and shao, and the predatory animals, including wolf, snow-leopard and fox. The wolves especially create great havoc among the flocks, to guard which the Tibetan herdsmen keep huge mastiffs, which are trained to be fierce. To protect the necks of their dogs from the fangs of the wolves thick padded collars are placed on them. Tibetan antelope and the wild yak are not found near Gyantse or Yatung, but I have seen the former to the west of Khamba Jong. Small game abounds, such as hare, partridge, sand-grouse, pigeon, with occasional snipe. The big lakes during the summer are literally black with countless thousands of duck and geese, which come there to breed.

Stalking in Tibet is, however, a most strenuous business, as it has to be done at an elevation of anything up to eighteen thousand feet above sea-level. One must, moreover, have experience in the country of judging distances, as at first, owing to the extreme clarity of the atmosphere, one is prone to underestimate distances.

In the Chumbi Valley, and in the gorges leading down from Pharijong, we got the monal, the blood and the tragopan pheasants, as well as snipe, rock-pigeon and snow-cock. Bear had their habitat above Lingmathang and Yatung, and were considered vermin, dozens being killed each season. Their skins, rough-dried, kept well in the cold dry climate of Tibet, and made excellent rugs. On many occasions we have had peasants and woodcutters brought into the little hospital at Yatung suffering from terrible wounds due to having been mauled by bears, which always seem to attack the face. The best time of the year for bear shooting was at the ripening of sweet buckwheat, for these animals love this grain.

Two or three families of Nepalese would come from their country every year and poach immense numbers of the beautiful monal pheasant, sending the skins down to India for sale, through Bhutan. So heavy were their depredations that there was danger of this magnificent bird becoming extinct in the Chumbi Valley. I, therefore, in conjunction with the Tibetan Trade Agent, took all possible steps to put a stop to this wholesale slaughter, and after a long time managed to catch the poachers red-handed. I fined them heavily, and told them that if they were ever caught poaching in the valley again they would be handed over to the Tibetans for punishment, which frightened them considerably. They never, as far as I am aware, returned to worry us after this. In southern Tibet and in Bhutan is found the rare takin, and I saw two live specimens of this beast, a male and a female, which were presented by the Maharaja of Bhutan to Major F. M. Bailey, then Political Officer in Sikkim. This officer had a fine collection of local birds and animals

Fishing

at the Residency in Gantok, and I heard later that he
presented them to the Edinburgh Zoological Society,
in whose gardens they are now to be seen.

When I first went to Tibet I occasionally fished in
the Amo river above Yatung, and caught many pounds
of small fry, which were excellent eating. In fact,
during the children's holidays, my family made it a
weekly picnic to go fishing at one or other of the
picturesque spots on the river. One day we landed
some tasty specimens, and after they had been fried
and eaten I happened to wander along the bank looking down into the water, and came upon hundreds of
similar fish feeding on a human corpse, which had
been thrown into the river as a form of burial. We
never ate local fish again! In Gyantse fairly large fish
are caught, sometimes weighing as much as fifteen
pounds. The Tibetans stretch nets across a shallow
part of the stream, where the water is slow, and their
companions go upstream and frighten the fish into
the nets by throwing stones into the water. The fish
caught at Gyantse were too insipid and bony for
eating.

The Government of India established an outside
clinic in the Gyantse Bazaar, where anyone could on
application receive free medicines and treatment. Free
vaccination was given to any who applied, for smallpox
is a national scourge, and every third person, of both
upper and lower classes, whom one meets is pock-
marked. Once started, in a town or monastery, this
disease spreads with astonishing rapidity, fostered by
the insanitary and crowded conditions in which the
people, and especially the lamas, live. No isolation of

infected cases is practised. At first the Bazaar clinic
was an absolute failure, for the Tibetans mistrusted
anything new in the form of medical treatment, and
the lamas were strongly opposed to it, as every patient
who went there meant so much financial loss to themselves. In Tibet the practice of medicine is a Church
monopoly, and is inextricably bound up with the
affairs of the soul. Very few cases came to the hospital
from the town, unless the lama doctors had given
them up as incurable. As a rule, when this happened,
the sick were too far gone for anything to be done. In
spite of this, however, the clinic soon became quite
popular, especially for the treatment of eye cataract,
for which hundreds of successful operations have been
performed in Gyantse and Yatung.

During the Great War medical charge of the Gyantse
and Yatung posts devolved on two Sikkimese youths
who had been trained in India, and appointed to the
Tibet Agencies to assist the British Medical Officers.
These two young men proved very satisfactory, especially Bo Tsering, the one stationed at Gyantse. This
man had a genius for the treatment of eye complaints,
which are very common among the Tibetans, due
to the severe weather conditions and duststorms of
the plateau, as well as to continual attacks of snow-
blindness. These two young doctors were also in charge
of the meteorological observation stations in Tibet. Bo
Tsering has recently been given the title of Rai Saheb
by the Government of India for his good work at
Gyantse.

In 1914 Tibet offered her troops to Great Britain, an
offer which, while deeply appreciated as a demonstration

BLESSING THE PEOPLE IN THE CHUMBI VALLEY

1. HIS HOLINESS, THE DALAI LAMA, IS STANDING UNDER THE UMBRELLA. EACH SUPPLIANT
PLACES A SCARF AND MONEY OFFERING AT HIS FEET AND IS TOUCHED ON THE HEAD BY HIS
HOLINESS' TASSEL.

2. THE DALAI LAMA'S THREE CHIEF LONCHEN, OR MINISTERS, AND THE AUTHOR, IN 1912.

of the good will then existing between the two peoples, could not, for obvious reasons, be accepted. Many Tibetan subjects did, however, enlist independently in Indian corps, and they rendered excellent service. During the war we received daily Reuter's Press Telegrams direct, so that in far-off Gyantse we were aware of what had happened even before the news was printed in the Calcutta newspapers. The messages usually came through in the evenings, and every day, after tea, a group of anxious officers would gather in the tiny telegraph office to hear of the latest developments.

In April 1916 Major W. L. Campbell, C.I.E., R.A., was appointed as the British Trade Agent at Gyantse, where he remained until the end of March 1918, when he took over the duties of Political Officer in Sikkim, from Mr C. A. Bell. Beyond routine work, and ordinary dealings with the Tibetans, nothing of particular interest occurred during those years in Yatung, to which Agency I reverted. In March 1918 I again took over charge of both Gyantse and Yatung, which I held till my retirement from Government service in 1925.

CHAPTER FOURTEEN

*The Death Roll—A Sad Affair—Situation in Kham—Military Honours
—Some Amusing Incidents—Mrs Bell—Schary's Story*

DURING my time in Tibet, apart from the Younghusband Mission we had very few deaths among British officials stationed there. Conductor Hann, of the Indian Supply and Transport Corps, died in Gyantse in 1915, and being the only qualified person I had to read the Burial Service over his body, which is interred in the Gyantse cemetery. His death was due to pneumonia, contracted after a chill due to going about insufficiently clothed in the bitter weather of the Tibetan plateau.

A very sad affair occurred in Gyantse in 1917. An ex-military telegraphist, who was employed as the Trade Agency head clerk, was found one afternoon dead in his quarters. A shot had been heard from the direction of his room. The door was forced open, and it was discovered he had blown out his brains.

The last death among officers of the Agencies was that of Lieutenant Chatterjee, an Indian who was for a short time the officer commanding the escort in Tibet. This unfortunate gentleman suffered greatly from insomnia, probably the effect of the height, which affects some people that way. He had contracted the habit of taking a sleeping draught each night. One night he must have taken an overdose, for he was found dead in his bed the next morning. He was one of the officers commissioned under the scheme for the

Indianisation of the commissioned ranks of the Indian army, and was very popular. We were all very sorry to lose him.

Owing to the increased number of Chinese troops that were being employed on the Sino-Tibetan frontier the situation in Kham, the Tibetan province on that border, became serious. It was feared in Lhasa that China, if successful in that province, might be able to resume her former powers in Tibet, and to prevent this the Tibetan Government decided that some of their troops should be trained in modern methods of warfare. To this end, the permission of the Government of India having been obtained, batches of Tibetan soldiers, fifty at a time, with their officers, were sent down to Gyantse for training under the British and Indian officers of the Trade Agents' escort. With only a few intervals, Tibetan troops were being thus trained up to 1924. I became friendly with many of the officers attached to these Tibetan troops, among others Changlochen Kung, a descendant of the family of a former Dalai Lama, Doring Theji, the son of a great landowner near Gyantse, who, incidentally, was of higher rank than his father, Tsoko Depon, and Kyipup Kusho. The Kung and the Theji, officers of the third rank, proved very apt pupils. Unfortunately, when they returned to Lhasa, they became involved in a scandal over Government rifles, which they had been keeping in their private houses instead of in the State armoury. They were degraded and dismissed from Government service, in addition to losing all their titles.

About this time another grave scandal in the capital

brought about the downfall of many of the most promising young officers in the Government employ. The excuse for their degradation was that they had adopted European dress and manners, and had cut their hair short, but the real reason lay deeper than this. Several of the younger military officers had signed a pact to assist each other, in every way, in the conflict that was even then brewing between the civil and military powers. One person, however, though present at the conference at which this compact was drawn up, refused to sign it, and revealed the matter to the Government. This informer, Dzasa Trumpa, was afterwards appointed as Commander-in-Chief of the Tibetan Forces, displacing the Tsarong Shap-pe, who was alleged to be at the head of the military faction. The Dzasa, however, did not hold his position for long, for he became an opium addict, and was dismissed, being succeeded by Tsipon Lungshar, now the most influential man, after the Dalai Lama, in the country.

Tsoko Depon, a general officer in the Tibetan army, paid me a unique tribute on the occasion of my final departure from Gyantse in 1924. He turned out all the Tibetan troops then in that district as a guard of honour, and ordered his buglers to sound a valedictory fanfare—an honour usually reserved for the Dalai Lama alone. On asking him why he had done this, he replied that it was to do honour to so great a friend of Tibet, and to register appreciation of my help in arranging for the training of his men by the British. This officer made a great name for himself by subduing and settling the disputed Po province, on the eastern

Tibetan marches. Eventually he was recalled to Lhasa, and his colleague, the Garra Lama, was arrested, but managed to escape in an ingenious manner. He was imprisoned in southern Tibet, and one day, feigning death, was buried. That same night some of his friends dug him up, and he was able to make his way to China. His gaoler, Phangdong Chhondze, another army officer, of the fifth rank, may have aided him, at least the Tibetan Government thought so, for this man was brought to the capital and his goods confiscated. In addition he was given fifty lashes a day for some time, after which he was made to perform the lowest menial work as a sweeper in the Summer Palace of Norbhu Lingka.

During the training of the Tibetan troops in Gyantse many amusing incidents occurred. Most of the Tibetans learned a few words of Hindustani from their instructors, though all words of command were given in English. General Pereira, when he came through from China to India, *via* Lhasa, told me that he had been amazed to hear English words of command used by the Tibetan troops on the far-off Kham frontier. This showed that the Tibetans still remembered something of what they had learned at Gyantse.

It must be mentioned that the Tibetans had adopted the British style of uniform. One morning we found that each Tibetan officer had paraded with British war medal ribbons on his left breast. When requested to take them down it transpired that, having seen our own officers wearing them, they assumed that the ribbons were part of the uniform. In the place of our medal ribbons they later wore some of their own devising, each one selecting the colour scheme that pleased him most. They considered a " brightening-up " effect as necessary to the sombre field-service kit that was worn in Tibet !

In 1917, though still in charge of the Yatung Agency only, I visited Gyantse in company with Mr Bell, then the Political Officer in Sikkim, who was making his annual visit to Tibet. Mrs Bell (now Lady Bell) accompanied him on this, and indeed on several of his tours, and proved herself a good traveller, and keenly interested in the Tibetan people, especially the women-folk. Mrs Bell is the most travelled European woman as far as Tibet is concerned. The Political Officer visited Tibet every year, arranging his tour to avoid the worst of the rainy season in Sikkim, which can be very trying. He usually spent a couple of months or so in each of the Tibetan Agencies, though on two occasions he spent eighteen consecutive months in the country. He sometimes visited Bhutan to pay over the subsidy granted to that country as rent for the Dooars. He travelled in Bhutan also from time to time, his chief visit to this Himalayan state being in 1910, when, on behalf of the British Government, he concluded a treaty by which Bhutan placed her foreign relations under British control, in return for a guarantee of non-interference in her internal administration. His visits to Tibet made a welcome break for us. Beyond the inspecting officers of the Public Works Department, and of the Post and Telegraphs, very few visitors came to Tibet during most of the time I was in that country. It is only of late years that occasional tourists have been permitted to enter Tibet.

October 1918 was marked by an unusual occurrence. I was in Yatung at the time, but I had the story from the Gyantse men and met the chief actor therein afterwards when he passed through the Chumbi Valley on his way down to India. As I have already described, the British Trade Agency at Gyantse was located in a small fort garrisoned by Indian troops. One evening, at dusk, a begrimed and filthily clad figure, covered with festering sores, crawled up to the main gate of the fort. In Hindustani he asked the sepoy sentry to let him in. The sentry, taking him for a Tibetan beggar, refused, and ordered him away from the Post. The man sank down on a stone by the gate, and said to the sepoy: "I am a white man! You must let me in!"

He pulled up the tattered sleeve of his robe, and showed the sentry a rather dirty and very brown arm. The sepoy was sceptical, thinking that if the wanderer was a sahib he was very different from any other he had ever seen, and again ordered him away from the gate. At this stage the senior Indian officer of the detachment, a subadar, came along, and took the affair out of the sentry's hands.

The wanderer again insisted that he was a white man, and asked if there were any of his race in the fort. When he heard that there were he asked the subadar for a piece of paper and a pencil, and wrote a note, which he begged should be given to one of the sahibs. This note was handed to my head clerk, Mr Martin, and read as follows:

"I am Schary, an American, and have arrived starving and sick at your gate. The sentries will not let me in, and I ask your help. If you do not assist me I shall die here, as I can go no farther."

The note was signed " S. G. Schary."

As soon as this letter had been read Schary was, of course, brought into the fort, and given some food and tea. Afterwards he was bathed and his sores attended to by the doctor babu. He was in a terrible condition, verminous, ill-nourished, and really very ill. After he had been clothed in borrowed garments, and had rested for a while, he told his story.

Several months before he had been employed in Kashmir by a timber concern, and, having saved a few hundred rupees, decided that he would cross Tibet from Ladakh to the Chinese frontier, for the experience of the journey, which had never been done before. He intended to write a book about his adventures. His funds were small, so with only one servant, a pony, and with few rations, he set out from Leh, the capital of Ladakh. A fortnight out from this place his pony died, and he was forced to continue his journey on foot, as he would not turn back. A few days later his servant decamped with the bulk of his money, leaving him with less than a hundred rupees for his two-thousand-mile journey. Still he refused to retrace his footsteps, and made his way onwards, begging at the villages and monasteries he passed on the road. For weeks he existed on the hospitality of the nomads, for his money was soon exhausted. Gradually he was reduced to rags and semi-starvation, for Tibet is an inhospitable country for the destitute foreigner, especially when the latter can speak only a word or two of the language. Moreover, the Tibetans living in the outlying parts of the country fear severe punishment should they assist any unauthorised interlopers, who might be spies.

By the time Schary had been on the road four or five months he had given up all idea of reaching China, and his sole object then was to get out of Tibet as soon as he possibly could, as the severe winter of the Tibetan plateau was fast approaching. He then found that, for anyone unprovided with the necessary letters of authority, leaving the country was not an easy matter.

He made his way to the Nepal frontier, only to find that the Nepalese frontier guards would not let him pass. Disheartened, and by this time desperate, he attempted to force his way past the guards, but was turned back with violence. Then he somehow got the idea that there was a British Post at Shigatse, and determined to make his way thither, and throw himself on the mercy of the officers in that place. He travelled from the Nepal frontier to Shigatse, by marches that must have been terrible ordeals, only to find that his information was incorrect. Starving, ill, and with cut and bleeding feet, he told us that he had literally crawled the last few miles into that city.

In Shigatse he got correct information of the Gyantse Trade Agency, sixty miles away to the south. For three or four days he was unable to move, but at last he dragged himself away, and arrived, after dreadful sufferings, at Tsechen, a monastery four miles from Gyantse, from which the British fort could be seen. After a rest there he crawled painfully on, until he was able to see the Union Jack flying over the fort.

L

He said that he broke down at this sight, for he knew that his troubles were nearly over. Will-power alone carried him along to the fort gate, only to find that he was denied entry. Schary said that had he not been given admittance he would surely have died at our gates, as he was unable to move another yard. He could never have got back to the Tibetan city, even though it was only a mile or so away. This, from the state he was in, was evidently true. Several weeks of careful attention and dieting nursed him back to health. His craving for anything sweet-tasting was pathetic, for the Tibetan of the poorer class very seldom uses sugar, and Schary had been deprived of this luxury for several months. We had to watch him carefully or he would have finished a full tin of jam at every meal. He was eventually sent down to India, and after he left Yatung I never saw or heard from him again. While he was convalescing in Gyantse Schary used to play the violin to the men, who said that he was a very fine musician. How a violin happened to be in Gyantse I do not know, but someone unearthed it from some godown.

Schary's story, in so far as it related to his visit to the Nepal frontier, was afterwards proved to be true in a peculiar manner. Just before Christmas 1919 I was travelling down from Gyantse to Yatung to spend that festival with my family. As was my custom, I halted in Pharijong, where the local officials and headmen called on me to pay their respects. Among them was a former headman of a village on the Nepal frontier. This man produced a sheet of coarse European-made paper, on which there was writing in English. He asked me what it was about. To my surprise it was a letter written by Schary, and bore out his statements regarding his movements on that frontier. In it he damned the inhospitality of the Tibetans, who had evidently received him with coldness. Apparently it had been written on a page torn from the report-book of the Nepal frontier guard.

JUNE and July are the months of the outdoor festivals in Gyantse, as the weather is then at its best. Little work remains to be done in the fields, as the crops are then ripening. Early in June a horse-race is held, which brings the people out in their thousands to make holiday. Certain of the great houses must, by custom, enter one or more ponies for this race, under penalty of a fine. The origin of this custom is obscure, the only information that I could get being that "it had always been done."

One peculiarity of this race is the belief that if a pony belonging to the house of Phala should win, no good fortune will come to the city or to its people during the ensuing twelve months. Steps are therefore taken to make sure that such an animal does *not* win, although it has to be entered regularly every year. On race-day thousands of spectators throng the slopes of the hill on which the Tibetan jong is perched. All arrangements for the race are made by the representatives of the houses of Gabshi and Phala.

The course is about six miles long, starting at a place called Rinang, and finishing below the jong. At the start the ponies are ridden by small boys, specially trained, but these riders invariably contrive to fall off before half the distance is covered, leaving the riderless ponies to be driven by relays of mounted men for the remainder of the course. Never within human memory has a horse finished other than riderless. The winning pony is decorated with strips of silk of the five sacred colours, the second receiving only a white silk ceremonial scarf. At about eight o'clock in the morning the race is over, for it starts at daybreak, and the spectators spend the rest of the day picnicking and playing games in the open air. Strangely enough, the Tibetans, who are very fond of gambling, do not bet on the result of this race.

When the Chinese were in Tibet we used to have regular race-meetings at Gyantse, with a proper course, and a totalisator, which was largely patronised by both Chinese and Tibetans. The former, of course, were inveterate gamblers, and were very prompt in settling their debts of honour. Should a Chinese not be able to meet his liabilities on the spot he would give an IOU, which would be redeemed faithfully the next morning. The Tibetans themselves are not so keen on the actual racing, though races similar to those of Gyantse are held at various centres all over the country. They have some allegorical meaning, but I could never find out what this was.

What really delights the heart of a Tibetan is a picnic. He never misses an opportunity of spending a day in the open air, and makes the most of a short summer. At this time of the year, wherever one went, one would see, in the vicinity of the towns and large villages, little parties, usually consisting of the members of one family, spending the day out of doors. Each party takes a small tent, for shelter from the wind, and after partaking of a meal they while away the time playing the Tibetan guitar, dancing and singing.

Archery is one of the favourite sports of Tibet, and is practised at many of their outdoor festivals and picnics. Their bows are fairly short, about four feet long, and are made of a tough wood imported mostly from Sikkim, or from the Abor country, which borders on the southern frontier of Tibet. They are strung with twisted gut. When not in use, the bows are kept in decorated leather sheaths, arrows being carried in a quiver holding about twenty. For competitions two kinds of arrows are used, steel-tipped for long-distance shooting, and for short distances a somewhat shorter arrow fitted with a wooden whistle. The ordinary arrow is a yard long.

For use with the whistling arrows, the target, which is placed about thirty paces distant from the archer, consists of a wooden disc, nine or ten inches in diameter, suspended from the middle of a cord stretched between the tops of two poles, six feet high. In the centre of this disc is a loosely fitted wooden plug, three inches across. The object of the competitors is to knock this plug out of the disc. With practice one can become surprisingly accurate if the same bow is always used. I could myself, after a year or two, reckon on hitting the plug squarely once in every three shots, and not to miss it by very much any time. At parties where there are several archers present it is customary for each of them to place a small stake in the pool, which goes to the first man to dislodge the plug, lots having been drawn for the order of firing. As a variation of this procedure each successful competitor takes out of the pool a sum equal to the original stake, in which case the pool lasts longer. When it is exhausted each man renews his stake. For long-distance shooting a target, some twelve feet square, is marked out on the ground four hundred paces from the firing-point, and the man who drops his shaft nearest the centre of this takes the pool, or is awarded the prize. At fixed intervals, competitions in archery are held at the big centres, under the patronage of the Tibetan Government, which provides small rewards for the winners.

Early each June a great open-air festival is celebrated at Gyantse, near the paper factory, during which archery contests figure on the programme of events. All the townspeople turn out for this, and picnics on a grand scale are held for three days, the time being spent in various sports and trials of strength and skill. In the evenings follow gambling, singing and feasting. This occasion coincides with a bathing festival for the townspeople, who take the opportunity of having a thorough bath in the Nyang river, which flows quite near. All bathe together, men, women and children, for the Tibetan has no false modesty. Afterwards they all don their finest apparel, so that the festival becomes a kaleidoscope of colour, for Tibetans, especially the ladies, do not err on the side of sombreness when selecting material for their gala robes. The brightest coloured silks and brocades are chosen by the more well-to-do people.

Apropos of bathing, one is told that the average Tibetan is a dirty person. This is to a great extent true, especially of the lower classes. Still, they have some excuse. In a cold country like Tibet it is impossible for people to bathe in the icy waters of streams and lakes except during summer. At other times of the year fuel is so scarce that, after providing for cooking purposes, there is no surplus available for heating bath-water. The better-class Tibetans do bathe frequently. When I first went to Tibet I was told by a humorist that there was no need to carry a razor. All one had to do to get rid of a beard was to rub a little water on one's face, and go outside for a few minutes, after which, by passing one's hand over the face, all the hairs, being frozen, would break off short! This, fortunately, was not literally true, but when coming along the trade route in the winter, between the two Agencies, the breath from the nostrils would cause lumps of ice to form on one's moustache. The Tibetans consider that dirt is lucky. Accumulations on sacred images are often washed off and the cleansing water drunk as a medicine for certain diseases.

The lamas of the Palkhor Chhöde Monastery attend the festival at the paper factory *en masse*, and participate in wrestling, jumping and skipping competitions. Each monk brings his own cup and bag of barley-flour. For meals they are seated in two long rows, two yards apart, facing each other, and much laughter is caused when one of the more greedy priests produces an outsize in bowls for the free tea-ration. Before commencing their meals the lamas chant a most impressive grace, led by their precentor. At the midday meal large quantities of rice and meat are cooked for them in huge iron cauldrons. The younger monks gorge themselves with this until they can hardly stand, for it is not often that the ordinary lama gets rice to eat. The main article of diet in the monasteries is tsampa, or parched barley-flour, eaten in the form of dough made into balls with butter-tea. I noticed at this festival that some of the elderly lamas were not averse to assisting their digestion by occasional helpings of barley-beer.

On this occasion everybody is on pleasure bent. Each of the local notables had his own large tent, comfortably furnished with cushioned seats, pitched on the scene, and here he entertained his friends. We of the British Trade Agency would also have our tent, and would spend the afternoons and evenings joining in the festivities. Our tent was specially popular, as each evening we provided dinner in European fashion for any of the Tibetan officials who cared to come along. We invariably had a tent full of curious Tibetans, who wished to taste the kind of food we ate. The amount of barley-beer consumed at this festival was prodigious, and there was a continuous procession of small boys and women carrying large earthenware vessels of beer from the town to the scene of the feasting. This barley-beer is quite wholesome, and if not allowed to ferment for too long is very mild.

The festival is held at the paper factory, which is the main centre of the industry in this part of Tibet. Large quantities of paper are made there, mostly for the Tibetan Government, which uses it for the printing of sacred works for distribution to the monasteries, especially the Kangyur and Tengyur, the Lamaist scriptures and commentaries. These works consist of one hundred and eight and two hundred and twenty-five large volumes respectively, and are very expensive. The paper is sent from Gyantse to the printing-houses at Narthang, near Shigatse, which have the wooden carved blocks from which these and other sacred works are printed. There is no such thing as type in Tibet, each page of a book is laboriously carved in reverse characters on wood, from which the impression is made. The blocks for such a work as the Tengyur occupy several large buildings, each set of blocks being kept in separate racks. There is only one set of iron blocks, for the Kangyur, in the whole of the country, and these are, or used to be, kept at Derge, in Kham.

When anybody desires a copy of one of the more uncommon works, for which blocks exist, it is customary first of all to order the paper, and when this has been made, and delivered, to place instructions at the monastery which holds the blocks for printing. For each page, according to size, a charge of one to two trankas, or threepence to sixpence, is made for the actual printing, which is done by lamas. If no blocks exist the work must be copied in manuscript, which is more expensive than printing. Except in the case of small and popular religious works and calendars no retail trade is done in books. The more common pamphlets are bought from the monasteries, which print them, by wandering book-pedlars, who may be seen displaying their wares in the market-places of the bigger towns and villages. Such publications usually contain recipes for repelling demons, and the ritual in certain religious ceremonies, and are mostly bought by lamas.

The actual method of paper-making is very crude

and unpractical, but the results are satisfactory to the Tibetans, who seldom use any paper but that made in their own country, either for correspondence or for printing. The thicker and coarser kinds are used for printing and packing, while the finer qualities are used for letter-writing. From the hills around Gyantse large quantities of the bark from a species of a small poisonous shrub are collected by forced labour, each village, according to its size, having to send out so many workers. This bark, having been steeped in water for several days, is pounded by foot in a specially constructed trough. The resultant glutinous mass is then spread on one side of a fine gauze net, stretched on a wooden frame, about four feet square, and then washed in gently running water to remove impurities. It is then respread to the required thickness, and the frame is placed in the open air to dry. After the moisture has evaporated the sheet of paper is peeled off, trimmed, and is then ready for use. It is a peculiar fact that few insects will attack Tibetan-made paper, owing to its poisonous content, and for this reason also one must be careful not to remain too long in a room where large numbers of Tibetan books are stored, or severe headaches will result.

In July is held a semi-military rally, the venue being an open space of ground a mile from Gyantse town. All who can ride and use a bow or gun may come to test their skill in open competition. From all the countryside, and from the town, people flock to see the fun. The local notables pitch their tents facing a course about two hundred yards long, while the common people seat themselves where they can get a good view of the proceedings. They bring with them provisions for the day, not forgetting the inevitable barley-beer.

The rally opens with an inspection, by the senior official present, of the equipment, dress and general turn-out of the competitors. Some of the ensembles are quite good, the pony trappings being very ornate, and sometimes costly. One often sees saddlery mounted with silver, and with cloisonné enamel work, and turquoise-studded bridles. The finest Tibetan saddlery I have ever seen belonged to a Gyantse landowner. It was of supple leather, decorated with real gold cloisonné, and showed exquisite workmanship.

Two targets, about fifty yards apart, are set up on the course. Each is mounted on a tripod, five feet in height, one being for arrows, the other for bullets. From a given point each competitor in turn has to get his mount into a gallop, loose his arrow into the first target, and, on the return run, fire his prong gun into the second, without slackening speed until he has crossed the starting-line. Marks are given for style and speed, as well as for marksmanship. The winner receives little by way of a monetary reward, but enjoys the admiration and respect of his fellows. Local Tibetans told me that this affair was in olden times of much greater importance than at the present day, every able-bodied man in the district having to turn out with his weapons. Apparently it was a form of annual training for the levies which have always formed the bulk of the Tibetan army. The meeting is becoming smaller every year.

In mid-June the lamas of the Palkhor Chhöde

Monastery in Gyantse hold a three days' dance, which is well supported by the townspeople. Held in the main courtyard of the monastery, this festival portrays with all hideousness the devils that the Lamaist will meet on his way through Bardo, the Valley of the Shadow of Death. In order that the ordinary layman may not be terrified at these dreadful shapes, the lamas encourage their followers to see the devil-dances whenever possible, so that they are always assured of a good audience. The biggest dance of its kind is held every year at the monastery of Ten-Chok Ling, which is about twelve miles from Gyantse. Every twelfth year a specially elaborate show, with new masks and robes, is given, and I was fortunate in being able to be present at two of these special functions. The dance will be found fully described in my book, *The Land of the Lama.*

CHAPTER SIXTEEN

*Sino-Tibetan Treaty—Signing of the Armistice—Tibetans & Trade
Agencies—Official Calls*

DURING the summer of 1918 I was busy with the matter of the Sino-Tibetan Treaty that was then being negotiated by Mr Eric Teichman, the British Consular Officer on the Sino-Tibetan frontier. All communications and correspondence in this connection were sent through me for encoding and telegraphic communication to the Government of India. It was quicker, and certainly more reliable, to send dispatches across Tibet to Gyantse than through China to India. Both parties to the dispute had been carrying on desultory fighting for several years, and were tiring of guerrilla warfare. The Treaty was finally signed on 19th August 1918. During the conflicts which preceded the peace negotiations the Tibetans had demonstrated their superiority over the local Chinese troops, and finally established supremacy in eastern Tibet by the capture of the stronghold Chiamdo.

As far as we in Tibet were personally concerned, the great event of 1918 was the signing, in November, of the Armistice ending the Great War. In far-off Gyantse the news reached us at practically the same time as it was generally known in India, thanks to the excellent Press telegram bulletins received by the British Trade Agents in Tibet. The evening we received the information will always be remembered by those five of us there at the time. The following day, however, we decided that the event should be commemorated in such a manner that the Gyantse Tibetans would not soon forget our joy, and we planned a celebration on a scale the like of which had never been seen before in that city. Invitations were issued to every Tibetan of any standing at all, whether private or official, lama or layman. We fixed the date of the entertainment a week ahead, and sent a crier round the town to summon the poorer people to witness our happiness. It was our intention to provide a feast for the poor people and the beggars, and to give lunch and dinner to the official and private families.

The beggars began to arrive on the scene a couple of days before the appointed time, determined not to miss anything. Just outside the Gyantse fort we had a large polo-ground, round three sides of which were pitched tents and marquees, the latter borrowed from the monastery, for our guests. The abbot very kindly lent us many low cushions, used as seats in Tibet, and carpets to cover them. The common people and beggars sat wherever they could find room. Sports events open to everybody, and archery competitions, were carefully arranged. The fun of the fair included a casino, from which all profits were to be devoted to charity. I should estimate that at least three thousand people gathered on the appointed day. We built special fireplaces, on which rice was cooked, in bath-tubs, for the masses! Maunds and maunds of this cereal were boiled, and proved a great treat for the majority of the people. For the accompanying curry we used yak-meat, bought on the hoof. The cooking was done by sepoys of the escort, and the menials of the Agency garrison. The beggars had their feed at eleven o'clock in the morning, and they literally gorged themselves. What they could not eat they carried away.

An arrangement was made with several of the local hostelries for six hundred gallons of chang, or barley-beer, at sixteen gallons for the equivalent of fourpence. For the townspeople we gave much the same food as for the beggars, except that we put mutton curry in place of the yak-meat. They received also a portion apiece of potatoes, considered a luxury among the poorer Tibetans. The citizens were no more backward than the beggars in surfeiting themselves with curry and rice, nor did they neglect the beer, of which everyone, except the lamas, drank their fill. The latter enjoyed similar fare to the townspeople, but were served separately. Officials and local gentry lunched, and later dined, with us, in English fashion, at long tables set out under a marquee. We had insufficient available space within the fort to entertain our guests, and had to make the best of things outside. No one seemed to mind that chilly November evening, as we were all securely wrapped up in furs.

As already mentioned, it was decided to take this opportunity of raising funds for war charities, and as it solved the problem of amusing the guests between meals, and in the intervals of sport, roulette-tables and " lucky dips " were arranged. The former were placed in a large tent, and the latter out in the open, on the polo-ground, where everyone could " dip " in comfort.

For roulette was fixed a maximum stake of thirty rupees—about two pounds sterling at the then rate of exchange. The officer commanding my escort, assisted by one of the military telegraphists, ran this, while the lucky dips—at one tranka, or threepence, per chance— were supervised by my head clerk and the commissariat conductor. I spent most of my time entertaining the lamas and higher Tibetan officials, who did not take an active part in the fun of the fair.

These two side-shows yielded a substantial sum for charity, the wealthier Tibetans seldom staking less than the maximum on the roulette. They staked on the colours only, and would have nothing to do with the numbers or combinations, which they do not understand. The Tibetans had seen roulette before, for during the Chinese occupation it was played considerably in Gyantse. The lucky dip was most popular. As prizes we had collected cows, calves, goats, sheep, yaks, fowls, pigs, sacks of rice, flour, bags of potatoes, boxes of dried fruits, bottles of wine and liqueurs, soaps, matches, tins of kerosene oil, candles, biscuits, bottles of sweets, hair-oil, hurricane lanterns, empty bottles, packets of cigarettes (this was before smoking was prohibited in Tibet), cloth, sugar, salt, penknives, scissors, and innumerable other small articles that we could get in the fort and the bazaar. The little shop run by my head clerk more than justified its existence on this occasion, for we cleared its entire stock. Altogether there were over a thousand prizes, some small, some large, and these having been numbered, corresponding tickets were placed in a large box, with a suitable number of blanks.

M

Everyone was attracted by this novelty, for nothing quite like it had ever been seen before in Tibet. Fortunately the first few tickets sold drew one or two of the larger prizes. As a result, a steady demand was kept up until the last chance had been sold.

At dusk the townspeople returned to their homes, but the officials and gentlefolk remained on till the early hours of the morning, entertained by a party of professional actors and actresses that we had engaged. Altogether it was a most successful affair.

The Tibetans delighted in visiting our Trade Agencies, and none of our invitations was ever refused. They liked English food, with the exception of fish, against which they are somewhat prejudiced on religious grounds. They believe that the souls of lamas who fail to maintain their set standards of purity while on earth enter at death into the bodies of fish. Consequently they prefer to avoid the risk of offending the gods by complete abstinence from all forms of fish diet. Many of the poorer class Tibetans, however, especially those living near lakes or rivers, have no such qualms. Some of the lakeside villages do an extensive trade in dried fish. Indian tea as made in European fashion was found by the Tibetans to be insipid, though they would drink it, sweetened to a sickening degree, out of courtesy. Lay officials and private persons were very fond of European liquors, especially in liqueur form, their great favourite being *crème de menthe*, probably on account of its warming properties. Ginger-wine was also popular.

When a Tibetan official came to call on me he invariably would be accompanied by a number of servants, according to his rank. In Tibet prestige demands that one must have as many retainers as possible. While the master was being entertained in my quarters, his servants would be provided with refreshments in the servants' lines. In Gyantse I had set aside a special room for this purpose. Of course, when I went calling, my servants were entertained in return. Officials of every rank made a point of calling at the fort when passing through, sometimes bringing their womenfolk with them, and it was a pleasure to entertain them. They displayed the keenest interest in everything that they were shown, especially in our manners, customs and mode of living. Their first attempts at using our cutlery were often amusing, as much to themselves as to us, for the Tibetan has a lively sense of humour. One does not meet with the caste prejudice in Tibet that so greatly limits intercourse between Indians and Europeans, nor is there anything in the nature of purdah for Tibetan women. For instance, should one be visiting a Tibetan gentleman, and he be not at home, his wife and daughters will always entertain one until his return. Ladies will sometimes make calls unaccompanied except by a maid-servant. This degree of freedom is rarely met with in India.

CHAPTER SEVENTEEN

A Visit from the Tashi Lama—The Tashi Lama's Mother—Incarnation of Amitabha—The Tashi Lama's Brother—Appearance of the Tashi Lama

EARLY in 1919 I had a letter from His Serenity the Tashi Lama informing me that he was going to Lhasa, and that on his return from the capital he intended to travel *via* Gyantse, in order to meet me again. He mentioned that he was visiting Lhasa at the request of the Dalai Lama. In due course news of his approach was received, and I, with my mounted escort, accompanied by the British officials in the Gyantse Trade Agency, rode out about six miles to meet him, as far as the mansion of my friend Gyalse Kusho, the head of the Tering family. Every Tibetan official, in his robes of office, who was then in the city, was also present to welcome His Serenity.

Gyalse Kusho had refreshments ready for us, and entertained us while we were awaiting the prelate's arrival. He had prepared a special room for His Serenity's reception, and he asked me to intercede on his behalf should his humbly proffered hospitality be refused by the Tashi Lama.

The Tashi Lama arrived at about eleven in the forenoon, escorted by a brilliantly equipped retinue of about a hundred persons. He dismounted, and greeted me warmly. We had not met since 1912, the occasion of his first flight from Shigatse, and he seemed very

1. THE MOTHER OF HIS SERENITY THE TASHI LAMA
TAKEN AT GYANTSE DURING A VISIT TO THE AUTHOR.

2. ARRIVAL OF THE TASHI LAMA, IN HIS SEDAN CHAIR
TAKEN ON THE OCCASION OF HIS VISIT TO GYANTSE IN 1911.

pleased to see me again. After our greetings were over, and I had introduced the other British officers who were with me to him, the higher rank Tibetan officials who had come to meet him advanced and paid their respects. His Serenity stated that he wished to move on to Gyantse immediately, as he was tired, and wanted to get the journey over. Gyalse Kusho then made his request that the Tashi Lama should enter his house, and sanctify it by remaining there a few minutes; but he was met with a refusal. I could see that the old man was bitterly disappointed, for the Grand Lama might never pass that way again, and as Gyalse Kusho was a very special friend of mine I persuaded the Lama to make a short halt, and thus honour the house of my friend. Should a High Lama, and, above all, should the Dalai or Tashi Lama, enter a layman's house, and remain there even a few minutes, it is considered a mark of great honour and a certain harbinger of good fortune for the entire family, even ensuring for its members high and more worthy reincarnations. Hence the keen desire of my friend that the Tashi Lama should cross his threshold. This piety left Gyalse Kusho poorer by two thousand rupees, which he offered as a gift to the Lama. His Serenity blessed every member of the Tering family, who knelt before him one by one. I noticed during his visit to Gyantse that the Tashi Lama would bless a priest by touching his head by hand, while all others, except laymen of the highest rank, were blessed by being touched with a tassel of red silk cloth attached to a short rod, called tar-chang.

After half-an-hour at Tering the Tashi Lama

mounted his horse. The procession was re-formed, and we moved off to Gyantse. I rode on the Lama's right hand, the officer commanding my escort on his left. At the head of the column were two mounted infantry sepoys carrying the Union Jack, which always preceded me on official excursions. The mounted infantry of my escort followed. Next came the Tibetan officials of Gyantse, the lowest in rank riding first, the highest last, and immediately behind these came the Tashi Lama. The rear was brought up by the Lama's own people, and the remainder of my escort. *En route* the Tashi Lama pointed out to me a very fine white riderless pony, which he said he had brought for me from Lhasa.

On either side of the road, at intervals of a hundred yards or so, from Tering to Gyantse city, reverent citizens had erected large earthen incense-burners. As His Serenity approached these were lit, so that for several miles we rode along in a mist of fragrant incense. Approaching the city, crowds of people lined the track, and as we passed at a walk they joined in behind the procession. By the time we reached the Palkhor Chhöde Monastery, where the Tashi Lama was to stay, almost every able-bodied person in the city and its vicinity was following us, a wonderful testimony to the reverence in which the Tashi Lama is held in that part of the country. The Tibetans believe that certain spiritual reward is gained even by merely gazing upon the persons of either of the two Grand Lamas. They never miss an opportunity of acquiring merit, so necessary in obtaining rebirth on a higher plane. This rebirth depends entirely on the amount of spiritual merit accumulated during their sojourn on this earth.

Having escorted the Tashi Lama as far as the monastery, I accepted his invitation to lunch, and arrived back at the fort in the late afternoon. His Serenity promised to lunch with me at the fort the next day. I had specially requested the Tashi Lama to bless the Lamaists in the Agency personnel, and for this purpose I had prepared an audience-chamber. The throne itself was formed of large square cushions, piled to a height of four feet from the floor, and draped with silk brocade of the sacred yellow colour.

Next morning His Serenity arrived at about ten o'clock, with a large retinue, which of course also had to be entertained. He inspected the guard of honour drawn up to receive him, and having exchanged ceremonial scarves we sat talking for an hour or so. He then intimated that he would bless the people in the fort, who were all ready, dressed in their finest clothes. Taking his seat on the throne, the people filed past him, each being touched with the red silk cloth. Every suppliant bowed at the foot of the throne and placed on the ground before him a monetary offering tied in the corner of a scarf. The senior among my Tibetan clerks were specially honoured by being touched with the Lama's finger-tips.

After this ceremony was over, lunch was served in the mess dining-room in English style, only the Tashi Lama, among all the Tibetans present, seating himself at the table. No Tibetan would dream of seating himself in the presence of this god on earth, as such an action would be considered sacrilegious. Some of his officials stood behind his chair throughout the entire meal. He partook of every dish offered, but drank only water. I was careful to see that no fish was served. He seemed especially fond of tinned fruits, of which, before he left Gyantse, he obtained a supply from the small shop in the fort run by my head clerk. When lunch was over we retired to my private sitting-room and discussed various matters.

I gathered from his conversation he was not at all certain of the future, and that the Lhasa Government were pressing him very hard in the matter of revenue, of which they alleged that he was in considerable arrears. He stated that the Dalai Lama's ministers were likely to deal very harshly with him, and that during his recent visit to Lhasa only a temporary settlement had been arrived at between the Central Government and himself. Altogether, he seemed very despondent, and I was unable to comfort him. He professed his utter inability to meet the revenue demands of the Central Government, as his province, that of Tsang, could never raise the sum levied. The Lama asked me to use my influence on his behalf in the event of an open breach between himself and Lhasa. He almost broke down when telling me of his position, and he seemed to feel the attitude of mistrust against him. As a matter of fact, these two Grand Lamas always insist that they personally are friendly, and blame all their differences on the intrigues of their respective ministers.

To honour the Tashi Lama I sent my escort with him as far as the monastery, on his departure from the fort. I knew that every single detail of his visit would be reported to Lhasa, as well as the attitude I had adopted towards him. Before taking his leave the Tashi Lama told me that he intended to start for Shigatse before dawn the next day, so at three in the morning, with my mounted escort, I rode out to the Palkhor Chhöde to bid him farewell. It was a bitterly cold morning, and snow was falling heavily, so that I and the officer commanding my escort were very grateful for the steaming hot butter-tea that was provided on our arrival. At that moment His Serenity was engaged in performing a ceremony in one of the temples, and we were informed that we could watch this from a balcony. Thus for over half-an-hour we listened to the deep impressive chanting of the assembled lamas below us, and observed the ceremony being conducted.

This over, the Tashi Lama received the homage of the Gyantse monks, blessing each one by touching his bowed head with his finger-tips. His Serenity looked very weary, and had obviously had little or no sleep, but when he finished in the temple he came straight to us and partook of tea. He conducted us to his room, where small bowls of rice, cooked in butter, and dried fruits were passed round. Before we ate, the Lama solemnly blessed the food. My confidential Tibetan clerk, a devout Lamaist, who was also present, instead of eating his portion surreptitiously emptied his bowl into the pouch formed by his robe and waist-band, to take home to his family, for once the Lama had blessed it this food was sacred. Such food is considered a very potent talisman as protection against all ills and misfortunes.

After the repast, during which the Tashi Lama drank his tea from a wooden handleless cup, lined with heavy gold plate, he drew us aside and, seating himself between my escort commander and myself, took one of our hands in each of his, and continued his conversation of the day before. Although I was not at the time able to interpret some of the things he said, I now know, in the light of later occurrences, that he was even then considering the advantages to be gained by fleeing from his country.

At about half-past five in the morning he brought the conversation to a close by blessing both of us, laying both his hands on our heads—a very great honour indeed, and one that I am certain had never before been given to any European. As dawn was breaking we rode out of the monastery, through the sleeping town, on to the broad Shigatse plain. The Lama was robed in furs, over which he wore a long, yellow, quilted silk cloak. A yellow fur-lined cap with long earflaps covered his head. I and my escort accompanied him some six miles on his way, and then bade him farewell. I never saw him again. To-day he is a refugee in Manchuria, whither he was eventually forced to flee owing to the persecution of the Lhasa Government. Whether he will ever return to his country is problematical, but a large percentage of the Tibetan people are anxious from religious motives to see the Tashi Lama reinstalled at Shigatse under any conditions.

On this occasion I met the Tashi Lama's mother, a venerable old lady of over seventy. Since her son's selection as the incarnation of Buddha Amitabha she has taken the vows of a nun, and she accompanies her son, now literally a living god, wherever he goes. She has unfortunately been deaf and dumb from birth, but she is able to communicate her thoughts by signs. The old lady, like her son, gave me to understand that she was much perturbed over the trend of political events in Lhasa, and by signs besought me to protect the Tashi Lama from harm. As a parting gift she presented me with a beautifully worked bead-mat, the work of her own hands.

The story of the birth and discovery of the present incarnation of Amitabha, the Buddha of Boundless Light, is interesting. His mother was of very humble birth, a shepherdess, and was otherwise employed as a menial on the estate where she was born, a slave. She would be away in the hills tending the cattle sometimes for weeks at a time. When the last incarnation of the Buddha passed away she was found to be with child, but she either could not, or would not, reveal who was the father. There is a story, which is widely credited, that the infant's father was a High Lama of Takpo, from which district the present Dalai Lama also comes. Some people have professed to have detected similar physical peculiarities on the persons of the present Tashi Lama and Dalai Lama. They assert that these are hereditary in the latter's family. At the time of the Tashi Lama's birth unusual phenomena were in evidence. The crops that year were exceptionally fruitful, and the numbers of cattle and sheep increased beyond the average. It is also said that the first time the infant placed its foot on a stone its footprint remained indelibly engraved. The committee appointed to discover the child into whose body the incarnate soul of the Buddha had entered without hesitation adopted the herdswoman's child as the next Tashi Lama. The old lady died in 1926.

I also met, and later became very friendly with, the Tashi Lama's younger brother, who had been ennobled and given the title of Kung, or Duke, as is customary in Tibet where relatives of the two Grand Lamas are concerned. The family of the present Tashi Lama seems doomed to misfortune.

In appearance the Tashi Lama is a little below the average height, and of medium build. He has a meek, retiring nature, and dislikes intensely being involved in the political intrigue so noticeable in Tibet. He is very timid, as is evidenced by his desire to fly from the slightest danger.

AN instance of the ungoverned brutality sometimes displayed by the Tibetans is afforded by
an occurrence in the Chumbi Valley that came
under my direct notice. Fortunately such incidents
are not frequent. One day the Tibetan Trade Agent
at Pibithang, then the Depon Lheding Se, the same
man who was later concerned in the trouble arising
from the withholding of rations from the Chinese
prisoners from Chiamdo, invited me and my family to
spend the day at his house. As was the custom, we
arrived there at about eleven o'clock in the morning,
as soon as I had finished my office work. A few other
local Tibetan notables were present, and having par-
taken of the inevitable butter-tea the menfolk of the
party settled down to play " Ba," the Tibetan domino
game.

My wife and daughters were entertained in another
room by the Depon's wife, who showed them her
household treasures, silks and embroidery, and so forth.
We amused ourselves thus until lunch was served, a
light repast consisting of thukpa, a kind of spaghetti,
cooked with chopped meat and soup, handed round
in small bowls. A few curries and cold-meat dishes
were also offered, everything, of course, being eaten
with chopsticks, in the use of which all my family

were proficient. After a short rest and a smoke—the Depon himself indulging in the usual Tibetan smoking-mixture of tobacco and chopped rhubarb-leaves, cupped in a small, brass-bowled, long-stemmed pipe—we were told that a very special entertainment had been arranged for us. Ushering my wife, daughters and myself into a small courtyard near by, where seats had been placed for us, the Depon dramatically pointed to the scene that met our eyes. Pegged out, face downwards, on the ground was a man, naked, his back and thighs badly lacerated, obviously as a result of whipping. Standing by were two brawny Tibetan soldiers, with raw-hide whips in their hands, ready to begin on him again. My wife and daughters, of course, promptly fled inside the house, while I asked the reason for the affair, and pointed out to the Depon the impropriety of inviting them to see such sights. Not a whit abashed, he told me that the prisoner had deliberately burned down the village of Phema, in the Lower Chumbi Valley, and having been caught he had sentenced him to be flogged at the rate of three hundred lashes a day until he died. The victim of this cruelty turned his eyes towards me—he was obviously past all speech—and I could see from the glare in them that he was a madman.

I had heard about the burning of this village, and it was, as I knew, a serious matter for the people who had been rendered homeless, and who had lost all their household goods and stores of grain for the winter. In the Chumbi Valley the houses are nearly all built of wood, which is plentiful there, with shingle roofs. In the dry autumn weather they burned like tinder, once the fire had started. But from what I had heard, the burning of this village was as much the result of accident as of design. I explained to the Tibetan Trade Agent that it was nothing less than sheer barbarity to punish a madman in the manner he was doing, and worthy only of uncivilised savages. No matter what he had done, if they wanted to kill the man they should behead or shoot him, and have done with it, and not torture him. I, moreover, told the Depon that I would certainly not be a witness to any further flogging. The whipping was then stopped, and the man placed under guard in a prison chamber attached to the Trade Agent's house. This place was not strong, and I was not surprised to hear later that he had escaped to Sikkim, from whence he could not be brought back, as there was no law of extradition between that country and Tibet. The Tibetan authorities pressed for some time for his surrender, but without success.

Tibetan officials have almost unlimited power over the subjects in their districts, and by bribery and flogging in many cases amass comfortable fortunes during their tenure of office. Magisterial work is done by the Jongpens and depons of the fifth and fourth rank respectively. They are responsible for the collection of revenue, and for the maintenance of law and order in their districts. Jongpens are usually appointed for a period of three years, but in some cases they hold office for longer terms. In the Tibetan courts there are thirteen grades of legal fees, payable according to the status of the persons concerned in the cases, and according to the matter under dispute. These

" costs " must be paid before a case is heard, and when fines are inflicted a certain proportion of the money thus realised becomes the perquisite of the judge and of his court subordinates. According to the size of his district each magistrate has to remit a certain amount of fine-money every year to Lhasa, any excess of this amount realised being divided among the court officials —three-quarters to the magistrate, and one-quarter to the clerk of the court. It will be seen therefore that it is in the officials' interest to encourage litigation.

Revenue for each district is also fixed, and any excess collected goes into the local officials' pockets. Every year the Central Government at Lhasa circularises every official—possibly tongue in cheek—to perform his duties faithfully, exhorting him to refrain from oppressing the people. Law principles are contained in a code called " The Thirteen Judgments," of which each magistrate has a copy. Confession and evidence are extracted by flogging. In the courts each party to a case first of all files a written statement, and witnesses are examined after this has been deposited. There is a Tibetan proverb that runs : " The sheep that has wool, fleece him ! The fish that has no hair, beat him ! " And the magistrates faithfully follow this saying when dealing with litigants.

Each official above the sixth rank keeps a register in which every event of importance occurring in his district is recorded. I was fortunate in obtaining that of the Pharijong magistrate at the time of the British expedition to Tibet in 1904, in which the last entry is : " This year the enemies of religion, the British, arrived here, and war resulted." In this register was also written down the code of the "Sixteen Laws" by which officials are supposed to govern their conduct. I still have this book of records, the only one in existence as far as I know, outside of Tibet. Much of the recent history of the country would become clearer if all these records could be collected and examined. The code of the "Sixteen Laws" runs as follows:

1. To have faith in God, to worship Him, and to make offerings at all times.

2. To believe in the doctrine of retribution, and to refrain from sin.

3. To honour and serve one's parents.

4. To return kindness with kindness.

5. To follow the example of the virtuous, and to avoid imitating the vulgar.

6. To behave with becoming modesty.

7. To acquire knowledge from the learned.

8. To pay no heed to the words of women.

9. To deal with true weights and measures.

10. To pay taxes and debts when due.

11. To serve the public and to harm nobody.

12. To respect age and superiors, and to obey them.

13. To pay heed only to the calls of duty, and not to engage in outside pursuits.

14. To keep promises, and never break oaths.

15. To be loyal to superiors and to obey their orders.

16. To perform all duties with conscientiousness, and to administer justice and truth.

I am sorry to say that these precepts are more often honoured in the breach than in the observance, in Tibet as elsewhere.

N

TOWARDS the end of the summer of 1918 the
influenza epidemic sweeping the world came
to Tibet, carried in, it is believed, by the mails
from India. Later, returning traders also brought the
infection. Two days after the first case, Gyantse was
as a city of the dead. In our own fort, people were
lying ill all over the place, and the few Europeans,
before they themselves caught the disease, carried the
sick into the hospital and sepoy barracks, which was
used as a sickroom. The small hospital was hopelessly
inadequate to cope with the emergency. In Tibet the
danger came not so much from the influenza itself
as from pneumonia, that almost invariably followed.
The sub-assistant surgeon in Gyantse, although he
was unacquainted with the complaint, worked un-
ceasingly, until he himself contracted influenza. We
isolated the fort, cutting off all communication with the
Tibetan city, which suffered terribly. The monastery
especially was a death-trap, owing to the insanitary
conditions in which the lamas herded together. The
Tibetans had no knowledge of suitable treatment, nor
did they appreciate the necessity of isolation. All they
did was to hold services in the temples, burn immense
quantities of butter in their altar-lamps, and beseech
their gods to save them. My friend the Nepalese

agent in Gyantse dropped dead from heart failure
brought on by influenza. All communities suffered
alike. We had many deaths in the fort, and, following
the dictates of their religion, the Hindus naturally
burned their dead, on pyres erected by the river-side.
As time went on, and the burnings grew more frequent,
a deputation arrived from the Tibetan city requesting
us not to burn any more dead bodies, as the smoke
from our funeral pyres was wafting across the city and
thus conveying the disease to the Tibetans! Fortunately for all concerned, we had no more Hindu deaths
after the arrival of this deputation, so that question did
not arise again. The whole of central Tibet, one of the
most thickly populated parts of the country, suffered
severely. The deaths were so many that the local
Ragyapa, or cutters up of dead bodies, could not deal
with the number of corpses, which eventually had to be
buried, and later dug up a few at a time and disposed
of in the usual manner in Tibet.

Before the epidemic really got a hold in Gyantse
I was called to Yatung to meet His Excellency Lord
Ronaldshay (now the Marquis of Zetland), then
Governor of Bengal, who was visiting Tibet. It was at
one time thought that His Excellency's tour would
have to be abandoned owing to the influenza epidemic,
but he decided to take the risk of infection. When I
arrived in the Chumbi Valley from Gyantse I found
that the influenza had already got a firm hold on the
community. Every other person appeared to be affected.
Unfortunately, as soon as I arrived in Yatung, I myself
became the victim of a very mild attack, but was soon
about again. I was followed down from Gyantse by

the officer commanding my escort, who, failing to get any response either by telegraph or telephone from his Indian officer in Yatung, was naturally worried, and decided to come down to that place by forced marches to see what had happened. His presence was also required for the occasion of Lord Ronaldshay's visit. I recovered sufficiently to struggle out and meet His Excellency at Old Yatung, six miles from the Agency. I took my escort with me, and accompanied the Governor to the dak-bungalow in Yatung, where he was staying with his staff.

Captain Perry, the officer commanding my escort, then became very ill. He had had to vacate this bungalow to make room for His Excellency's party, and he was staying in a house in the Yatung Trade Mart Bazaar. As soon as he left me, after seeing Lord Ronaldshay to the dak-bungalow, he must have returned to his quarters and gone straight down with a very bad attack of influenza and malarial fever. I did not realize what had happened until the next day, when his orderly told me that his officer was very ill, and dying. I at once went down to the bazaar, and there found this unfortunate young officer delirious with fever, and attended by some lamas, whom his Tibetan servants had called in! The Yatung sub-assistant surgeon was down with influenza at this time and could not move from his house. Two lamas were seated in one corner of Captain Perry's room, one tapping a drum while the other clashed cymbals, both intoning passages from the Lamaist Scriptures the whole time, the idea being to prevent the sufferer from sleeping. It was believed that all sickness was caused by the action of malignant demons, and if a sick person slept too much, more devils would enter his body. The officer was being given only cold barley-beer to drink, and no food—not that he wanted any—was allowed. I turned the lamas out and placed the orderly in charge, with instructions to forbid anyone's entry to the sickroom, and undertook the treatment myself. It was some time before this officer was himself again, and I consider that only his exceptionally fine constitution and stamina pulled him through alive.

On this occasion Lord Ronaldshay remained only a few days in the Chumbi Valley. Accompanied by myself and Mr Gourlay, I.C.S., his private secretary, His Excellency visited the Tungka Monastery, six miles above the Trade Mart, and there consulted the lama oracle, or Choje, the medium through which Chokyong, the Defender of the Lamaist Faith, makes manifest the matters on which inquirers seek information and guidance. This particular oracle was famous throughout central Tibet, and was occasionally called to Lhasa, to deliver his oracles regarding affairs of State policy.

I knew this Choje very well indeed, as he was a constant visitor to my house in Yatung, and I was able to arrange a séance for Lord Ronaldshay's benefit. After looking over the monastery we were offered refreshments, consisting of butter-tea, dried fruits, and biscuits. We then proceeded to the main temple hall, which had been prepared for the occasion. We found the Lama Oracle ready seated on his throne, dressed in gorgeous silken brocades, and with a large polished metal breastplate edged with a row of turquoises, with the mystic sign "HRI" devised in the centre. His head-dress was a kind of casque, edged with small skulls fashioned from metal. In his right hand he held a heavy two-edged broadsword. Lamas seated to one side of the throne chanted invocations, while others, placed opposite them, beat drums and clashed cymbals, this service being conducted to induce the controlling spirit to enter the Choje's body.

After a while slight tremors began to shake his frame, increasing as the music swelled in volume until his whole body was violently agitated. Suddenly the Choje rose to his feet. Swaying from side to side he began to flourish the sword round his head. The spirit had now taken full possession of him. As soon as this happened, the crowd rushed forward and prostrated themselves before him, worshipping the Chokyong, the spirit that was in him. Gradually the oracle's face became suffused with congested blood, and he began to gasp out guttural monosyllables, which were written down on a slate by a lama scribe, specially trained for the purpose. No one else could understand their meaning. After a brief spell the Choje's body grew slack, and he dropped back exhausted on his throne. Yet again he worked himself into a frenzy, and answered questions put to him by the scribe at his side. The lama orchestra played and chanted during the performance. After he had pronounced his last oracle the seer quickly returned to normal, and shortly afterwards disappeared to disrobe. Among other questions put by Lord Ronaldshay was one as to when the Great War, which was then raging, would end. The reply gave November of that year, 1918, as the month in which hostilities would cease, a surprisingly accurate statement, coming as it did from one who could have had no knowledge whatever of world politics, or even of the progress of the war.

The spirit immediately controlling this oracle is said to be that of a departed lama, Shong Ton by name, and who is regarded as the Chokyong of the Tungka Monastery. The local priests believe that this deceased monk has taken this means of propagating the Lamaist faith.

While describing this visit to the Tungka Oracle Lama it may be of interest to note his career, which is typical of such seers all over Tibet. They rise from obscurity, flourish for a while, and then, either through jealousy or their own pride, they decline in power and return to the obscurity whence they emerged. I first met this Choje when he was a boy of sixteen, in 1912, shortly after his " discovery " by my friend the abbot of the Tungka Monastery, known and revered all over central Tibet as a " Geshe Rimpoche," a " Precious Teacher." It had been observed that this youth, then an ordinary village lad, would occasionally fall into a trance, during which he would utter cryptic sentences, which certain of the lamas professed to be able to understand and interpret. The boy was sent to Lhasa, where the priests of the Karmashar Oracle, then the State Seer, after careful examination and observation, decided that the youth was controlled by spirits. He was trained to pass under their direct influence at will.

After several years of careful instruction the young oracle returned to the Chumbi Valley a fully fledged

"Choje," or "Lord of the Faith," and was installed in the Tungka Monastery, being given a house just outside the institution proper, as he was considered to be outside the priestly orders. The Chokyong, or controlling spirit, was believed to have taken up its abode in a tree near by. This particular spirit marked its entrance into the medium's body by shaking his frame to an excessive degree. By this he became known as the "shaking oracle." His fame rapidly spread to Bhutan and Sikkim, from which countries people flocked to consult him, at a price. Thus wealth began to flow into the coffers of the monastery to which he was attached, and of which he became the greatest attraction.

Choje Kusho was an interesting young man, and we became great friends. I suspect, however, that he was an epileptic. He paid frequent visits to the Agency, and was always pleased to entertain me and my family whenever we went to the Tungka Monastery, which is situated above the beautiful Lingmathang plain, one of our favourite picnicking places when the children were home for their holidays. A keen student of everything Occidental, he would listen for hours to descriptions of European countries and the customs of their peoples.

The Tungka oracle took an almost childish delight in mechanical toys, and in photography. I gave him a folding Kodak, with which he eventually became quite proficient. In due course he brought me the first roll of films for developing, properly sealed, and requested me to send it to Darjeeling for development. It came back a blank. I therefore called the Choje down, and checking his method of operation found it correct, and got him to take some pictures with my own camera, which, on development, proved quite satisfactory. He took another unused spool from me and went off to try again. A few days later in came the used film, but again it turned out a failure. Clearly something was wrong, and it was only by accident that I found out what he was doing. One day, while he was with me, I had occasion to change the spool in my own camera. While I was fitting the new spool I happened to look round, and found the Choje carefully unrolling the used film to see what was on it. On inquiry I found that he had been doing this with his own spools, and carefully sealing them up again.

During one of my periodical visits to Yatung, in 1922, a messenger arrived post-haste from the Tungka Monastery and informed me that the oracle had died. Accompanied by the doctor babu, I rode up the valley the same morning, and saw the corpse, robed in ceremonial garments, laid out on a bench. After condoling with the abbot, I came away.

I was very surprised when, four days later, I received another message that the Choje had come to life again ! Once more I rode up to see him, and this time found him sitting up on his bed. He told me that his spirit had been wandering in Bardo, the Lamaist limbo where souls await their judgment by Shinje Cho-Kyi-Gyalpo, the King of the Dead. I suppose this must have been a case of suspended animation, for no other explanation would fit the circumstances. I refused to believe, with the Tibetans, that the Choje had been really dead. They call such a person a " delok," and by becoming this the Choje vastly increased his prestige and influence. I heard of one or two similar instances while I was in Tibet.

Eventually he was summoned to Lhasa to assist the Government in deciding important questions of policy, in which an oracle is invariably consulted. The Choje remained in the capital for several months, and returned to the Chumbi Valley a very important personage indeed.

I met him on his way down from Lhasa, at Dochen, and we travelled together for several stages. Later he fell in love with the beautiful sister of the Tibetan Trade Agent at Yatung, and married her. For this offence against the gods the Choje was unfrocked, and compelled to retire to his brother-in-law's estates, where he now leads the life of a country gentleman. The possession by an oracle of a wife, I gathered from my friend the abbot of the Tungka Monastery, raises the jealousy of the gods. A Choje having once disregarded the celibate state is adjudged incapable of being a reliable medium between gods and mortals.

The Bonpo priests, followers of the old pre-Lamaist faith, long jealous of his popularity, were well pleased with his downfall.

One of my greatest friends among the Tibetan priesthood was, and still is, the saintly abbot of the Tungka Monastery, near Yatung. He holds the title of Geshe Rimpoche, or "Precious Teacher," which roughly corresponds to the western Doctor of Divinity. This title is conferred only on very learned lamas, after years of study, and after very searching examinations. Not infrequently twenty years or more must be passed at one of the great lama colleges before a candidate is

BABY'S BATH
TAKEN IN THE MEDICINAL HOT SPRINGS AT KHAMBU, NEAR PHARI.

A PICNIC PARTY
THE WOMEN OF HIGHER SOCIAL STANDING MAY BE DISTINGUISHED BY
THEIR HEAD-DRESS.

THE LARGE URN IN THE FOREGROUND CONTAINS CHHANG, A BARLEY
BEER, VERY POTENT AND ONE OF THE MOST POPULAR BEVERAGES IN TIBET.

judged fit even to appear at one of these tests. The Chumbi Valley Geshe Rimpoche was trained in the priesthood at the Tashilhunpo Monastery, where the Tashi Lama formerly had his residence and head-quarters. He has dedicated his life towards bringing about a revival of Buddhism among the hill peoples of the eastern Himalayas. He is one of the very few missionary monks that are to be met with in Tibet, and has established monasteries at Kalimpong and at Ghoom, near Darjeeling, which he periodically visits, even though he is now an old man. The Geshe is greatly revered among the people with whom he works. He is a good, earnest man, and exceptionally tolerant where other faiths are concerned.

I once spent a week with him at the hot springs of Khambu, some fifteen miles west of Pharijong. Visiting these hot springs is a favourite form of holiday among the better-class Tibetans, who can thus combine medical treatment with their favourite recreation of picnicking. My family, and a few of the other British officials stationed in Tibet, used to visit these springs every other year. The spa of Khambu consists of nine springs, the waters of which vary in temperature. Several of the springs are enclosed in large stone huts, with an aperture in the roof for ventilation. Visitors either live in one of these huts, or camp near by.

On the occasions of our visits the Pharijong Jongpen would send word ahead to the caretaker, who would specially clean out one of the largest huts for our reception. I and my family were able to make this quite comfortable with thick rugs and a profusion of the thick Tibetan cushion-seats. The Tibetans and others seldom intruded on our privacy, although among themselves privacy is a thing unknown, men and women bathing together in the same pool.

Large numbers of afflicted persons came to these hot springs. The temperatures vary, some being quite moderate in heat, while others are too warm to remain in for more than a minute at a time. The hottest of the springs are not enclosed, and at these, in the winter, it is possible to sit on a block of natural ice with one's feet in almost boiling water. My family and I used to visit Khambu as a rule in September, remaining there about a week. The weather at that time of the year is dry and brilliant. Our days were spent in shooting, and exploring the neighbouring hills, and in visiting local notables. We bathed morning and evening in the medicinal spring enclosed by our hut, and it was very pleasant on our return from a strenuous day in the mountains to plunge straight into the hot water, and then laze about in dressing-gowns till dinner-time. The health baths would eradicate all fatigue. Dinner over, we would amuse the other comers to the springs with the gramophone, while they in turn would sing and dance, accompanying themselves on their Tibetan guitars. These springs are patronised by people from Sikkim and Bhutan as well as by Tibetans.

At the springs there is nothing but the bare huts, everything for food and comfort must be taken along by visitors. Each particular spring is believed to possess its own peculiar virtues in the cure of various diseases, and a small booklet describing these may be obtained in Gyantse from one of the local booksellers.

CHAPTER TWENTY

The Maharani of Sikkim—The Rakasha Depon—The Visit of a
Shap-pe—Loss of Favour in Tibet—Friction between Lamas
& Lay Officers

I FIRST met the present Maharani of Sikkim when
she passed through Gyantse in 1919 on her way to
be married. She was then only fourteen years of
age, and had never before been out of Lhasa, nor had
she previously met any European. For many genera-
tions it had been the policy of the ruler of Sikkim to
seek his bride in Tibet, and this procedure was not
altered in the case of the present Maharaja. The
bride and her escort of Sikkimese nobles, sent to conduct her safely to Gantok, stayed in the Gyantse dak-
bungalow for a couple of days, during which time
British officers stationed in that place and I paid our
official calls. She lunched at the fort with me. Since
her marriage she has attended a college in Musoorie,
where she learned English, and became conversant
with Western manners and customs. She is a very
gracious lady, and is an undoubted asset to the Sikkim
State, in the welfare of which she takes a deep interest,
besides being devoted to her children.

Years before I had met her father, the Rakasha
Depon, head of the great Lhasa family of the same
name, and which has in the past given several chief
ministers to Tibet. When he first called on me at
Gyantse I remember that he would on no account seat
himself in one of our ordinary English chairs, but

205

insisted on taking his seat on one of the low Tibetan divans, of which I had several in my sitting-room. His reason for this was that he would not presume to place himself on an equal with me by occupying a chair of the same height, but desired to demonstrate his respect by taking a lower seat. One seldom sees this nowadays among the younger generation of Tibetan officials. Rakasha had been a successful army commander on the Sino-Tibetan frontier, and he had come to ask me to use my influence with the Dalai Lama to obtain promotion for him. In Tibet all advancement is dependent on gaining and retaining the ruler's personal favour. After some hesitation, for I did not care to presume on my friendship with His Holiness, except in really deserving cases, I did eventually write to him about this matter, as I felt that General Rakasha deserved reward and encouragement.

The Dalai Lama replied, saying that while he fully appreciated the services rendered by Depon Rakasha, to promote him at that time would create much jealousy among the other army officials, and that this would benefit neither party. His Holiness stated, however, that he would bear this officer's name in mind for promotion when opportunity occurred. At Lhasa, in 1921, I was very hospitably entertained by the then Rakasha Depon, son of the officer referred to above. This young man is the full brother of the Maharani of Sikkim.

During the many years I have known the ruling family of Sikkim, I have been privileged to enjoy the friendship of the present Maharaja's sister, Rani Choni Wangmo La, now the wife of Raja Sonam Tobgay

Dorji, the popular young Prime Minister of Bhutan. Rani Choni, a charming, highly educated and accomplished lady, at present resides in Kalimpong, where she assists her husband in the management of his vast estates, for he is a wealthy man, holding large grants of land in Bhutan as well as a considerable amount of property in British India. In addition to his appointment as Prime Minister of Bhutan, he is assistant to the Political Officer in Sikkim for Bhutanese Affairs. While Rani Choni is interested in every phase of modern life she is yet a devout Buddhist, and has had a great deal to do with the establishment and endowment of the Buddhist monastery in Kalimpong, founded by another of my Tibetan friends, the Geshe Rimpoche of the Tungka Monastery in the Chumbi Valley. This young couple are most popular in every society.

For the Tibetans in Gyantse the great event of the year 1919 was an official visit of one of the four Shap-pe, or chief ministers, of Tibet. The officer who came down was Kunsangtse Shap-pe. Strictly speaking, the Lhasa Government should have had nothing to do with the internal administration of the Tsang Province, of which Gyantse is the second city, since this town lies within the province of the Tashi Lama. Gyantse being a Trade Mart, however, Lhasa supervised its administration, and appointed its officials.

As was customary in the case of high dignitaries, I rode out with my escort, some four miles, to meet the Shap-pe. Only for the Tashi and Dalai Lamas did I go out farther. Kunsangtse thanked me profusely for the courtesy shown him. In appearance he was a fairly tall, thin, ascetic-looking man, highly cultured according to Tibetan standards. His manners were perfect. He had the reputation of being a difficult man to work with, and of being very high-handed, and was therefore intensely unpopular among the lower rank officials with whom he came into contact. He was always courteous towards me, and would often accept my advice. During his visit he lunched with me at the Agency, and was much impressed with the guard of honour ordered for his reception.

He inspected every detail of the sepoys' equipment, and asked innumerable questions regarding their training and cost of maintenance in European style. He impressed me as an able administrator. At his first visit to the fort, Kunsangtse Shap-pe presented me with gifts sent by the Dalai Lama. These consisted mostly of Chinese porcelain and carpets.

The Shap-pe was staying in a large house lent for the occasion by a wealthy landowner of Gyantse. When I called on him it surprised me to find sentries posted at various unexpected corners. As one came round a corner in a passage, a sentry, stationed round it just out of view, would present or order his rifle with a crash, which being quite unexpected nearly made one jump out of one's skin. I had never met with such procedure in Tibet, and it spoke well for the discipline maintained by Kunsangtse. One of the sentries, as he ordered his weapon after saluting me, did so with such enthusiasm that the rifle went off, alarming the entire household. Luckily no one was hurt, but I noticed a neatly drilled hole in the ceiling, and wondered who was in the room above. Each sentry had a neat little tuft of red yak-hair in the muzzle of his rifle, which, even if not good for the weapon, was at least decorative.

Kunsangtse Shap-pe had his eldest son with him, who entertained us with an exhibition of Tibetan dancing, by a professional party that he had brought down from Lhasa. The Shap-pe remained in Gyantse for a fortnight, during which time every local notable called on him and paid his respects. After his return to Lhasa he wrote to me, and I had the pleasure of meeting him again when I visited that city in 1921. I again had many talks with him, and was confirmed in my opinion of his abilities. His strictness, however, had made him many enemies. In 1922 I heard that he had been suspended from his high office of chief minister. He again managed to get back into favour, and was appointed as the Minister of Agriculture, with the rank of Theji. He died in 1923. His son is now an officer in the new Tibetan army.

In Tibet it is fatally easy for an official to lose favour with the Dalai Lama, or with the Government, which consists mainly of the four chief ministers and the Lonchen, or Prime Minister. The slightest friction that arises causes the lesser man to lose his place. Lama officials of high rank, with the influence of their monasteries behind them, are not in so precarious a position as their lay brethren. It sometimes happens that loss of position is not the only punishment that befalls a deposed official. He often suffers confiscation of property, and in some cases imprisonment, and even flogging. For more serious offences the whole family of a disgraced official may suffer, women as well as

o

male members being mercilessly flogged if there is the slightest suspicion of their complicity.

Intense jealousy is rife among the lay officials in Tibet, and enemies will resort to any means of undermining a rival's influence with his ruler, or with his Government.

There is, moreover, constant friction between lama and lay officers, of whom more or less equal numbers are employed. The lama element in the Government has of recent years become very powerful. The actual excuse made for disgracing the Tsarong Shap-pe was that he ordered a soldier's leg to be amputated, and the ears of another to be cut off, for attempting to fight with the then newly raised Lhasa police. The Tsarong managed, probably owing to his influence with the ruler of Tibet, to retain his appointment as chief minister. The Dalai Lama had sworn that in return for the Tsarong's devotion in fighting the Chinese at Chaksam, in 1910, he would always protect him. Without this protection the latter would have had to endure much more than he did.

CHAPTER TWENTY-ONE

CHIAMDO, the Chinese post on the eastern Tibet frontier, having been besieged for several months, finally capitulated to the Tibetans in the autumn of 1913. The Chinese troops evacuated on the promise of considerate treatment and assistance in reaching their own country. This promise was faithfully kept, but the Tibetans took the precaution of repatriating their prisoners *via* India and Burma, so as to keep them out of the fray for some months at any rate. Disarmed, but still under the control of their own officers, about two thousand Chinese began their long march to the Indian frontier, being fed *en route* by the various Tibetan officials through whose jurisdiction they passed. On the whole they were fairly treated, and all went well till their arrival in the Chumbi Valley.

At that time Lheding Se, a Depon or fourth-grade officer, was stationed in Yatung, as Tibetan Trade Agent. Yatung was the last halt of the Chinese prisoners before they crossed into Sikkim, which is included in British Indian territory. The Depon considered that he could safely refuse to give rations to the Chinese, who would be anxious to hurry out of Tibet. The Chinese however refused to continue their march forward until they received suitable supplies, sufficient to last them till they could get into touch with their consul in Calcutta. Starving persons recognise no restraint, nor are they respecters of persons, as this emergency proved.

The Chinese were under the command of a major, their general having died during imprisonment in south-eastern Tibet. This major, with his second-in-command, called at the Agency to enlist my aid in procuring food for his men. Dispensing with formality I invited them in, as the matter had become urgent. They asked me to influence the Tibetan Trade Agent to give them supplies, failing which they suggested rations be given them from my own store. The British officer commanding my escort was in Yatung at the time, and together we gave, from our own reserves, several sacks of flour and rice, and other items such as tea and salt. For so large a number we were unable to give more than would suffice for one meal. The materials were not available, and only a limited amount of rations may be obtained for private use on payment.

However, little as we could do, the Chinese major was very grateful, and sent the foodstuffs at once to his men, who were in the Agency Bazaar. He and his junior officer accepted my invitation to lunch. Meanwhile the Tibetan Trade Agent rashly rode through the Agency Bazaar on his way to visit me. The Chinese, realising from the richness of his raiment, and his mounted servants, he was some high Tibetan official, ran into the road, and two of them seized his bridle.

The Chinese afterwards asserted that they merely wished to ask him about their missing rations. The

Depon slashed at them with his riding-whip, without giving them a hearing. At this the remaining Chinese closed in, the situation being further aggravated by the Depon's servants, who promptly bolted, their ponies knocking down several of the Chinese. Knives flashed, and the situation looked grave, when I hurriedly arrived with my sepoys. Holding off the Chinese we escorted the Depon to the Agency. There he actually demanded I should call out my escort and shoot the Chinese down. Naturally his mind was soon disabused of this idea, and I pointed out to him that the affair was really his own fault, owing to his withholding the rations, and suggested that a hint to Lhasa of what had taken place would probably result in serious trouble for himself. This brought about an immediate change in his hitherto uncompromising attitude. He spent the night at the Agency, and before leaving the next morning he promised the Chinese officers, in my presence, that the full quantity of rations to which they were entitled would be forthcoming. The Tibetan Trade Agent carried out his promise, and the Chinese left the valley in batches of five hundred or so.

The influenza again visited Tibet in 1919, but this year, fortunately, it was nothing like as virulent as in 1918. Many hundreds of people did die, but the country did not suffer as it did in the previous epidemic. It was during the 1919 outbreak that my youngest daughter, Bettine, was born, in Yatung. Altogether five of my children were born in Tibet; only four are now living, one being buried in the little cemetery established at the time of the 1904 mission. Among others, this God's acre contains the grave of

the first casualty of that expedition in the Chumbi
Valley, an officer who died from the effects of exposure
while crossing the Jelap Pass. Beside his grave are
those of two unknown British private soldiers. I did
my best to trace their names, but met with no success.
The cemetery is situated about half-a-mile above the
Agency on the Gautsa road.

One night in 1912 the graves of the British privates
were broken open, probably by Chinese soldiers, who
at that time were evacuating the valley. They must have
been under the impression that the British, like the
Chinese, bury valuables with their dead. On inspection I found the skeletons and a few rags of clothing
in the tombs. These were properly and reverently recovered, and I guarded against further molestation by
enclosing the cemetery with a high stone wall, having
glass set in cement on the top. Outside Choten Karpo,
the Chinese post in the Upper Chumbi Valley, is a
large Chinese cemetery, and I found that the graves
there had also been rifled.

In Gyantse and Yatung, all marriage, burial and
christening services were conducted by myself, in my
capacity as a magistrate and registrar. There were a
fair number of Christians among my clerks and
servants, who had their own little church community,
over which I presided.

In Gyantse the cemetery is situated a couple of
hundred yards from the fort, on the bank of the river.
Whoever selected this site showed very little fore-
thought, for the Nyang river changes its course almost
every year. On several occasions the fort itself has
been threatened, and only by rapid revetment, and

sandbag reinforcement, has it been saved. The fort would be better placed on the other side of the river, thus avoiding the necessity of a bridge, which at present constitutes a strategic weakness in case of siege or attack. The site, however, was the only one obtainable at the time.

In the cemetery are buried the casualties which occurred during the storming of the jong in 1904, and those Christian and Mohammedan British subjects who have since died in Gyantse. This cemetery is firmly believed to be haunted by the ghost of one Johnson, a former head clerk of the Trade Agency, who blew his brains out in the fort and who is buried there. The local people assert that his ghost sits on the cemetery wall on dark nights, calling out to passers-by for cigarettes. The tale probably arose as the result of some practical joke played by some-one in the fort. Not one of the native followers, however, will pass the place at night alone, preferring to make a wide detour through the fields to reach the fort.

During the winter months grave-digging was a problem. Fires had to be lit on the surface of the ground before picks and shovels could make any impression on the earth, frozen to rocklike hardness. The fact of the ground being so hard in the winter, coupled with extreme scarcity of firewood, probably accounts largely for the Tibetan custom of air burial. Lamaism recognises four means of disposal of the dead; by air, fire, water and earth. These are four of the Lamaist elements, to one of which the body must return after the soul has left it. Air burial, by far the most common, is carried out by dissecting the body, breaking the bones, and feeding the pieces to vultures and ravens. Fire burial is, of course, carried out by burning, while water burial merely consists of dismembering the corpse and throwing it into the nearest lake or river. Earth burial is seldom practised, for reasons already given.

We were always very fortunate in the British medical officers who were stationed in Gyantse, and several studied the Tibetan language. All of them were enthusiasts about Tibet. They were good companions socially, always working in harmony with our small community. When the permanent British Trade Agent was absent from Gyantse, either on other duty or leave, the medical officer would be appointed to act for him by the Foreign Office in Delhi. The first medical officer posted to the Gyantse Agency was Captain Steen, I.M.S., who remained there after the departure of the Younghusband Mission. He stayed until 1909, when he was relieved by Captain (now Lieutenant-Colonel) Kennedy, I.M.S., from whom I took over charge in that year.

Captain Kennedy was keenly interested in the peoples of the eastern Himalaya, visiting Bhutan and Lhasa in company with Sir Charles Bell, when the latter was deputed on special duty to the capital of Tibet. Captain Macgregor, I.M.S., was associated with me during the Chinese trouble in 1912, when he rendered many services to the wounded Tibetans and Chinese. He was relieved by Captain Harland, who was the last British medical officer to hold charge in Tibet until the close of the Great War. After the war Captain Lee was posted to Gyantse. He remained for only one year, being relieved in 1923 by Major Hyslop, I.M.S., who in his turn gave place to Major Vance, who officiated on more than one occasion as British Trade Agent at Gyantse.

CHAPTER TWENTY-TWO

ON the advice and with the assistance of the Government of India, the Tibetans sent four boys to be educated in England. They left India in charge of Mr B. J. Gould, I.C.S., for some time British Trade Agent at Gyantse, and Mr Laden La, of the Bengal police. The latter, a Sikkimese, spoke Tibetan fluently, and was a suitable guardian for the youths. A young Tibetan army officer, the Tsipon Lungshar, who at the time of writing is Commander-in-Chief of the Tibetan Army, also accompanied them. I had the pleasure of entertaining the boys in Yatung. They were bright lads, but I wondered if they would take kindly to the routine of an English school. Soon after their arrival in England they were received by the best schools in the country. It was hoped that the boys would absorb Western methods and ideas, and, after completing their training in different branches of modern enterprise, would afterwards be useful in developing the resources of their own country.

Three of the boys were laymen, the fourth a priest, for in Tibet it is the custom for boys intended for holy orders to enter the monasteries at very early ages. Two of the boys were sent to Harrow and two to Rugby, where they remained several years. Later, one was sent to Sandhurst for army training, one was apprenticed

to a firm of electrical engineers, another was sent
to a mining college, while the last was given a general
training in modern business methods and engineering.
In due course they completed their studies, and returned to Tibet in 1920, when I met them again. I
was surprised at the change in them all, though, of
course, I realised that the most impressionable years
of their lives had been spent in Britain. They went
away shy, uncouth children; they came back speaking
perfect English and polished men of the world. None
of them had displayed any marked brilliancy, but
neither were they reported to be backward. They were
completely Westernised, and had almost forgotten their
mother tongue.

On returning from England, Kyipup, one of the
laymen, was trained in telegraphy by the Government
of Bengal. He was later placed in charge of the
development of telegraphic communications in Tibet,
which had begun with the construction of a line
between Gyantse and Lhasa. So little encouragement
did he receive from the authorities, however, that he
has now resigned his position. He is now living
at his family estate, and it is doubtful if he will be
employed again by his own Government.

Gongkar, the youth trained at Sandhurst, who should
have been given an administrative post, was sent to
the Sino-Tibetan frontier as a subaltern officer. He
found that money for training expenses and for practice
ammunition was very limited, and any attempt he
made to introduce modern and efficient methods was
balked by the old-fashioned superior officers under
whom he had to serve. When he came back from

England he told me that he had fallen in love with a girl there, but that his Government would not allow him to marry her and bring her out with him. I was glad for the girl's sake that they had objected, for a British woman domiciled in Tibet would have been another complication to be dealt with by the Trade Agent. Gongkar told me that he disliked returning to Tibet, and wished he could travel all over the world. He died very soon after being sent to the Sino-Tibetan Frontier.

Mendong, the lama, and the most likeable of the four, had been trained as a mining engineer. He was a delightful fellow, of most engaging manners and appearance, and we expected that he would do well, and make a great name for himself in his own country. Unfortunately, a motor-bicycle which he used in the streets of Lhasa made him unpopular. Men and animals alike were scared by the roar of its exhaust. One day a high official was thrown from his mule owing to the animal being frightened by the cycle, and Mendong was forbidden to use his machine again. He made a present of it to the Dalai Lama, and it is now stored in a godown, where it is rusting away.

Mendong was sent to the country north of Lhasa to find gold, where he soon located this precious metal in paying quantities. He told me later that he had not progressed far with the work of excavation before a deputation of lamas from the local monastery arrived on the scene. The abbot solemnly warned him to desist from his mining operations, as these were annoy-ing the earth spirits, who would be certain to bring ill-fortune to Tibet, either by causing the crops to fail or by visiting the people with epidemics. The angry prelate also said that, if he failed to replace all the earth and ore he had dug out, Mendong himself would suffer harm, and probably death, at the hands of the demons of the locality. Moreover, while turning up the ground, his men had found a toad, which was looked on by the lamas as a very bad omen. Mendong appealed to Lhasa, but the objections of the local priests were upheld, and he was compelled to abandon his mine. Disappointed and disheartened, Mendong asked to be retired to his monastery, but he was recalled to Lhasa, and placed on duty as a police officer, with the title of Khenchung, of the fourth rank of monk officials. Later he found himself in disgrace, and was degraded, being sent to serve as an ordinary Jongpen at Tsaprang, in western Tibet. Now he is in Lhasa again, where I am sure his natural ability will be recognised.

The fourth and youngest of the English-educated youths, Ringang, the electrical engineer, has had the best fortune of all. He enjoys the favour of the Dalai Lama, and is in charge of the electrical plant in Lhasa.

Owing to the desire of the Tibetan Government for Western education in Tibet, the Government of India co-operated in establishing a school at Gyantse in 1923, for the sons of the Tibetan officials and wealthy landowners. The school was opened with forty Tibetan youngsters, whose families had received orders from the Dalai Lama to send their sons for education. Most of the lads came from Lhasa, and were accommodated in the paper factory, and the dak-bungalow was lent for classrooms, pending the erection of suitable buildings by the Tibetan Government.

The first, and only, headmaster was Mr F. Ludlow, a member of the Indian Educational Service, who was lent to the Tibetan Government, which undertook to pay his salary. He had a Tibetan assistant master for the kindergarten classes. Eventually the new school-buildings were erected, close to the paper factory. As far as was possible, Mr Ludlow endeavoured to organise his school on the lines of an English public school, but from the beginning there was constant friction between the English head and the Tibetan master, the latter having been appointed by the Tibetan Government without consulting Mr Ludlow. This Tibetan master is now the abbot of the Gyantse Monastery.

Mr Ludlow was enthusiastic about the venture, and his one thought was for his boys. So as not to tire his pupils he would not allow them to study long at one subject. The Tibetan master thought nothing of keeping the boys working for seven hours at their Tibetan lessons. In Tibetan schools it is usual to keep the pupils constantly at work from dawn to dusk, with the result that the boys and girls detest their school. At Gyantse games formed an important item in the curriculum, as Mr Ludlow wished to create in his young charges an early appreciation of the team spirit. This noble aim met with considerable resistance, for the lads were required to attend Tibetan classes for several hours after their games, which resulted in fatigue and poor work the next day. Eventually a compromise was arrived at, by which the boys should study English in the mornings, and Tibetan in the afternoons up till four o'clock, after which they were to be free for organised games. After dusk, not more than two hours were to be spent in study.

The school continued for three years. It was then closed. Among other official reasons given by the Tibetan Government for thus abandoning the project was that the parents of the pupils were averse to sending their sons so far from their homes. The lamas were against the school as they considered that if the boys' time was divided between English and Tibetan they would learn neither properly. Lack of study in Tibetan meant to them lack of knowledge of the tenets of the Lamaist faith. Actually, however, the school was closed because the Tibetan Government was unable to keep up the regular payment of the headmaster's salary. There is no likelihood of this school being reopened.

After the closing of the Government school in Gyantse several of the army officers who were in training at that place invited a teacher, by the name of Tharchin, a man from Kulu, who was then in the city, to hold a daily class for them. He undertook this work, his pay being subscribed by his pupils, who were mostly of adult age.

Tharchin was a Christian, and he spoke and wrote Tibetan and English quite well, and was able to teach the rudiments of the latter language to his pupils, who, it will be noticed, had no prejudice on the matter of his religion. They were so well satisfied with their progress that these officers, their military training in Gyantse over, persuaded Tharchin to return with them to Lhasa, so that they could continue their studies there. He remained for some time in the capital, but found the life there very trying, and not very remunerative, as living expenses for a person not of the country are high. Finally he tried to augment his income by trading in a small way, but still found that he could not make ends meet. He is now with me in Kalimpong, where he is employed as a lay teacher by the Tibetan Mission in that place.

In 1912 my wife started a private school, at the request of several headmen of the villages, and of a few of my clerks. A few details may here be given. It was opened in 1912, in a building specially erected in the Agency Bazaar, funds for the teacher's pay being met partly by my wife, partly by a grant from the bazaar funds, and partly by the mission in Kalimpong. No fees were charged, and the school was well attended by children from the Trade Mart and neighbouring villages. The subjects taught were English and Hindi, reading, writing and simple arithmetic. Those children for whom further education was desired were sent down to the Boys' and Girls' High Schools run by the Guild Mission in Kalimpong. At one time there were over forty pupils in regular attendance, necessitating the employment of two teachers.

When I first arrived in Yatung there were not more than twenty people permanently resident in the Agency Bazaar. When I left there were over three hundred. My wife started various enterprises to give employment to the local people, among these being rug and carpet making, knitting, and so forth. Hearing that there was regular and well-paid employment to be had in Yatung, artisan immigrants came and settled there from various parts of the Chumbi Valley. Since my departure, however, the school has decayed, and the bazaar has returned to its former emptiness, for there has been no permanent Trade Agent stationed in Yatung, nor anyone to take an interest in the place. I felt that it was good policy from the Government's point of view to have the Agency Bazaar well populated, as by this an adequate revenue could be raised from bazaar taxes to keep the place clean and in proper repair.

CHAPTER TWENTY-THREE

WHEN at Gyantse in December 1920 I received word from Mr Charles Bell, I.C.S. (now Sir Charles Bell, K.C.I.E., C.M.G.), then in Lhasa on special duty as the Viceroy's Agent, asking me to join him at the capital. At this time I was appointed by the Government of India as his assistant. I was able to leave immediately, as there was no pressure of work in Gyantse at the time, nor was my presence required at Yatung. I was delighted at the opportunity of visiting Lhasa once more. With a small party, consisting of my confidential Tibetan clerk, Rai Sahib Norbhu Dhondup, and the sub-assistant surgeon of the Gyantse Agency, Dr Bo Tsering, I took the road to Lhasa. Being December, it was very cold, but dry, and we made normal progress over the one hundred and fifty-six miles from Gyantse to Lhasa. On the way we passed the monastery of Ralung, "The Country of the White Goat," so called because long ago a white goat is said to have spoken and to have indicated the site on which the monastery should be built. According to the Tibetans, Ralung contains thirteen most excellent objects of reverence and wonder, among which is a picture painted in pure gold, and also the head of

A TYPICAL TIBETAN FORT ON THE BANK OF YAMDOK LAKE IN FRONT OF PEDE VILLAGE

the original white goat from which the place takes its name. The collection includes a jade cup formerly used by the hermit saint, Mila Repa.

In Ralung, which houses a hundred monks and nuns, the priests are permitted to marry, their children being brought up in the Church.

The next halt was Nagartse, consisting of a fort and a few houses. It is noted for the large horse and mule fair held annually, attended by traders who come from as far as the Chinese frontier. Samding Monastery lies three miles from this fort. I called in here hoping to meet Dorje Phagmo, the only female incarnation in Tibet. She was sitting in meditation, however, and sent a message through her secretary saying she would be delighted to entertain me on my return journey.

After Nagartse we reached Pede Jong, most picturesquely situated on the great Yamdok lake. Here are only a few hovels, used as rest-houses by travellers. We crossed the Chaksam Ferry in a hide coracle, our ponies and pack-mules being rowed across in a large and unwieldy wooden punt. From Chaksam through Nyethang to Lhasa is an easy march, and we arrived at the capital on Christmas Day, 1920. Nyethang is interesting, as the tomb of the Indian saint, Atisha, may be seen here. Atisha was one of the earlier Buddhists to leave a lasting impression on Tibetan Lamaism.

As we passed through the city my friend the Tsarong Shap-pe came out of his house, and pressed me to take lunch with him. According to Tibetan custom I could not refuse without slighting him, so accepted his invitation. Looking up at the building known as the

Chensa Linka, as I entered, I saw the Dalai Lama on the roof, looking down at me. Saluting His Holiness by raising my topee, I was honoured with a little bow. The only other instance I know of when the Dalai Lama has ever come out to see a visitor enter Lhasa was in the case of Mr Bell.

After lunch I went to Dekyi Lingka, where Mr Bell was staying, and there met with a warm welcome. Two rooms were set aside for me, one of which I used as a bedroom, the other as a reception-room. The Tibetan Government had offered me the use of a large house near by, but I preferred to stay with Mr Bell and Colonel Kennedy. The next morning I took a ride with Colonel Kennedy, round the Parkhor, the road that encircles the Potala Palace, and found him a delightful companion, an interesting conversationalist, and an Omar Khayyám enthusiast.

On returning to my quarters I found many of my Tibetan friends waiting to see me. First came His Excellency the Tsarong Shap-pe, who, after a while, was followed by the Dronyer Chhembo, the Dalai Lama's private chamberlain, and the most powerful man in Lhasa at that time. The latter brought with him a breakfast of which I had to partake, ready cooked in the Dalai Lama's own kitchen. After the meal was over he carefully collected all the remains and, with the exception of a few fragments of food begged by my servants, took them back to the Norbu Lingka, or Jewel Park. This food is blessed by His Holiness, and is considered by the Tibetans to be luck-bringing, and to possess magic properties.

I had sent a messenger to Norbu Lingka early in the

1. CROSSING THE BRAHMA PUTRA

ROUGHLY 50 MILES SOUTH OF LHASSA. THE AUTHOR AND HIS RETINUE EN ROUTE TO VISIT
HIS HOLINESS AT THE HOLY CITY.

2. THE AUTHOR JOINING AN ARCHERY COMPETITION IN BHUTAN

(AND WITH A FAIR MEASURE OF SUCCESS TOO !!!)

morning, informing His Holiness that I would call
on him during the forenoon, and so, after breakfast,
having obtained permission from Mr Bell, I proceeded
to the Jewel Park. After a few minutes I was ushered
into the presence by the Dronyer Chhembo. His
Holiness received me in the audience hall. On entering his room I presented him with a large white silk
ceremonial scarf, together with several gifts I had
brought. These he graciously accepted. The chamberlain then offered me a chair beside His Holiness, who
was seated on a high dais, and placed a small table in
front of me for the teacups. In front of the Dalai Lama
was a large square table.

When I was seated he asked after my health, and
inquired whether I had had a good journey. I made
appropriate answers, and thanked him for the interest
he had shown in my affairs. The Dalai Lama told me
that he had been praying that I might come to Lhasa,
and that he was extremely gratified that his prayers
had been answered. After tea we talked on various
subjects for about a couple of hours, mostly about
our last meeting and the existing conditions in Tibet.
Before I took my leave he asked me how long I was
staying in Lhasa, and when I told him only ten days
or so he was surprised, and desired me to stay longer.
I had to tell him that this was impossible. Before I
left his presence, His Holiness presented me with a
white silk ceremonial scarf, which he had kept by his
side during the interview.

As I was leaving Norbu Lingka the Dronyer
Chhembo told me that the Grand Lama had given
instructions that I should be received whenever I came

to see him, if possible every day. The chamberlain said that evidently His Holiness wished to do me great honour, and added that the favour shown me was partly on account of the shortness of my visit. He stated that other officers had to give three days' notice of their intended visits, high Tibetan officials a week or ten days, while ordinary people sometimes had to wait for months before His Holiness would consent to receive them. Early during my visit I called on the Silon, or Prime Minister, the Lonchen Shokang, whom I had met many years previously in Yatung. He was very kind, and greeted me by placing his forehead against my own, signifying that he regarded our friendship as unbreakable. I called on this influential gentleman several times before I left Lhasa. One day, when in company with Colonel Kennedy, he said that he had heard a rumour that I was to be transferred from Gyantse. He told the Colonel, if this was correct, to request Mr Bell to move the Government of India to retain me in Tibet, as the Tibetans felt that they would lose a very good friend were I to leave their country. The Silon, then an old man, was considered by his own countrymen as one of the ablest and most experienced of their administrators.

It appeared that the Tibetan Government had recently considered increasing the strength of their standing army from five to fifteen thousand men. This plan, however, did not meet with the approval of the powerful monasteries of Drepung, Sera and Ganden, who feared that their lamas would be recruited for the new regiments, and that they and other monasteries would be stripped of some of their estates, the revenue from which would be applied for the maintenance of the new troops. The proposal was first made just prior to the arrival of the Bell Mission in Lhasa. A certain section of official opinion in Tibet unjustly blamed the mission as the originator of the unpopular scheme. The trouble was that such persons as held this view would not publicly state their case.

I visited Sera Monastery, the senior abbot of which was an old friend of mine. He received me cordially. He too stated that the monasteries feared the loss of some of their estates, and also the loss of recruits to the priesthood. It appeared that Sera, at any rate, would oppose the proposed increase in the army with all means in its power. He concluded that the solution would be a gradual increase in army strength, rather than the recruitment of the full force immediately. In this way, he asserted, it would be possible for the differences to be adjusted. He insisted, moreover, that all new recruits for the army should be brought in from the outlying provinces, and trained outside Lhasa, so that the strain of maintaining them would not fall on that city.

When next I visited the Dalai Lama he said he considered that the suggestion to increase the army gradually was worthy of consideration. He realised that any innovation in this direction was bound to meet with opposition in his country, as his people, and especially the lamas, were ultra-conservative. That he had decided to introduce his proposals gradually was evident from the statement of my friend the abbot of Sera, who, when I next saw him, told me that everything had been amicably settled. The Dalai Lama's hand was being forced by the progressive party among the lay officials to make the sudden increase in the army, to which the monkhood and the ordinary people were opposed.

The next few days were spent in visiting other Tibetan officials. Lhasa, being the seat of Government, was full of these, every one of whom wished to entertain me in return for the hospitality I had shown most of them during their visits to Gyantse and Yatung. Some days, so hard was I pressed, and quite unable to refuse, I had to eat two lunches. When one realises that a ceremonial Tibetan lunch may consist of anything up to fifty courses the discomfort that I experienced may be imagined. Only the fact that I had to ride several miles every day saved me from indigestion. The chief ministers, the higher officials, and the abbots of the various religious institutions in and around Lhasa vied with each other in lavishing their hospitality. My visit, originally limited to ten days, had already stretched to three weeks. I attended to my routine work at Gyantse and Yatung by means of runners, who carried correspondence between those places and Lhasa.

Colonel Kennedy and I made many excursions into the country around Lhasa, and visited every place of interest in the city itself. Occasionally Mr Bell would accompany us, and on such trips we would lunch and spend the whole day in the open. Though it was January, and bitterly cold, the rarities we inspected and the glorious panoramic views we obtained more than repaid us for our trouble.

In the Mint, at Dode, we saw the processes of Tibetan

coinage manufacture. Only silver currency was struck here, from bar silver imported from India. The plant, with its stamps and dies, formerly run by water-power, is now worked by electricity, which, though more costly, is proving satisfactory. The officer in charge, Kusho Ngakwang Lobsang, whom I had met during the Chinese troubles in 1912, was delighted to renew our acquaintance. I asked him if he expected any further promotion, for since I had first met him he had been made a Khenchen, or third-rank monk official. He replied that the only promotion he expected was when he died, but I heard later that he had been appointed as Zimpon Khempo, personal attendant to the Dalai Lama. With two other monk officials, a Chhopon Chhempo and Sopon Khempo, correspond-ing to cardinals, he was in constant attendance on His Holiness, and in this confidential position wielded much influence.

When we were at the Mint an old Mussulman, nearly blind, came up to us and paid his respects. It appeared that he was one of the Indian armourers who years before had been lured to Tibet to help the Tibetans to manufacture rifles and ammunition. He said that having lived so long in Tibet he was not desirous of returning to his native land, even though he was free to do so. He was insistent, however, that he had retained his status as a British Indian subject. He had been down to India on various occasions during his service in Tibet, to purchase material for his work on behalf of the Tibetan Government.

My Lhasa visit was finally terminated on receipt of instructions from the Government of India that I should return to Gyantse. My Tibetan friends strongly pressed me to remain for a while longer, but this I could not do. Colonel O'Connor had been posted as Political Officer at Gantok, and wanted me to meet him in Kalimpong as soon as possible. I therefore paid farewell visits to my principal friends—there was not time to see everybody—and left Lhasa. The Prime Minister was visibly affected at our parting. He took both my hands in his and placed his forehead against mine. We never met again. I said good-bye to the Shap-pes at a farewell lunch they gave in my honour, my last morning being reserved for taking leave of His Holiness the Dalai Lama. I was received in the Durbar Hall, and, after greeting me warmly, His Holiness told me that he wished me to stay on with Mr Bell, but I had to tell him that this was impossible, as there was no responsible officer at either Gyantse or Yatung. The Dalai Lama expressed the hope that I would again visit him in his capital, not once but many times. All that I could reply was that I would endeavour to obtain permission from Government to do so.

Before taking my leave I asked His Holiness to bless my clerks and followers, and he at once acquiesced. He sent for the rod and blessing tassel. My servants were brought before the presence and were touched on the head with it, this being the customary form of benediction accorded to ordinary persons. Each man of my retinue prostrated himself three times, and then, with tongue respectfully protruded, approached for the blessing. After my servants had withdrawn I rose from my seat and offered His Holiness the parting ceremonial scarf. In return he presented me with a similar silk scarf. This was a very great honour indeed, for in Tibet only equals or the greatest of friends exchange scarves. After saying a few words of farewell the Dalai Lama blessed me with both hands laid on my head, and thus I left him. Very soon after I had gone His Holiness must have ridden to his country house, for as I rode by some time later I saw him watching me leave the city.

The Dronyer Chhembo informed me that the Dalai Lama had done me a very great honour by blessing me and my followers in the Durbar Hall, since custom decreed that blessings should be given there only on certain days, of which my visit was not one. My friend of former Gyantse days, Depon Neto, was detailed to escort me as far as Nyethang, while the very fine pony I rode was lent by the Tsarong Shap-pe, my own animal having been sent on ahead. Neto told me that the Dalai Lama had issued instructions to all officials stationed along my route to Gyantse that they should study my comfort in every way.

On arrival at Chaksam Ferry a severe sandstorm was raging, which forced me and my party to take shelter. The bulk of my baggage and followers had crossed the Brahmaputra earlier in the day, before the storm arose, so that I was stranded without kit of any description. The ferry-master at first refused to take me across, as the waves were running very high. When the wind had abated a little I was able to persuade him to attempt the crossing, but even then only because orders had been received from Lhasa to comply with all my instructions. Eventually we reached the opposite bank. In midstream we begin to ship water, and only constant bailing and skilful handling kept the unwieldy wooden boat afloat. I never want to go through such an experience again. Most of the boatmen's wives were in the boat helping their husbands, and invoking the aid of the gods for their safety. We were carried a considerable distance below the usual landing-place by the wind, against the force of which the boatmen's poles were of little use. I eventually got to dry land by being carried through the last fifty yards of shallow water on the back of a ferryman. Gladly and handsomely rewarding the ferry-master and his men, I immediately proceeded to the next halting-place.

Shortly after arriving at Gyantse I received a telegram from Colonel O'Connor, Political Officer in Sikkim, saying that he had received orders to hand over charge of that office to me, pending the arrival of Major F. M. Bailey, who had been posted to substantive charge of the Sikkim Residency. I received letters of congratulation on this acting appointment from the Dalai Lama and his Tashilhunpo confrère, the Tashi Lama. The Maharaja of Bhutan and all the principal officials of the Tibetan Government conveyed their felicitations. I deeply appreciated their kind thoughts, and was grateful to the Government of India for the confidence they had thus placed in an officer who, after all, was of the provincial service. Colonel O'Connor handed over by telegram on 26th March 1921. I held the office of Political Officer in Sikkim in addition to my charges of Gyantse and Yatung. As soon as outstanding matters in Tibet were settled I proceeded to Gantok, in Sikkim.

1. A VIEW OF THE POTALA PALACE, RESIDENCE OF HIS HOLINESS THE
DALAI LAMA

A NINE-STOREYED BUILDING, IN WHICH THE AUTHOR WAS PRIVILEGED TO INSPECT PRICELESS
TREASURES DATING BACK TO THE SEVENTH CENTURY.

2. STUDY OF A SIKKIM LAMA, ATTENDED BY MONKS

ONE DOES NOT FIND IN SIKKIM THAT RIGOROUS AUSTERITY OF RELIGION SO PROMINENT IN TIBET.

CHAPTER TWENTY-FOUR

*The Palace of Potala—Famous Warrior-Kings—Choten—Scriptures—The
Treasury—Officials in Charge—The Potala & the Chokhang—A Holy
Tree—The Chokhang—Assembly Hall—Side Chapels—The Holy
of Holies—The Cathedral Armoury & Chapels—Lings—
Summer Palace — Ladakhis —The Monastery of
Drepung—Figure of Champa—Discipline in
Drepung—A Sacred Dagger—Fighting
Lamas—Ganden—Tsethang*

DURING my visit to Lhasa in 1921 the Dalai
Lama issued instructions I should be shown
all over his Potala Palace, as well as any
other monasteries or buildings I wished to see. I had
cursorily glanced over the Potala at the time of the
Younghusband Mission, but owing to the then somewhat strained relations between Tibetans and ourselves
it was possible to make only a superficial examination.
Accordingly, accompanied by Mr Bell and Colonel
Kennedy, I spent several hours among objects few
Western eyes had seen before—the treasures of the
Potala. At the hour of our visit the lamas of the
Namgyal Tatsang, the royal monastery within the walls
of the palace itself, were engaged in a religious ceremony, which we watched a while. This institution has
one hundred and seventy-five monks in residence, and
is attended by the Dalai Lama himself, who worships
there as an ordinary priest.

In the temple hall is a silver image of Chenresi, the
spirit incarnate in the person of the Dalai Lama. It
has a golden head-dress, twelve feet in height. On the

door is an effigy in relief of the fifth and, up to the present, greatest Dalai. This pontiff was the real founder of the line of priest-kings who have ruled Tibet for several centuries. The ceremony we watched was an ordinary temple service, but one never fails to be impressed by the deep chanting of the monks, and the general atmosphere of devotion present on such occasions.

Passing through a reception or durbar hall, on the walls of which is inscribed in gold letters the name of a former Chinese emperor, we came to a room in which is placed a group of figures representing the most famous of Tibet's warrior-kings, Srong Tsan Gampo, with his Chinese and Nepalese queens, and his two famous ministers, Gar and Thonmi Samhota. To Thonmi is ascribed the letters now used in Tibet. He journeyed to India, and having learned the Devanagri characters of that time adapted them for the language of his own people. One of the most striking relics in the Potala is an immense choten of the fifth Dalai Lama. This huge edifice, within the building, rises in tiers through several storeys, the floors having been cut away to permit its erection. It is richly decorated with gold and precious stones, while behind it, hidden from the casual visitor, are stored many old, priceless specimens of Chinese porcelain and valuable silken religious banners.

Among other chotens is a large one dedicated to the seventh Dalai Lama, but this is not nearly so magnificent as that of his predecessor. Solid gold butter-lamps stand on every altar, and images of the Buddha and the saints are to be seen everywhere, some of gold, some of silver and some of copper. The image considered the most holy of all, however, is said to be made from sandalwood, and portrays Lokeshwara, the God of the World. The image is large, and of obvious antiquity. On the Potala roof—the building is nine storeys in height—are the famous roof-pavilions, the gift of a former Chinese emperor. These pavilions have gilded roofs, and are visible for miles around, being the first objects in Lhasa to catch the eye of an approaching traveller. The apartment occupied by the fifth Dalai Lama is still preserved as he left it three centuries ago. On a table therein I saw one of the most wonderful pieces of porcelain it has ever been my good fortune to handle. It was a kylin, or symbolical lion, and had been presented to the Tibetan prelate by the contemporary Chinese emperor. We were taken through room after room filled with the most gorgeous objects of Oriental art silks and banners, carved jade of all colours, porcelain, gold and silver images and lamps, until our minds ceased to comprehend the beauty of each individual piece.

Now that the treasures of the Chinese royal house have been dispersed, the Potala collection of Chinese art must without doubt be the finest in the world. It is customary for each Dalai Lama to leave some lasting memorial covering his occupation of the pontifical throne of Tibet. The present ruler has had made a large silver image of Chenresi, the reflection of the Buddha incarnate in his own person. This image has eleven heads and one thousand hands and eyes, an eye being graved in the palm of each hand. He is also having prepared, on stiff black paper in letters of pure gold, silver, turquoise, coral and brass, the Kangyur, or Lamaist scriptures, a tremendous work, contained in one hundred and twenty-two huge volumes. Each page has five lines. Each line is completed in one of the above-named substances. It will take twenty men four years to do the work. On the lower floor of the Potala are the offices of the Prime Minister, his secretary and other clerks, who are thus near their ruler should he wish to consult them.

In the treasury within the Potala, known as the Namse Bangdzo, are stored the accumulated gifts of centuries, presented to the Dalai Lama by the Chinese emperors and pious pilgrims from all over Lamaist Asia. At Labrang Teng, on the upper storey of Chokhang, can be seen the stores of butter, some of it years old, also tea, and other supplies, collected for the use of the Dalai Lama and his followers domiciled within the palace. From this store the priest-king issues rations to all the monks in Lhasa on certain occasions, such as the great Monlam, or prayer festival, for which over twenty thousand lamas come into the capital.

The lamas and other officials in charge of the various shrines and rooms were most courteous towards us, and really put themselves out to make our visit interesting. The Potala is of considerable antiquity. It was first built as a fortress-palace by King Srong Tsan Gampo, in the seventh century, though the great central block is of somewhat later date. It ranks as one of the most imposing edifices in Asia, if not in the whole world. Compared to it, Chokhang, the "cathedral of Lamaism," appears insignificant, though it is not less holy in the eyes of the Lamaists. By special permission of His Holiness I was able thoroughly to inspect this temple. I had entered its gate in 1904, but at that time anything in the form of a detailed examination was impossible.

The Chokhang, while a large building, is not imposing, partly on account of the meaner houses huddled round it, and partly because of its unpretentious approaches. Nearing the main entrance one sees two doring, or edict pillars, of stone. On one of these is an inscription recording a Tibetan treaty between China and Tibet, while the other, badly disfigured, publishes regulations for the segregation of smallpox cases. Close by the latter is a very old weeping willow, called " The Lord's Hair."

In 1924 this tree was badly damaged during a heavy storm, losing many of its main branches. The superstitious Tibetans took this as an indication of troublous times to come. The Government had all the broken branches tied to the parent tree, and ordered special religious ceremonies to be performed in all monasteries to avert or lessen the coming misfortune. In the stone-flagged approach to the main gates of this temple deep grooves bear witness to the millions of pilgrims who have walked here. Their bare feet have worn away the solid stone. The Chokhang has been a centre of pilgrimage for over a thousand years, and this, too, is said to have been built by Srong Tsan Gampo, to house certain images of the Buddha brought from China and Nepal as dowries by his wives.

In the outer porch of the main entrance are painted the customary four guardian kings of the quarters. One also notices here two stone plaques let into the

Q

wall, on which are inscribed the record of the marriage of King Sron Tsan Gampo with the Princess Kong Jo of the Chinese royal house. In addition to the four guardians of the quarters there is a picture of a monkey seated in a tree. I noticed that while the four kings had recently been painted, the colour of the monkey had faded. I was told that it was inauspicious to renew its colouring.

From the porch one walks straight into the main assembly hall. Here the great annual prayer festival is held. The hall is very large, its roof being supported by over one hundred pillars. At one side is the raised throne occupied by the Dalai Lama when he attends service. Facing this is the seat of the abbot of the Ganden Monastery. It is the custom each year for some wealthy trader or pilgrim to present himself before His Holiness and, having offered princely gifts, to request the Dalai Lama to lead the prayer festival in the Chokhang. His Holiness is not supposed to proceed to this function without such invitation. The walls of the assembly hall are decorated with many frescoes, depicting saints, demons and heroes of olden times. To one side, before a small altar, is a loose stone, and pilgrims believe that every prayer uttered while they are balanced on this will rise straight to the gods. I also noticed a bell hung from the roof near this shrine. This is rung by each passing pilgrim to attract the attention of the gods.

Many side chapels open off the main hall, one of the most interesting being that dedicated to Thuk Je Chhempo. In front of this altar is a large hollowed-out stone, said to have been the bath of Princess Kong Jo, the Chinese consort of King Srong Tsan Gampo. In another chapel is a large, wooden-covered book, which every pilgrim tries to lift. The Tibetans believe that if any person succeeds in raising it from the ground, unaided, his sins are few, while if he fails his sins are many, and his hopes of rebirth in a higher plane meagre.

The Holy of Holies of Lamaism lies in a chapel immediately behind the main temple hall of the Chokhang. It contains on its altars three images. The foremost of these was brought from China in the dowry of Princess Kong Jo, while the second was made in Tibet. The latter is said to have moved back on the altar, of its own accord, to make room for the more potent images from China—a delicate way of hinting to the Tibetans of those days that when China came on the scene they had to take a back seat. A still smaller image is said to have been presented to the shrine by King Srong Tsan Gampo on the occasion of his conversion to Buddhism. Almost every object in the Chokhang has its own history, for which there is no space here. Before the altar in the Holy of Holies are many golden butter-lamps, which are kept burning day and night. Among others I noticed one presented by Mr Bell. It was thoughtfulness displayed in this and in similar ways that made Mr Bell so popular with all classes of Tibetans.

A rough wooden ladder takes one to the second storey of the Chokhang. In one of the chapels on this floor are the relics of Srong Tsan Gampo, as well as his effigy. Placed before the latter is a large, silver wine-jar, and pilgrims believe that, if their prayers are to be granted, wine will miraculously flow from this. A finger of this image bears a gold ring said to have belonged to this king's Chinese wife.

On the upper floor of the cathedral is the armoury, where old-time weapons and armour are stored. In one of the chapels on this storey, dedicated to the fierce goddess Lhamo, identical with the Hindu Kali, are numerous mice, which are quite tame. These are fed by the pilgrims, who believe the spirits of human beings to be reincarnated in their tiny bodies. On the roof are gilded pavilions and small chapels. The Chokhang, hub of Lamaism, is visited by pilgrims from all over Buddhist Asia, and derives considerable revenue from their gifts. During my visit, however, I was particularly impressed by the air of depression that seemed to pervade the place. Even the priest in charge seemed despondent, though they showed me every possible courtesy. They even permitted my entry to the main altars, and allowed me to examine closely the images thereon, and even to handle them. They knew, of course, that I was visiting the temple with the acquiescence of the Dalai Lama. Moreover— and this was the case wherever I went—I had a command of their language equal to their own, a qualification rarely met with outside Tibet. High Tibetan officials have frequently requested me to write letters for them to the Dalai Lama, as they considered my knowledge of Tibetan, especially of the honorific dialect, to be greater than their own.

Four of the most famous, though small, monasteries in the whole of Tibet are what are known as Lings, in Lhasa. These institutions gave, in olden times,

several regents during the minorities of the various
Dalai Lamas. Each "ling" provided a regent in turn.
They are named Kundeling, Tengyeling, Tsomonling
and Tsecholing. Of these the most interesting, and in
former times the most powerful, is Tengyeling, and
though all its former glories had departed at the time
of my visit, in 1921, there were still many things of
interest to be seen there. Tengyeling was suppressed
by the Tibetan Government in 1900, its monks dispersed, and its abbot imprisoned until he died. The
main charge brought against its lamas was conspiracy
aiming at the downfall of the Dalai Lama. The monks
of this monastery were alleged to have prepared, and
presented to the Dalai Lama, a pair of boots into the
soles of which they had sewn death-bringing charms.
Falling out among themselves, however, the bootmaker,
who had been taken into their confidence, divulged
the secret to the Tibetan Government. Examination
proved his statement to be correct, and the abbot
and his immediate satellites were arrested and thrown
into prison. The monastery was sealed, and its estates
confiscated. Daily torture was practised on the monks
who had been arrested, until they all died, and the
wealth of the institution was seized. Tengyeling did
not again raise its head until 1910, when the Dalai
Lama fled to India, when for three years it again
flourished, receiving back at the hands of the Chinese
its former estates and treasure. On the Dalai Lama's
return to Lhasa in 1912, however, it was again suppressed, only ten monks being permitted to remain in
the monastery to conduct the worship ceremonies of
a fierce deity enshrined there. The latest news from

Lhasa, however, is that Tengyeling is to be rebuilt
and re-established by the Tibetan Government, and I
should not be surprised if this is being done at the
request of the Chinese.

I saw some of the treasures formerly owned by
Tengyeling, and they are priceless. Wonderful
examples of Chinese porcelain, gold-work, carved jade
and turquoise, and many very finely painted and
embroidered religious banners were stored in godowns
sealed by the Devashung. Many pieces have been
stolen by traders, and have found their way to India,
but there are still several hundred old Chinese carpets
stored there. No Tibetan monastery, as a rule, will
sell its property, which finds its way on to the market
only when stolen by the lamas.

For several years past the outbuildings of Tengyeling
have been used as a Post and Telegraph Office. Now
that proposals are afoot to re-establish it as a religious
institution this office will have to be moved elsewhere.
A few years ago an attempt was made to induce a
spirit controlling an oracle attached to Tengyeling to
change its residence to Norbu Lingka, but without
success. While the medium was in the Jewel Park
the spirit refused to enter into him.

During the warmer months of the year His Holiness
spends much of his time at his summer palace, called
Norbu Lingka, and it was there that he, as a rule,
received me during my visit to Lhasa. Norbu Lingka
consists of a large walled enclosure, in which, besides
the Grand Lama's quarters, are offices and residences
for the ministers, secretaries and servants of the Tibetan
ruler. The bodyguard, consisting of five hundred

soldiers, under command of a depon, or general, are also quartered within its walls. The present ruler is very fond of animals, especially dogs, of which he has many and various breeds presented to him from time to time. His Holiness once accepted from me a pair of greyhounds, a gift which delighted him. He also has a stable of over five hundred picked horses, and a small menagerie. When the Dalai Lama travels between the Potala and Norbu Lingka the scene is one of great magnificence. Escorted by high officers of State, and by lamas carrying sacred emblems, all dressed in their finest ceremonial robes, His Holiness passes between lines of troops. Behind these thousands of townspeople and pilgrims cluster to catch a glimpse of his holy person.

Domiciled in Lhasa is a small community of Mussulmans, the descendants of immigrant traders from Ladakh and Kashmir. They are known as Ladakhis. Their forefathers have been trading in Tibet for hundreds of years, and for the past two centuries they have had a permanent settlement in Lhasa. They are a prosperous people, and are well treated by the Tibetan Government, to whose jurisdiction they are entirely amenable, possessing no extra-territorial rights. The late headman of the community, Ghulam Mohamed—for whom I obtained the honorary title of Khan Sahib from the Government of India, in consideration of the assistance given by him from time to time—and his son, Faizulla, were always friends of mine. I was able to assist them and members of their community in many matters, such as permitting them to occupy our dak-bungalows when travelling between Gyantse and

India, giving them cheques on Indian banks in exchange for cash, which is difficult to carry in large quantities in Tibet, and in arranging their transport and supplies. In former times their headman was elected by the community, but recently he has been selected and appointed by the Tibetan Government. The Ladakhis are a law-abiding people, and shrewd business men, dealing principally in wool and furs. They also export Chinese brick-tea to Ladakh. For some years past they have claimed rights as British subjects, but without success. This cannot be so long as they are domiciled in Lhasa and Shigatse, in which latter city a few of them reside.

On one of my excursions I was able to visit the great monastery of Drepung, the largest in Tibet— indeed in the world. It has a nominal complement of seven thousand seven hundred lamas, but this number is frequently exceeded. Naturally, its abbots wield immense power in the conduct of Tibetan affairs. Drepung belongs to the Gelukpa sect, the Reformed Church of Tibet, of which the Dalai Lama is the head. Divided into three large colleges, each has its own abbot, the monks being housed in numerous hostels, called khamtsan, lamas from each district congregating together as far as is practicable. The poorer priests herd together in the larger halls, while those with means have separate rooms. In this monastery are many relics of the fifth Dalai Lama, and here is kept, as he left it, the room he occupied while in residence. This practice of retaining undisturbed the habitations of holy lamas is common throughout Tibet. Many nobles, in whose houses one of the Grand Lamas may have spent a few hours, will show visitors the room, usually furnished as a chapel, in which the Pontiff sat. They spend much money and labour on the decoration of such places. Many a time, when staying at a Tibetan's house, I have slept in one of these chapels. Besides being the cleanest room in the house, it is generally the only one in which privacy is possible. I remember that in the private chapel of a Tibetan Trade Agent at Yatung was the skull-top of his only son, a gruesome relic to keep on one's family altar.

Drepung is noted for its great figure of Champa, the coming Buddha, who is shown seated in European fashion, not in the squatting attitude of all other Buddhas. The lamas of this monastery also show five images of the goddess Drolma, each of which they state has spoken. This great institution is, of course, a town in itself, its temples, colleges and residential buildings covering hundreds of acres. It is supported to a great extent by the Government, which has allotted estates farmed out for its benefit. A considerable bazaar has grown up in the vicinity, in which most of the shops and stalls are run by women. Near the monastery is the temple of the Nechung oracle, its roof being marked by a gilded pavilion. After the Younghusband Mission of 1904 this oracle fell into disgrace, for several of its prophecies failed to come true. It was therefore abolished, and its hundred attendant lamas dispersed. Recently, however, I hear that a new oracle has been installed there, and the institution reopened. The Choje, as the oracle is called, is not permitted to reside within the limits of the monastery proper, but must live at a

distance, in a separate establishment. The spirit
believed to control this oracle dwells in a tree near
his temple.

Discipline in Drepung is very strict, as indeed it has
to be, considering that at least two thousand soldier-
monks are domiciled there. It is maintained by two
lama officials, called Shengo, assisted by a staff of
priestly police. These Shengo are elected, and hold
office for three years. They are all-powerful where the
lamas are concerned, for, in any event, no monk may
ever be tried by a civil court in Tibet. On the occasion
of my visit I was cordially received by the senior
abbot, who gave me lunch and showed me round.
He naïvely told me that there was at Drepung in
years gone by a goblet of dragon's milk, but that it
had been stolen by some sacrilegious person. Sera, the
second of the great monasteries near Lhasa, with over
five thousand monks in residence, is the deadly rival
of its brother institution of Drepung. Their lamas are
constantly at feud, and I ascertained that much of the
existing jealousy is due to the fact that the Sera priests
are very usually successful in any contest that takes
place between the two monasteries. The word " sera "
means "hail," while "drepung" means "heap of rice,"
and the Lhasa people say that, as hail can destroy rice-
crops, so Sera can always overcome Drepung. I visited
this monastery for the second time in 1921.

The most sacred object in its temple is an iron
phurba, or dagger, which reposes in the shrine dedicated to Tamdrin, a fierce horse-headed deity. This
phurba is believed to have miraculously flown from
India, and to have been picked up by a lama on a hill

near the monastery. It is taken once a year in procession to Lhasa city, at the time of the Losar, or New Year festival. The Dalai Lama himself reveres this dagger by placing it upon his head and blessing it. All other phurbas used in religious ceremonies in Tibet are modelled on this one.

There are two companies of fighting lamas in Sera, who have made the name of this monastery almost synonymous with quarrelling. They pursue no course of study, but spend their time in exercises, with a view to increasing their bodily strength. They follow none of the disciplinary rules laid down for the conduct of the ordinary priests. If no outside opponent offers, they fight among themselves. Every seventh year companions selected from the fighting lamas of Drepung and Sera meet in contests of strength and skill in arms, and these occasions are always attended with considerable bloodshed. Every December, despite the bitterly cold weather, the fighting priests of Sera race stark naked across the bed of a river, and along its banks for several miles.

Ganden, possibly the most influential of the three great monasteries, though the smallest, I was unfortunately not able to visit, as it lies some distance from Lhasa. Ganden is noted, among other things, for the large numbers of " self-sprung " bas-reliefs of the gods on the rock faces in its vicinity. It has a nominal complement of three thousand three hundred lamas, divided into two colleges. Here also is to be seen a golden choten, containing the remains of Tsong Kapa, an opening being left through which the face can be seen. The body is mummified, and the lama in charge takes impressions of the saint's teeth on paper, which are distributed to the faithful for use as charms. Tsong Kapa was the founder of the Reformed Tibetan Church, and is revered throughout the country. Fifteen famous religious banners are kept at Ganden, painted in gold, and these are exposed only once a year to the faithful, who worship them. The priests state that these were painted by the gods.

I wanted very much to visit Tsethang, to the south of Lhasa, where the Tibetans assert that their race had its origin, but again lack of time prevented me. They state that the mother of their people was an ogress of the rocks, and their forefather a saint, who had assumed the form of a monkey. The local people still point out the meadow where these early ancestors of the Tibetan race grew the magic grain on which they fed their children. Here also is a fort built by the first historically known King of Tibet, Nya Thri Tsempo. In one of its temples are beautiful frescoes, which are renewed often, at the expense of the local people. I would also have liked to visit the Chho-Khor-Gyal-La-Tso, in Kongbu, where the Dalai Lama retires once during his lifetime, to see reflected in its waters his future heavenly home, but this, too, was impossible.

CHAPTER TWENTY-FIVE

*The Monastery of Samding—The only Female Incarnation—Story of the
"Thunderbolt Sow"—Taking over Posts in Sikkim—Reconnaissance
Party to Mount Everest — Customs of the Sikkimese — The
Lepchas—The Pao—Talung Monastery—British Officials
at Gantok—Hon. Mary Scott—A Wedding Ceremony*

ON my return journey from Lhasa in 1921 I
visited the famous monastery of Samding, the
home of Dorje Phagmo. I arrived, as arranged
on my upward journey, soon after ten in the morning,
and was at once shown by an attendant lama into the
private sitting-room of the only female incarnation in
Tibet. I presented her with a silk ceremonial scarf,
and with certain gifts I had specially selected for her.
These consisted of soaps, face creams, powders and
scent, all of which she greatly appreciated. She offered
me a seat, and during the inevitable butter-tea interlude
I had an opportunity of observing my hostess. She
was very fair, and rather below the average stature of
a Tibetan woman. A highly cultured woman, I enjoyed
her animated conversation. She is very well born, being
the daughter of the great Lhasa family of Lhalu. At the
time of our meeting she was twenty-seven years old.

She asked after my health, and hoped that I had
had an enjoyable time in Lhasa, which she herself
had not visited for several years. She inquired after
Mr Bell, whom she had met before. This gentleman,
Colonel Kennedy and myself were the only Europeans
she had seen up to that time. She told me that she

was specially delighted at my ability to converse with her in her own Lhasa dialect.

After a while I asked her to bless my followers, which she was pleased to do. Each one of them, as he was blessed, placed a small money present, tied in the end of a scarf, at her feet. Her blessing is considered of great benefit. Dorje Phagmo was specially interested in my meetings with the Dalai Lama, and I had to describe His Holiness's appearance and state of health at great length. She was also interested in Indian and Chinese affairs, and asked many questions about Great Britain, our King and Queen and the Royal Family. She told me that the monastery of Nenying, about four miles from Gyantse, was under her administration, and that she hoped to be visiting there shortly, as she was collecting funds for its repair.

It was snowing hard, so Dorje Phagmo requested me to lunch with her. This was served in Chinese fashion, with many little dishes of stews and curries, with spaghetti boiled in soup and served in small bowls. Being a monastery, no wines were served with the meal, only tea. When the storm had passed over I bade farewell to my hostess, and left the monastery. Before departing she presented me with a silk ceremonial scarf. There is a room in this monastery in which I saw the mummified remains of all the bodies of former incarnations of Dorje Phagmo. The monks told me that once during her earthly life each incarnation is taken to look on these remains, with the object, I suppose, of demonstrating to her that life can end in only one way, and that the soul goes on from existence to existence.

DORJE PHAGMO AND HER SISTER

THE ABBESS IS THE ONLY FEMALE INCARNATION OF THE GODDESS DORJEE PHAGMO OR "THE DIAMOND SOW"
WHO RESIDES IN SAMDING MONASTERY AT THE NORTHERN END OF YAMDOK LAKE.

Samding is one of the very few institutions of the Reformed Church in which lamas are presided over by a lady abbess. At the time of my visit about fifty priests were in residence. Dorje Phagmo's sister, also a nun, but not an incarnation, lives with her at Samding. The legend concerning the first Dorje Phagmo, which means the "Thunderbolt Sow," arose as follows. In 1716 central Tibet was overrun by Jungar Tartars, who roamed the countryside, looting every village and monastery they came across. In due course they arrived outside the gates of Samding, and their leader, a Mohammedan by faith, having heard that there was treasure concealed in this monastery, demanded entrance. This was refused by the abbess, and the order was given to break down the gates. This was soon done, but the invaders were astonished to find the courtyard occupied only by a large herd of pigs, headed by a huge sow. Disgusted at this sight, which was particularly abhorrent to a Mussulman, the Jungars left without entering the monastery buildings. No sooner were they out of sight than the herd of swine resumed human forms, while the gigantic sow became the lady abbess. By her magic powers she had preserved her monastery and its lamas from harm. Since that day she has been venerated by all Tibetan people. Her spirit is reincarnated in each succeeding abbess of the institution. The Dorje Phagmo is accorded privileges shared only by the Dalai and Tashi Lamas.

When a new incumbent takes over any of the posts in Sikkim or Tibet he arrives in a kind of triumphal progress, and when I took over the acting appointment as Political Officer in Sikkim there was no exception to this rule. Many local kazis, or noblemen, of Gantok came out several miles to meet me, and offered ceremonial scarves and refreshments in a tent they had pitched by the roadside. On nearing the Residency I was met by a guard of Sikkim police, and by my friend Kumar Palden, the Maharaja's Judicial Secretary. I had known his father many years before, when engaged in settlement work at Kalimpong. The morning after my arrival I called on Their Highnesses the Maharaja and Maharani, who received me with great cordiality. They returned my call the next day, and invited me and my daughters to dinner at the palace, an invitation which was repeated on several occasions during my stay in Sikkim. Once settled at the Residency all the kazis and headmen paid their official calls. I was happy in re-establishing former friendships.

Shortly after my arrival in Gantok I received instructions from the Government of India to assist members of the reconnaissance party then proceeding to Mount Everest. They had to pass through Sikkim and Tibet to reach their objective. For this purpose I visited Kalimpong, where I again enjoyed the hospitality of Dr Graham and his family. Dr Graham, the well-known missionary and philanthropist, had, I consider, the finest character I have ever met, and his broad-mindedness, tolerance, sympathy and Christ-like life have gained for him a unique and lasting place in the hearts of all with whom he has come into contact. This gentleman is the founder and superintendent of the world-famous St Andrew's Colonial Homes, where poor and destitute British and Anglo-Indian children are cared for and brought up and equipped to face life

and earn a respectable means of livelihood. Dr and
the late Mrs Graham were always kindness personified
to me, and later to my family. I used to stay with them
at the Mission House in Kalimpong whenever I visited
that place, and was thus privileged to know the whole
Graham family. I found that an old acquaintance,
Colonel Howard Bury, whom I had met previously
in Tibet, was the leader of this expedition. It was a
pleasure to help him and his party. Among the
members were Mr Mallory, afterwards to lose his life
on Everest; Dr Kellas, who died on the way to the base
camp; Major Wheeler, one of the surveyors, and Mr
Wollaston. Even in Kalimpong, Dr Kellas was not a
fit man, and he should not have continued. It was
impossible for me to accompany the expedition through
Sikkim and Tibet. Being in charge of two Trade
Agencies in Tibet, as well as Sikkim and Bhutan, it was
necessary to remain within easy reach of Gantok. The
party was provided with Indian army transport mules,
and these, as I had seen proved time and again, were
utterly useless for work in the eastern Himalaya. Unfit
for climbing and unacclimatised to great heights, they
could not carry their own saddlery, let alone a useful
load. A few days out from Kalimpong, Colonel Bury
had to return all these animals and carry on with those
he could hire along the road.

The customs of the Sikkimese are very interesting.
The original inhabitants of this little Himalayan state
were Lepchas, whose origin is obscure. They are
thought by some authorities to have emigrated there
from Upper Burma several centuries ago. They have
been displaced gradually by the more energetic and

R

pushful Nepalese immigrants, who for some years
poured into Sikkim by thousands. The Lepcha is
essentially a shy, retiring person, by religion Animist,
and a dweller in the forests, worshipping the spirits
of the mountain, river and tempest. Of recent years
many of them, however, have embraced Christianity.

The original kings of Sikkim were Lepchas, but
constant intermarriage with Tibetan women has elim-
inated practically all trace of Lepcha strain from the
ruling family. For centuries now Rajas and Maharajas
of Sikkim have gone to Lhasa for their brides.

The Lepchas have no organised priesthood, the
simple rites of their faith being conducted by exorcists,
who are termed "Bongthing." In times of stress—
during crop failures or when epidemic disease threatens
the people—the Bongthing is called in to diagnose what
particular evil spirits are responsible for the calamity.
His co-religionists provide various animals and birds
for sacrifice, including buffaloes and bullocks, cows,
pigs and fowls, according to the wealth of the individual or of the village calling for his services. The
Bongthing, having slaughtered the sacrifice, examines
its entrails, and thus divines the cause of the trouble,
and suggests the remedies necessary to appease the
angry spirits. In the case of very poor consultants
the Bongthing has to satisfy himself with a few eggs,
which he breaks, and examines the yolks. Providing
the necessary sacrifices are forthcoming, the Bongthing
will undertake to divine any matter, from the cause of
simple stomach-ache to the failure of the crops in a whole
district. Flesh of sacrificed animals becomes the property of the Bongthing and his assistants, the suppliant

1. RAJA SONAM TOBGYE DORJE, DEB ZIMPON OF BHUTAN

AN ABLE SUPPORTER OF BRITISH ADMINISTRATION.

2. HER HIGHNESS THE MAHARANI OF SIKKIM AND NOBLES

(TAKEN JUST PRIOR TO HER MARRIAGE).

THE DAUGHTER OF A FAMOUS TIBETAN GENERAL, HER HIGHNESS IS NOW TRULY LOVED BY HER SIKKIMESE SUBJECTS.

party being strictly forbidden to touch it. The Bong-thing sometimes has a female counterpart, called " Mun." This lady sings for hours at a stretch to keep evil spirits away from sickrooms and distressed areas. In return for her services she receives her food, lodging and a small fee.

Yet another exorcist, termed a " Pao," is sometimes met with in Sikkim. This person specialises in casting out demons from houses. When engaged at his work he dances round twirling a skull drum, and tinkling a small bell, until the evil spirit enters into his body, and while thus possessed the Pao discovers how to counteract the demon's machinations. Having given his advice, the Pao finds that the spirit leaves him. This individual, of course, also receives a fee for his services, sometimes in cash, sometimes in kind. I was fortunate in seeing the Bongthing and Pao at work on several occasions, and I found that the Lepchas have implicit faith in them. The kazis and well-to-do classes in Sikkim, who are greatly intermarried with the Tibetans, are Buddhists, and owe spiritual allegiance to the Dalai Lama. There are several important monasteries in the country, the best known being Pemayangtse, where only the scions of noble houses are admitted as monks. The High Lamas of these institutions wield a very considerable influence in the conduct of State affairs.

The most interesting monastery in Sikkim is that of Talung, where relics of the old-time kings, saints and heroes of the country are stored. Very few Europeans have visited this place, which lies somewhat off the beaten track of the ordinary tourist. As a holiday, touring in Sikkim is yearly growing in favour among Europeans in India. No more health-giving or interesting form of spending leave can be imagined than a trip through some of the finest river and mountain scenery in the world such as Sikkim affords. All the routes are provided with excellent dak-bungalows, which tourists may occupy on the payment of a small fee. *Touring in Sikkim and Tibet*, a small book I have specially prepared, will save intending tourists much time, trouble and unnecessary expense.

The few other British officials stationed in Gantok while I was there completed a very cheery little community. I must mention the name of the Honourable Mary Scott, who for many years has conducted missionary work in Sikkim. She is one of those missionaries who believe in saving people's bodies, and then caring for their souls. She has done much excellent work in teaching the elements of hygiene to a large number of the Sikkim cultivators. Her cottage industries provide work for converts, and a Girls' School is well attended by many of the Gantok girls.

I handed over charge of Sikkim to Major F. M. Bailey on 21st June 1921. After paying farewell calls on the Maharaja and Maharani, and the leading Sikkimese officials, I returned to Tibet, reverting to the post of British Trade Agent at Gyantse and Yatung.

I got back to Gyantse just in time to attend the marriage ceremony of my young friend Kyipup, the youth who had been educated in England. He was desired by his family to marry his elder brother's wife, in accordance with the Tibetan custom, but this he refused to do. He told his parents that if he was to marry he would share his wife with no one. At length his father and mother fell in with his views, and decided to find him a wife.

Having consulted the local Astrologer Lama as to whether the horoscope of the damsel they had selected was in agreement with that of their son, and having ascertained from the same source that the proposed union would be fortunate, preparations for the wedding were put in hand. The ceremony was to last three days, and invitations were issued to all friends and relations for the occasion. In accordance with the Tibetan custom, a messenger carrying a silk scarf arrived at the Trade Agency in Gyantse to bid myself and all the British officers stationed there to the marriage. We rode out to the Kyipup mansion the next day, taking my escort, and were received by the bridegroom's elder and younger brothers, who conducted us to a room where the bride and groom were seated.

Unfortunately we missed the ceremony of bringing the bride, which is done by the bridegroom's friends, dressed in their gayest clothes, and mounted on fiery little ponies. This party escorts the lady from her own home to that of her future husband. Strictly speaking she should ride a pregnant mare, and should be followed by a maid-servant mounted on another mare with a foal trotting behind. This is said to ensure a fruitful union.

When the girl arrives at her bridegroom's house she is seated with him on a low divan, having a swastika design worked on it for luck. Their relatives and friends are gathered round them. When all are settled a professional " praiser " sings the virtues of everyone

11234567890

present, even of the furniture and of the house. Then the parents of the happy couple bless them and place a scarf round the neck of each. This act constitutes the legal marriage. Barley-flour is then offered to the gods in the family chapel, and afterwards to everyone present. After a few months the bride's parents entertain their relations by marriage in their own house, and thus return the earlier hospitality of their son-in-law's parents. At the actual marriage, feasting goes on for three days. The dowry is paid over to the husband's parents after some months, while return gifts have to be made to the girl's people.

We arrived after the scarving ceremony, and found the happy husband his normal self and dressed in his best robes. His wife, however, was completely concealed by shawls and blankets piled over her. It was only after considerable persuasion that she was induced shyly to accept the scarves we offered. Our presents were placed on top of a pile of gifts from her relations and friends.

We then withdrew to a large sitting-room, with a wide window overlooking the courtyard, where a Bhutanese dance was in progress. This dance was introduced by the bridegroom's father, a Bhutanese who had settled in Gyantse, and married into a Tibetan family. During the whole three days' feasting eight professional wine-servers, four young men and four young women, beautifully dressed, plied the guests with locally brewed beer, or chang. When not actually occupied in serving they entertained the company with singing and dancing.

At about eleven in the morning, an hour or so after

our arrival, breakfast, consisting of thukpa, and six or seven meat, vegetable curries and stew dishes, was served. The guests then amused themselves by playing gambling games with dominoes and dice, and in watching the dancing, until three o'clock, when dinner was announced.

This was a most elaborate meal, and occupied about three hours. It was served on low, square tables, each accommodating about eight people, who, of course, used only chopsticks to convey the food to their mouths. Round the outer edge of the table were arranged about forty tiny saucers, each containing some kind of an appetiser popular in Tibet. These include nuts of two or three kinds, sliced hard-boiled eggs, orange quarters, lumps of raw sugar, small slices of liver, tongue, ham, beef and mutton, shredded turnips, currants, dried prawns, Chinese preserved fish and little rice-birds, bamboo-shoots, pickled kidneys, sunflower-seeds, and many other tit-bits. For a quarter of an hour or so the guests were left to sample these, until the first of the main dishes arrived. This consisted of some kind of fish cooked with green vegetables. Then followed at five-minute intervals other dishes, each served in a large porcelain bowl, and placed in the centre of the table. When four dishes had arrived, the one that had been on the table longest was removed, and a fresh dish brought in its place, so that there were always four courses on the table at the same time.

Mushrooms, sea-slugs, shark's fin, shark's stomach, bamboo-shoots, forcemeat balls, seaweed, frogs' eggs, sea-anemones, pork, beef, yak's meat, mutton—boiled, roasted and grilled—eels, turnips and pea-flour were only a few of the dishes that appeared. One takes only a morsel of each dish, otherwise it would be impossible to survive the meal. Half way through the repast a large bowl of hot water was placed on the table, in which everyone washed their chopsticks and china spoons. Following this came the sweet course, consisting of rice cooked in butter, with raisins, and little cakes made of barley-flour. After this had been consumed the meat, vegetable and fish dishes started coming again. The end of the meal was marked by placing a bowl of soup on the table, in addition to the four other dishes already there, and by passing to each guest a small bowl of boiled rice. Finally, hot, damp towels were passed round to cleanse the face and hands.

Then came for me the most trying part of the meal, refusing to drink barley-beer, of which I never partook. It is customary after one of these big feasts for each guest, except the lamas, to drink the contents of a half-gallon silver bowl, and the wine-maids stand over each guest singing until he has finished.

By the time this meal was over night had fallen, so we returned to the fort. We also attended the ceremony and feasting of the next two days.

Kyipup and his wife are now living on their estates at Gyantse.

CHAPTER TWENTY-SIX

MY second visit to Bhutan was made in 1921, in
company with the Earl of Ronaldshay, then
Governor of Bengal. He was a very keen
student of Lamaism, and deeply interested in the
peoples of the eastern Himalaya. Our journey was
full of interest. I went out to meet him as far as the
Kagyu Monastery, on the road leading from the Nathu
Pass and Gantok, and overlooking the Chumbi Valley.
His Excellency was a fast walker, and my short legs
found it difficult to keep pace with him. The Tibetan
Trade Agent had provided a Tibetan lunch for us at
his Trade Agency in Pibithang. The usual delicacies,
such as sea-slugs, frogs' spawn and sharks' fins, imported from China, were served, but Lord Ronaldshay
could be prevailed upon to taste only the more simple
dishes. The Tibetan Trade Agent did his utmost to
persuade His Excellency and his staff to drink quantities
of a very old and potent Chinese liqueur he had produced
for the occasion, but his efforts were unsuccessful.

That evening, Lord Ronaldshay, Mr Gourlay, his
private secretary, a very old friend of mine, and his
aide-de-camp, Captain Lyon, dined with me at the
Agency House, and after the meal we spent a pleasant
hour examining my collection of curios from Tibet and
Bhutan.

265

His Excellency, while in Yatung, inspected the tiny industrial and handicraft school established by my wife. He was pleasantly surprised at the quality of rugs and carpets woven by the Tibetan pupils.

After a day's halt in Yatung, to collect transport animals and porters, we rode up the Amo Chu gorge, passing across the Lingmathang plain, above which is situated the Tungka Monastery, and reached Gautsa, stopping there in the small two-roomed bungalow. Next day, six miles from Pharijong, we were met, according to Tibetan custom, by the local officials of that place, who came to welcome Lord Ronaldshay, and to escort him in to their town. A representative of the Maharaja of Bhutan was also present. The Tibetans were very curious as to why so important an officer as the Governor of Bengal had come to Pharijong, and insisted that there must be some ulterior motive in his visit. It was only after some considerable time that I was able to make them believe that he was there for pleasure.

An entire day was spent in exploring Pharijong and its environs, and we rode up the slopes of that wonderful mountain Chomolari, to a height of about eighteen thousand five hundred feet above sea-level. We had wonderful views across the tumbled peaks of Sikkim to the world's third highest mountain, Kinchenjunga. It may be of interest to note here, in view of recent controversy as to the origin of this name, that Kinchenjunga, or more properly Kangchen Dzönga, is purely Tibetan, and not Indian, as I have seen stated. Literally, it means the "Five Treasuries of the Great Snows."

DUG-GYE JONG IN BHUTAN

A FORTRESS IN BHUTAN, ORIGINALLY ERECTED AS A SAFEGUARD AGAINST MARAUDING TIBETANS. IT IS KNOWN AS THE FORT OF VICTORY, AS HERE
THE TIBETANS ONCE SUFFERED A GREAT LOSS.

Arriving at the dak-bungalow, in the late afternoon, we found Kumar (now Raja) Sonam Tobgye Dorje awaiting us. This young man is Prime Minister of Bhutan, an office he inherited from his late father, Raja Ugyen Dorje, Baron of Ha. He speaks English, and is perfectly at home in Western society. Kumar Tobgye was to conduct us through Bhutan. He told us that the Maharaja of Bhutan was prevented from meeting us at Paro owing to an epidemic of influenza there. We were naturally disappointed, especially as the Durbar which had been planned would now be abandoned. However, His Excellency decided to continue his tour. That night the thermometer on the verandah of the Pharijong dak-bungalow registered thirty-three degrees of frost, and was the lowest temperature we experienced.

Next morning, accompanied by Kumar Tobgye, we set out for Bhutan. Crossing the Tremo Pass, a sixteen-thousand-foot divide, on the Bhutan-Tibet frontier, we descended to the camping-ground of Shana, where everything had been prepared for our reception. From the Tremo La we had wonderful views of the snow-peaks of the eastern Himalaya, Chomolhari being especially magnificent. At Shana, His Excellency and party were accommodated in tents. The next day's halt was Duggye Jong, reached after a ride through a larch forest. The jong, or fort, is an imposing building, resembling the castles of Europe in the Middle Ages. Bhutan has a mediæval charm all its own. We visited the jong in the afternoon, and were shown round by the Jongpen, a jovial old priest, whom Lord Ronaldshay promptly christened " Friar Tuck."

He seemed to have stepped straight from the pages
of *Robin Hood*. The old gentleman dearly loved his
bottle of wine, and I had to entertain him at our camp
that evening. He so appreciated our company that he
left us only in the early hours of the following morning.

From Duggye Jong to Paro is two marches, and
on our way we passed the famous monastery of Paro
Taktsang. This is one of the most impressive institutions in Bhutan, and consists of a collection of small
cloisters clinging to the cliff face above the Paro
Valley. The Bhutanese believe it to be an earthly
prototype of the western paradise of Lamaism, over
which Guru Rimpoche, the " Precious Teacher,"
presides. They assert that this saint visited the site of
the monastery riding on a tiger, and from this incident
the place takes its name, which means the " Tiger's
Lair." At the time of our visit we were given light
refreshment by the lamas, which we greatly appreciated
after our steep climb from the valley below. About
twenty monks were in residence, and we saw one of
them seated in solitary meditation in an upper secluded
building. We also visited another monastery, called
Sangtok Pal Ri, supposed to represent a Lamaist
heaven. From this point a wonderful panoramic view
is obtained of the Paro Valley, with the river rushing
down over its rocky bed. On the altar of this monastery
are three dice, and pilgrims who cast these are told
their fortunes by attendant lamas.

We were escorted the last eight miles into Paro by
a detachment of Bhutanese men-at-arms, clad in steel
helmets and chain armour, closely accompanied by
musicians and dancers sent by the Maharaja. In

Bhutan, warriors dance in front of visitors of high rank as they approach the castle of a great chief. Two dancers on this occasion preceded us for no less than six miles.

Two miles from the camp we were met by the Paro Penlop, a powerful feudal baron, Governor of the Paro District. He was escorted by more men-at-arms, and was accompanied by the Jongpen of Punakha, an elderly man of grave demeanour. The Penlop himself was little more than a youth. He had had a tent pitched by the roadside, and, having dismounted, we seated ourselves, and were offered silk ceremonial scarves, similar scarves being given in return. After this little ceremony refreshments were passed round. The Penlop then went on ahead, ready to greet us again on our arrival at the camp.

When we reached our destination the Penlop received us in front of a large Durbar tent. He ushered us inside a shamiana, and offered us three different kinds of tea. First, tea mixed with cheese, then saffron-tea, and, lastly, a fine quality butter-tea, similar to that used in Tibet. Dried and fresh fruits were passed round and, following a short rest, the Penlop saw us to our quarters, neatly built little wooden houses, and tents. Later everyone wore full-dress uniform, in readiness for the ceremony of exchanging gifts, which was due to take place in the Durbar tent. Forming a small procession, headed by two Indian servants carrying His Excellency's gifts, and brought up in the rear by Lord Ronaldshay himself, we entered the Durbar. Here were gathered all the local Bhutanese officials and notables, with whom we sat down at a long table.

After a brief pause the Paro Penlop presented to Lord Ronaldshay gifts from the Maharaja. These consisted of two fine steel broadswords, in beautiful silver scabbards, a helmet, a shield, and a quantity of silk cloth. Mr Gourlay, Captain Lyon and I received swords of similar workmanship. A magnificent Bhutan stallion, of the famous Tangun breed, was then led into the Durbar, and presented to His Excellency.

Having thanked the Penlop for these handsome gifts, His Excellency requested him to convey our thanks to the Maharaja for his thoughtfulness and hospitality. In return, he sent His Highness, through the Paro Penlop, a silver casket, a pair of binoculars, and an autographed photograph of himself framed in silver. After this the Bhutanese officials offered their own gifts to Lord Ronaldshay, and the Durbar concluded. In the afternoon we entertained the Bhutanese officials in our camp, where they were very much interested in everything, especially our rifles.

The next morning was spent in visiting the jong, an imposing fortress, one of the largest in the country. It is a very handsome building, and even without artillery would be capable of resisting most sieges, were it not for the fact that, like most forts in Bhutan, it is dominated by its own outposts, from which, once they had been carried by an enemy, a destructive fire could be brought to bear on the jong itself. It contains some fine old Tibetan paintings, all of a religious nature, depicting incidents in the lives of the gods and the saints of Lamaism. His Excellency took many photographs of this place, some of which have been admirably reproduced in his book, *The Lands of the*

Thunderbolt. Very few Europeans have ever visited Paro, or indeed Bhutan itself, which has denied admittance to foreigners even more rigidly than Tibet, a policy likely to remain in force for many years to come.

The Penlop came to our camp and interested Lord Ronaldshay with a lengthy discussion on his country. Before leaving he gave me a silver-sheathed dagger and a silver supari-box. Until comparatively recent years the Penlops of Bhutan were always quarrelling among themselves for leadership. The late Maharaja, however, who was ruling at the time of our visit, succeeded in gathering the supreme temporal power into his own hands. He put a stop to the internecine strife ruining the country. He believed in keeping Bhutan for the Bhutanese, and would allow no European to settle or own land within his borders. A powerful personality, he was able to command the co-operation of the remaining Penlops in the maintenance of law and order. We were sorry to leave Paro.

Our next important halting-place was Ha, where Kumar Tobgye has his castle. This place is two marches from Paro. The new Ha Jong was built by Tobgye's father, after the burning down of the old fort some twenty years ago. A day was spent exploring Ha, after which I had to leave His Excellency's party and return direct to Yatung, three days' journey across the mountains. Lord Ronaldshay was going back to Calcutta *via* the Bengal Dooars, and therefore went straight through Bhutan to Banarhat. Before my departure he thanked me most cordially for the assistance I was able to render on the tour, in interpreting and in translation of letters from Tibetan and Bhutanese officials. But, as I told him, the pleasure I had derived from the trip was more than sufficient recompense for any little services I may have been able to render him.

Mr Bell passed through Yatung on his way down from Lhasa, where he had been practically a whole year. He told me that he was going on long leave preparatory to retirement, and was proceeding to England after making his report in Delhi, to the Viceroy's Secretary for Foreign and Political Affairs. This was the last occasion on which I saw Mr Bell in the East, and it was with deep sorrow that I bade him farewell. I had served under him for the greater part of my time in Tibet, and no one could have wished for a more kindly, conscientious and honourable chief with whom to work.

CHAPTER TWENTY-SEVEN

*The Second Everest Expedition—General Bruce—The Everest Expedition
—A Marriage—A Chieftainess—British Buddhists—Lake Dederich
—Dr McGovern*

THE second Everest Expedition came to Tibet
in the spring of 1922, and as I was stationed
at Gyantse and Yatung in that year I had the
pleasure of meeting most of its members, either on
their way up to or returning from the mountain. I
went out to meet them at Rinchengong, where the
track from the Jelap Pass meets the Chumbi Valley
proper. Some of my friends of the 1921 reconnaissance
were again present, and I was particularly delighted
in making the acquaintance of their leader, Brigadier-
General Bruce, of whom legendary tales are now re-
counted throughout the Himalayas. A wonderful
personality, he had the gift of endearing himself to
everyone, especially the hill tribes. To his personal
popularity, tact and intimate knowledge of the people,
and to his successful handling of the Tibetans along
his route of march, are largely due the achievements of
this expedition. As usual, my family entertained the
visitors. The inspiring enthusiasm of these moun-
taineers made us realise a newly found beauty in the
hills among which we had lived so many years. Mallory
especially, who afterwards died on Everest, was the
ideal mountain lover. He told me, as he regarded
Everest, he would never have a moment of real peace
until he had reached its summit.

Pharijong was, and still is, a difficult place in which to get large numbers of hired transport animals at short notice, but by sending word to the Jongpen and the headmen a week ahead I was able to ensure a minimum delay in getting the party's requirements. The attitude of the Tibetans towards the expedition, while not actively hostile, definitely was not cordial. They prophesied failure from the beginning, although certain High Lamas did bless the Buddhist personnel of the expedition, and this had an undoubtedly good effect on their *moral*. Sir Charles Bell, however, was primarily instrumental in securing sanction from the Tibetan Government for the expedition to enter Tibet.

My eldest son, John, joined the expedition later. He was employed as interpreter, and in the collection of natural history specimens, and as assistant to the transport officers. He was not permitted to attempt the ascent, and I have often wondered whether, had he been allowed to do so, he would not have succeeded in reaching the top of Everest. It must be remembered that he had lived for several years in Tibet, and was constantly at elevations up to twenty thousand feet, when out shooting, and was therefore absolutely acclimatised. Over six feet tall, with the tough, lean physique of the typical mountaineer, I feel that John would have won through.

The history of the expedition has been published elsewhere, and I will not enter into details of its accomplishments here.

On the party's return through Yatung one noticed a marked change in their appearance, and could see that their experience on the mountain had told on them all very severely. Everyone, however, was keen on returning to the attack the next season. We purchased much of their surplus stores and equipment. These were welcome on the occasion of my eldest daughter's wedding, which took place a month later, and at which we expected to entertain a very large number of people.

August 1922 saw the marriage of my eldest daughter, Anne, to a former colleague of mine, Mr F. W. R. Perry, who had spent nearly three years in Tibet commanding my escort. This was the first and, up to the time of writing, the only European marriage celebrated in Tibet. Quite apart from their interest in the affair as my personal friends, the curiosity of the Tibetans was aroused, since the ceremony was something entirely new to them.

We began preparations for entertaining our guests some weeks beforehand. Sheep, cattle and pigs had to be killed, quantities of flour, sugar, tea, Chinese delicacies, vegetables, and European stores of every kind had to be collected. Vast amounts of chang, or barley-beer, had to be brewed for our Tibetan guests, which procedure necessitated employment of dozens of men. The presence of all was requested, including the Dalai and Tashi Lamas. As a very considerable number of them attended, or sent their representatives, we had to entertain several hundred persons for many days. A few of our own personal European friends came up from India for the ceremony, for whom I was able to obtain permission to enter Tibet from the Government of India. To perform the marriage ceremony, a very old friend of mine, the Reverend

Evan Mackenzie, came up from Kalimpong, where he
had been in charge of the Tibetan congregation for
many years. Another very old friend, Miss Fredrickson,
accomplished a really wonderful feat in getting to
Yatung. Well over sixty, she walked all the way
from India, over the fourteen-thousand-foot passes,
disdaining the help of either pony or dandy. For forty
years she had been longing to visit Tibet, and by
obtaining her a pass to attend the wedding I was
able to gratify a heartfelt wish. We were glad to
have Captain J. B. Noel, F.R.G.S., the Mount Everest
photographer, with us at the time, and he was able to
get some unique pictures. He was passing through
Yatung on his way to India from Gyantse, where he
had been making cinematograph records of everyday
Tibetan life.

The wedding took place in the tiny schoolroom in
the Agency Bazaar. The bride and bridegroom had a
regimental guard of honour. After the ceremony the
party returned to the Agency House, where breakfast
was set out in large marquees on the lawn facing the
house. Perry and his wife sat outside, and received
the scarves of the Tibetan visitors, each of whom placed
a large silk ceremonial scarf round their shoulders, and
offered gifts of carpets or pieces of silk and brocade.
The Dalai and Tashi Lamas, and most of the high
officials in Lhasa and Shigatse, sent their representatives for the occasion. The Oracle Lama came down
from the Tungka Monastery and gave his blessing.
As the guests departed I presented each with a return
ceremonial scarf, as custom demands. We entertained
our visitors thus for three days.

A week after the wedding the Chieftainess of Duggye-jong, in Bhutan, with whom my daughters had gone through a blood-sisterhood ceremony, arrived for the festivities with eight stalwart retainers, two of whom were her husbands! She brought several mule-loads of gifts with her, mostly butter, chillies, vegetables and dried meat. She was not disconcerted at her late arrival, and stayed several days with us. She proved an entertaining companion, and made her husbands and followers perform Bhutanese folk-dances every evening. She always wore her national dress, and I have never seen another woman wear so great a number of coral and amber beads, each the size of a hen's egg, round her neck. She was a short, plump young woman, good-looking, while both of her male companions were brawny athletes well over six feet tall.

Some time before I had been notified by the Political Officer in Sikkim that a party of British Buddhists, calling themselves the British Buddhist Mission, was on its way to Tibet, their intention being to study the form of Buddhism practised there, and to make researches into its literature. The first member of the party to arrive in the Chumbi Valley was Dr William Montgomery McGovern. He called at my bungalow when he arrived. He was alone, the other British Buddhists having decided to travel from Kalimpong, with their stores and baggage. Dr McGovern was a scholar, and had spent many years in a Japanese monastery, where he had been ordained a priest. He was keenly interested in the Tibetan aspect of Buddhism, and hoped to spend some considerable time in Tibet, if possible in a monastery, studying Lamaism. He had a book-knowledge of the Tibetan language, but in my opinion he could never have passed as a Tibetan, since his pronunciation was very faulty. A fascinating conversationalist, we had many interesting discussions before the arrival of his colleagues. It is my personal opinion that Dr McGovern was sent on ahead to create a good impression on officials stationed in Sikkim and Tibet, both by reason of his culture and of his real Buddhist knowledge.

The remainder of the British Buddhist Mission arrived in Yatung a few days later, and called on me to present their credentials. The party consisted of Messrs Knight, Ellam, Fletcher and Harcourt. Mr Knight, a Fellow of the Royal Geographical Society, by profession a journalist, was secretary to the mission. Captain J. E. Ellam also was a writer, and like his colleague, Mr Knight, was a British Buddhist, and would spend hours translating Tibetan religious books at Dr McGovern's dictation. Mr Fletcher was in charge of the mission baggage and transport. Mr Harcourt, the youngest member of the party, admitted that he was not interested in Buddhism, and said that he had come to make a cinematograph film of the mission in Tibet.

Every member of this mission had his head close shaved, a custom observed by the more orthodox followers of Buddha. Someone had wrongly informed them that all Buddhists in Tibet shaved their heads. Only the lamas do this, and even then only at infrequent intervals. The mission, as British Buddhists, now wished to proceed to Lhasa and there pay their respects to the Dalai Lama. For this purpose they had prepared an address, purporting to come from the Buddhists of Britain, engrossed on parchment, and enclosed in a handsome silver casket. For lesser people they had brought an assortment of gifts, including gramophones and medicines. I noticed that many of their presents were of German origin.

At the request of the mission I telegraphed to the Government of India for permission for Mr McGovern and Captain Ellam to visit Lhasa, as their passports were valid only to Gyantse. The only hope of ever getting to Lhasa was by direct invitation from the Tibetan Government, but, despite their friendly overtures to the Tibetan officials stationed in Gyantse, the invitation never came. In these circumstances the Government of India requested the mission to return to India, as their passes were valid six weeks only from the date of crossing the Tibetan frontier. By getting an extension, however, the British Buddhists' Mission managed to remain at Gyantse for almost three months. Towards the end of this period they became impatient, and I had to watch their movements very closely, for I feared that they might make a dash towards the capital.

The mission spent their stay in Gyantse visiting the local monasteries, discussing Lamaism with the priests, and in translating Tibetan books. They were accommodated in the dak-bungalow. Eventually they decided to return to India.

On their return to Yatung they sold most of the presents they had brought for the Tibetans, as the cost of transporting them back to Europe would have been considerable. They were unable to obtain a

cinematograph film of anything new, the ground that
they covered having been previously visited by Captain
J. B. Noel earlier in the year. Disconsolately they
returned to Darjeeling, and I prematurely concluded
that I had seen the last of them.

Shortly after their departure from Tibet I was surprised to read in a newspaper that they had discovered
a new lake near Pharijong. It was most improbable
that such a lake, located quite near the trade route,
along which I and other British officers had travelled
almost every month, could have been overlooked, and
the report so intrigued me that I made a special journey
to Pharijong to investigate. I found that the new
" discovery " was very well known, almost dry in
winter, and formed by the melting snows of Chomolhari. Of little or no significance, it is not included in
any Government map. It was named " Lake Dederich"
by the British Buddhist Mission, in honour of their
financier, a London business man.

Several weeks had passed since the Buddhist Mission
had left Tibet when I was informed that Dr McGovern
had re-entered Sikkim, and all trace of him had been
lost. It was presumed that he would attempt to reach
Lhasa, and orders were issued to stop him if he came
to Gyantse or Yatung, or at any other point on the
main Indo-Lhasa trade route between the two towns.
McGovern, however, avoided these marts. Later, when
he passed through Yatung from Lhasa, he told me the
tale of his experiences.

It appeared that when the British Buddhist Mission
arrived back in Darjeeling they were labouring under
a sense of deep injustice at having been denied pass-

ports to Lhasa. It was finally decided that one of their members should attempt to reach the capital in disguise. The selection naturally fell to Dr McGovern, a profound Buddhist scholar, as he knew a certain amount of Tibetan. Accompanied by his local teacher, a Sikkim Bhutia, and two or three coolies, he crossed through Sikkim to Tibetan territory. At a place just below Gantok, the capital of Sikkim, McGovern adopted the guise of a lowly Tibetan, and, still accompanied by his men, managed to get past Gantok and into northern Sikkim without deception. His procedure was to act as the servant of his " teacher," nominally leader of the party. To complete the deception McGovern himself carried a small load. Sleeping in cowsheds and, when nothing better offered, in the open, he at length reached Khamba Jong, a Tibetan town just across the Sikkim-Tibet frontier. From this place right on to Lhasa he ran considerable risk of detection, for the route is well frequented. The guru (" guru "=teacher), realising this, took advantage of the position, assumed airs, and threatened exposure if his wishes were not complied with. He gave McGovern a great deal of trouble. However, the Doctor did eventually reach the capital of Tibet, where he disclosed himself to the Nepalese postmaster then in charge of the Lhasa Post and Telegraph Office. He was forced to take this step, partly due to failing health and partly to escape the tyranny of his servant. His arrival in Lhasa was immediately telegraphed to me. Whatever may have been written by others, I must state here that Dr McGovern during his journey was never in the slightest danger from the Tibetans. Had he been detected he would only have been sent back to Sikkim.

The rigours of the journey, however, reduced Dr McGovern to a physical wreck. A diet of raw dried-meat and parched barley-flour can play havoc with the toughest of digestions. He contracted dysentery, and it was nearly a month before he was able to leave Lhasa. Even when he got to Yatung he was by no means a fit man. One of the ministers, the Tsarong Shap-pe, did call to see Dr McGovern, as it was part of his duties to interview all foreigners who came to the holy city.

The Doctor managed to conceal a cinematograph camera in his kit, but he took no photographs in Lhasa, as this was forbidden by the Tibetan authorities.

CHAPTER TWENTY-EIGHT

IN June 1922 Major F. M. Bailey, C.I.E., then
Political Officer in Sikkim, was deputed to present
the insignia of Grand Commander of the Order of
the Indian Empire to the Maharaja of Bhutan, Sir
Ugyen Wangchuk. The Hon. Mrs Bailey and her
mother, Lady Cozens-Hardy, went with Major Bailey,
and I accompanied the party for some part of the
journey. We left Yatung, if memory serves me rightly,
on 15th June 1922, and reached Ha Jong after three
days' travelling. There we were entertained by my
old friend, Kumar Sonam Tobgye Dorje, to whom you
have already been introduced. We stayed one night
at his castle, and proceeded to Paro, which we reached
after a two days' march. I had been over this ground
before, but to the ladies it was new, and of great
interest. They were, to the best of my belief, the first
British women to travel in Bhutan, and those of the
Bhutanese among whom they passed were as interested
in the ladies as the latter were in them.

At Paro we were accommodated in the usual specially
built little wooden houses, as the guests of the Penlop.
He received Major Bailey with all the honour due to
an envoy of a Great Power. Soldiers and dancers
preceded our approach to the camping-ground, and the
full ceremonial of calling and returning calls, and the

283

exchange of gifts was completed. This over, we spent a couple of days exploring the countryside, and in showing the ladies over the castle of Paro.

From here the Major went to Tongsa, where he was to meet the Maharaja and conduct the investiture, while the Hon. Mrs Bailey and Lady Cozens-Hardy, escorted by myself, proceeded to Pharijong, *via* the Tremo La route, which I had gone over with Lord Ronaldshay the year before. We had just reached the top of the Tremo La, and were lunching in the shelter of a large rock, when a mounted messenger overtook us, and presented two letters from Major Bailey. One was for his wife and the other instructed me to return to Yatung. It appeared that he wanted the ladies to rejoin him in Bhutan as soon as possible.

All their baggage, however, had gone to Pharijong, so that they could not turn back from the Tremo La, but had to continue on to Phari. By the time of our arrival it was too late to start the return trip, and as Major Bailey had sent no escort for them, even though they would probably have been quite safe in travelling unattended, I did not feel justified in allowing them to depart alone. Accordingly, I got into telephonic communication with Gyantse and Yatung, and having ascertained that no matter required my immediate attention we set off the following morning for Paro. We met the Major on a shooting expedition at Chalimaphu. From there I returned to Yatung *via* Ha.

On the way I again visited Tashicho Jong, which was seen by Bogle in 1774. There I met the son of another old friend, the Thimpu Jongpen, who entertained me right royally. The lamas showed me over the local monastery, where I examined a very fine image of Zhab-drung Ngak-wang Rimpoche, the priest who is said to have introduced Buddhism into Bhutan. His successor in spiritual power, the Dharma Raja, was sitting in deep meditation at the time ; I did not disturb him, though he would have received me gladly. My friend, the late Maharaja Sir Ugyen Wangchuk, G.C.I.E., gradually gathered all power into his own hands, until, to-day, his son, the reigning Maharaja, controls both civil and Church parties in the country.

The Bhutanese received me during this visit with all kindliness, and accorded me the greatest honour. I am grateful also to Major and Mrs Bailey for all the kindness they showed me as their guest during the tour. They made me very comfortable. Later I received a cordial letter of thanks from Lady Cozens-Hardy on her departure from Tibet.

In this connection, it may be mentioned that Major Bailey is a noted explorer and traveller, having spent many years in Tibet and the North-Eastern Frontier of India. He visited Lhasa twice, in 1904 and 1924, being well received by the Dalai Lama.

A few months after my return, the Tsarong Shap-pe, then at the zenith of his power, decided to send his young sister-in-law to school in India. Always aiming at the betterment of his people, he set the example by sending a member of his own family, in the hope that others might follow his lead. It is regrettable that so many of the Shap-pe's national development schemes found so little favour in the conservative Church party.

He requested me to take the maid, Rinchen Drolma,

into my own home at Yatung for a few months before proceeding to India, so that by association with my daughters she might acquire some knowledge of English, and become acquainted with European manners and customs. She arrived, shy and nervous, with a large retinue and much baggage. We called her Mary, the nearest English equivalent to her Tibetan name, which means "Protectress." She had been with us barely a week when she adopted European clothes.

Most Oriental women appear awkward in Western dress, but not so Mary, who during the years she was away from Tibet continued wearing English clothes. Appreciating the then fashionable "bob," it was not very long before she had her own long black hair shorn. My wife, without avail, tried to dissuade her, because her hair was particularly beautiful. She learned English very rapidly, and was soon sufficiently advanced to enter a European school in Darjeeling, at the age of thirteen. Here she became very popular with both mistresses and pupils. Mary Tsarong remained there only three years, yet in that time she assimilated as much as an average girl would in six. Above all, she was taught to understand and appreciate the British interpretation of sportsmanship and morality. Her holidays were spent with my family, usually in Kalimpong, and each term the progress she had made was astounding. It was no small trial for Mary to submit to the strict discipline of school life. At thirteen a girl is considered as a mature woman in Tibet, and Mary, by virtue of her brother-in-law's official position, was one of the first ladies in the land. She was accustomed to having her every wish gratified. The

"MARY" TSARONG

friendship she formed with my family still exists, and we often hear from her.

When Mary returned from school she acted as her brother-in-law's confidential secretary, a very important position to occupy, and one not previously held by a Tibetan woman. In 1928 she married Kumar Jigmed Tering, the son of my old Gyantse friend, Raja Tsotra Namgyal of Tering. This marriage was most suitable in every way, as Jigmed also had been educated in Darjeeling. They have settled down at Gyantse, where Jigmed assists his father in the management of the family estates.

In 1923 a telegraph line was constructed between Gyantse and Lhasa. This made direct communication between the Tibetan capital and India possible, as a line already existed up to the Trade Mart of Gyantse. The Tibetan Government defrayed all expenses for construction, and the Telegraph Department of Bengal lent the services of one of their most experienced telegraph engineers, Mr A. King, who covered the one hundred and thirty-six miles in record time. All materials, including posts, had to be carried up from India, and skilled workmen also had to be imported.

Mr Rosemeyer, who for many years has been in charge of the telegraph system in Sikkim and Tibet, makes an annual trip to Lhasa to inspect that portion of the line. He has thus had the opportunity of seeing that sacred city more often than any other living European. Telephones were installed in all the important State offices in Lhasa, and these have proved satisfactory.

The telegraph office in the capital was placed in

charge of a Nepalese operator employed by the Bengal Telegraph Department, his services being lent to the Tibetan Government until a Tibetan could be trained for the work. Kyipup, one of the boys educated in England, went to India for training in telegraphy. On his return he was posted as superintendent of Tibetan telegraphs. At the same time, a Tibetan operator replaced the Nepali. One can now telegraph from Lhasa to any part of the world. The Tibetan portion of the line is being used more and more every year by traders, and, of course, by the Tibetan Government. For messages between Lhasa and Gyantse a charge of a shilling is made for every twelve words.

While on the subject of telegraphs, I remember that one of the Inspecting Telegraph Masters on the Gyantse line had a glass eye. He would cause considerable consternation among the Tibetans by removing his glass eye and showing it to them. He would often leave this eye to watch his property, and it is a fact that none of his belongings was ever pilfered.

One afternoon in August 1923, while I was resting, one of my chapprassis awakened me with the news that a woman in a white Tibetan dress, accompanied by a man dressed as a lama, urgently desired an interview. The chapprassi added that, although they looked like tramps, the lady insisted on seeing me, and that she spoke very tersely, "just like a European," to give his own words. Thinking this to be a practical joke by one of my daughters I instructed the chapprassi to show the lady into my bedroom. On her approaching I feigned sleep, and did not rise. After she had been in the room awhile I said, without turning, that I

THE WEDDING MASTERS OF CEREMONY AND THEIR ATTENDANTS

THIS PARTY OF TIBETANS ASSISTED IN THE CEREMONIES GOVERNING THE MARRIAGE BETWEEN "MARY" TSARONG OF TIBET AND KUMAR JIGME NAMGYAL OF TERING.

knew who she was, and told her to go away and not be silly. Imagine my confusion when a strange voice informed me that the speaker was Madame Neel. At once I conducted her to the sitting-room, where tea had been served, and there questioned her as to how she had come, and the reason for her wearing Tibetan clothes. She gave me a brief account of her journey from China to Tibet, a wonderful feat for a woman of her age and physique. She appeared very frail, and to succeed as she had called for immense courage and vitality.

Accompanied by a Sikkimese youth, Ongden, whom she had adopted as her son, she travelled as a beggar-woman all the way on foot from the Chinese frontier to Gyantse, visiting Lhasa on the way. She must have undergone incredible hardships, for, as a beggar, the houses of the better-class Tibetans, where *bona-fide* travellers frequently find some hospitality, were closed to her. Madame Neel told me she spent two months in Lhasa without being detected, nor was her identity revealed until she disclosed herself to Mr Ludlow, the headmaster of the Tibetan Boys' School in Gyantse. From him she had requested permission to occupy a room in the rest-house, but as this authority rested with me he had her sent on to the fort.

Madame Neel, by reason of the disguise she had adopted, unfortunately saw Tibet only from the view-point of a poor pilgrim. Before starting on her journey she had a very considerable knowledge of Lamaism and Tibetan habits. She has since written a book on her journey and adventures. At Gyantse she would say very little about these, frankly stating that she

T

preferred to avoid any discussion until her book was published.

After a short rest in Gyantse she went to Yatung, where my eldest daughter equipped her with clothing more suitable for travelling in India and Sikkim than the thick woollen robes in which she had crossed Tibet, and which were all she possessed.

Madame Neel was a Frenchwoman, but spoke quite good English, and Tibetan like a native. For several years before the Great War she had resided in Sikkim, but an unauthorised visit to Shigatse brought about her expulsion. The Government of India refused her permission to visit Tibet, and this apparently made her all the more determined to enter the forbidden land. She stated that she did not recognise the authority of Great Britain in denying nationals of other Powers the right to travel in Tibet, which is a completely independent country. In this connection it may be noted that the measures adopted by the Government of India for regulating entry into Tibet are in accordance with the wishes of the Tibetan Government. She went to China, and spent many years in monasteries along the Sino-Tibetan frontier, studying mystic Lamaism, and preparing for her dash to Lhasa, which was finally accomplished after several failures. With her adopted son, Ongden, Madame Neel has now retired to the French Alps, where she is engaged in literary and Buddhist research work. For some time she was associated with the organisation inaugurated by the famous Madame Blavatsky.

Soon after Madame Neel had gone to India, the Earl of Lytton, then Governor of Bengal, visited the

Chumbi Valley. This was in October 1923. He was accompanied by Mr Wilkinson, I.C.S., his private secretary, whom I had met before, and two aides-de-camp. The mounted infantry escort was brought from Gyantse by the officer commanding. We rode out to the Kagyu Monastery to escort the Governor into the Trade Agency.

Lord Lytton and his party spent a couple of days in the dak-bungalow in Yatung before going on to Pharijong. His Excellency did myself and my family the honour of lunching and dining with us. He proved to be very much interested in Tibet and the Tibetans. We visited the Tibetan Trade Agency at Pibithang, where the Depon Myeru Gyalpo entertained us to a sumptuous Chinese luncheon. The usual dishes appeared, but none of His Excellency's party would attempt the more gruesome delicacies. Another morning was spent visiting Tungka Monastery, residence of the famous Chumbi Valley oracle, who exhibited his powers on the occasion.

An Alpine sport enthusiast, Lord Lytton had brought skis with him, hoping to get a few runs. I hoped that there would be enough snow in Pharijong for this. We rode to the Khambu slopes only to find that the snow, where deep enough, was unsafe, and that in other likely places was too scanty. We reached sixteen thousand feet in a fruitless search. There were deep drifts on Chomolhari, but these were far too dangerous for ski-ing, and His Excellency unfortunately could not afford to wait for a heavy fall of snow.

When Lord Lytton and his party arrived in Pharijong all the local officials were there to greet him. The following morning they paid individual calls, offering ceremonial scarves and gifts, and receiving suitable presents in return. Before his departure I escorted His Excellency through the bazaar of Pharijong, which enjoys the dual distinction of being the highest and dirtiest town in the world. Lord Lytton did not linger long in its environs. I accompanied him back to Yatung. From there he returned to India.

CHAPTER TWENTY-NINE

Lhasa & Shigatse—Cause of the Quarrel—Flight of the Tashi Lama—
Pursuit of the Tashi Lama—The Tashi Lama at Mukden—The
Cause of the Flight—Hatred of the Police

FOR several years prior to 1923 relations between the Governments of Lhasa and Shigatse had been growing steadily more strained. Even in 1922 the Tashi Lama was very much alarmed at the turn that matters were taking, for in that year he wrote asking me to act as a mediator between himself and the Dalai Lama. This I was unfortunately precluded from doing by the regulations of the Indian Government, which rightly forbids its representatives in Tibet to interfere in any way with the internal affairs of that country. The people of the Shigatse province protested against having to supply free transport and labour to Lhasa officials travelling in their districts. They maintained that, as direct subjects of the Shigatse administration, these facilities should be supplied to their own officers only. It may be mentioned here that the central Government has since put a stop to this injustice, and all Tibetan subjects have to supply animals and labour alike.

Trouble between the two Grand Lamas finally came to a head because money was required for the maintenance of the army and for the defence of the eastern frontiers. At this juncture His Serenity the Tashi Lama was taking a cure at the hot springs of Je, a place four days' journey to the west of Shigatse. He returned to his capital at once. Certain of his ministers had been summoned urgently to Lhasa, and there had been thrown into prison.

At the first sign of really serious trouble between the Lhasa and Shigatse Grand Lamas I sent a man to the latter place, to His Serenity, to inquire after his well-being, and the very same night that he returned to his Shigatse headquarters the Tashi Lama, with his chief adherents, and about a hundred followers, rode away from the Tashilhunpo Monastery, heading for an unknown destination. Thus the Shigatse Grand Lama was following the example of his Lhasa confrère, who twice had to flee from his country, in 1904 and in 1910. I was not able to ascertain at that time exactly what information he had found awaiting him on his return from the hot springs, but that it was ominous is certain. I was later informed that the Tashi Lama had received word that a body of Mongolian troops were awaiting him not far from Shigatse, to escort him to their country.

The Lama headed westwards, where the country is very sparsely inhabited, but after travelling in this direction for a few days he swung off to the north, and managed to reach Mongolian territory. In crossing the Tsangpo, or upper reaches of the Brahmaputra river, he lost several animals and some of his baggage. After halting in Mongolia for some months the Tashi Lama went to Pekin, at the invitation of the Chinese Republican Government. There he was received with full honours. The Tashi Lama had, and still has, a large following in Tibet, which would undoubtedly be prepared to welcome him back on any conditions.

A fast courier can ride from Shigatse to Gyantse in twenty-four hours, with relays of ponies, and from the latter place to Lhasa there is telegraphic communication. It was therefore not very long before news of the Tashi Lama's flight was received in the capital. A body of five hundred troops was sent in pursuit, under the command of Tsipon Lungshar, now Commander-in-Chief of the Tibetan Army. These troops rode by a direct route to the Mongolian frontier, with the object of intercepting the Tashi Lama. They found, however, no trace of the fugitives, and, indeed, for some time were not certain that the Lama had fled that way.

Many rumours were current in Tibet as to the Tashi Lama's whereabouts, some alleging that he was still in the country, others that he had fled to India. Not long after the return of my own messenger from Shigatse, with the news of the Grand Lama's flight, one of the Lhasa Jongpens from that city arrived in Gyantse, and asserted that I was sheltering the fugitive prelate in the British Post, the friendly relations between myself and His Serenity being well known throughout Tibet. He wanted to search the British Trade Agency, and desisted from his inquiries only after being assured by the Khenchung Kusho, the local Tibetan Trade Agent, a very intimate friend of my own, that the Tashi Lama had not been near Gyantse.

The absence of that prelate from his country is causing great uneasiness among devout Lamaists. His own subjects of the Tsang province are groaning under the burden of the new taxation imposed by the central Government, which has now placed its own officers in charge of the districts formerly directly administered from Shigatse. In that city is stationed a Lhasa official of ministerial rank. He is assisted by four fourth-rank men. Orders have been issued that all taxes and arrears of revenue are to be exacted to the last farthing.

The Tashi Lama asserts that he wishes to return to his monastery, and the Dalai Lama replies that he is at perfect liberty to do so. The former, however, before he will return to Tibet, requires some substantial guarantee of his personal safety, and that of the ministers who are sharing his exile. He once asked if the Government of India would provide this guarantee, but this, of course, could not be done. At the time of writing, the Tashi Lama has left Pekin, and is resident at Mukden, in Manchuria, where he is well treated. He lives in a palace, specially built for his accommodation by the Chinese Government. There he receives sufficient funds from the gifts of pious pilgrims to maintain himself and his suite in comfort. He is also in receipt of an allowance from the Chinese, and still retains some of the treasures he took with him from Tibet.

Before he left Shigatse the Tashi Lama left a letter for the Dalai Lama, in which he stated that he was going to Mongolia for the purpose of raising money, and that he had no intention whatever of being the cause of starting civil strife in Tibet. Once he had left the country, the central Government published a bulletin to the effect that the Tashi Lama had gone away of his own accord, and that they had not threatened him in any way, nor could they take any responsibility for his flight.

The man who was responsible more than any other for the flight of the Tashi Lama was the late Dronyer

Chhembo, or Chief Chamberlain to His Holiness the
Dalai Lama. This official was formerly in the service
of the Tashi Lama, but had been punished and dismissed for certain irregularities. He obtained service
with the Dalai Lama, and rose to very high rank, but
he never forgave the Tashi Lama for his early disgrace.
Money had to be found for the army and the new
police, and this Dronyer Chhembo, having the ear of
the Tibetan Government, persuaded the latter to press
the Shigatse pontiff for considerable subscriptions,
which could not be raised.

A police force was inaugurated by my friend, the
Tsarong Shap-pe. He persuaded the Dalai Lama, in
the face of bitter opposition from the entire Church
party, to sanction his scheme. Having been approached
by the Lhasa authorities, the Government of India
lent them the services of Mr Laden La, of the Bengal
Police, to organise the police force. Mr Laden La, a
Sikkimese by birth, speaking Tibetan as his mother
tongue, and with considerable experience in dealing
with hill peoples, was peculiarly suited for this work.
He knew personally many of the high officials with
whom he would have to come into contact, and was a
great friend of the Tsipon Lungshar, a coming man
in Tibet, who had been associated with him in England
in connection with the education of the four Tibetan
youths sent to that country for schooling.

Mr Laden La proceeded to Lhasa, and began his
work, adapting Indian police methods to the conditions in Tibet. He was hampered, however, by the
peculiar customs of the Tibetan capital, whereby, at
certain times of the year, all administrative and executive

powers are withdrawn from the civil authorities, and placed in the hands of the lamas of the three great monasteries of Drepung, Sera, and Ganden. The material with which he had to work was not of the best. The rank and file of the new force were practically conscripts, sent in by owners of great estates, who, naturally, did not part with their good men. The pay of a constable was small, and offered no inducement to the ordinary citizen to join the force. Training the new police must have been terribly uphill work, and Mr Laden La is to be congratulated on the results he managed to achieve. His duties unfortunately told on his health, and after a year he was compelled to return to India to recuperate. Once he had left, the police force, for various reasons, went to pieces. Continual friction existed between the military and the police.

From its very inception the Lhasa townspeople hated the police force. The new police were unfortunately apt to be a trifle overbearing, over-conscientious in the performance of their duties, and prone to make arrests on the slightest pretext. The Lhasa citizens were unused to this kind of treatment, and naturally detested the new guardians of the law. To-day there remain less than fifty constables, who have now been placed under the control of the Mipon, or city magistrates. Almost every one of the commissioned ranks appointed to the police have been degraded or dismissed, so bitterly did the citizens, high and low, dislike the innovation, and those who had anything to do with it. One of the police officers, Pema Chandra, attempted to flee from Lhasa, owing to persecution, but was caught and shot by the soldiers sent in pursuit.

CHAPTER THIRTY

Third Everest Expedition—Mrs Noel—Brigadier-General Pereira—The Purchase of Mules—Visitors to Tibet—Transport of Heavy Plant to Tibet—Sir Frederick O'Connor—Motor-Cars

THE third—and, up to the time of writing, the last—Everest Expedition passed through the Chumbi Valley on their way to the mountain in 1924. General Bruce was again the leader, with Colonel Norton as second-in-command. This party seemed to me to be much stronger than any sent previously, not only in numbers, but also by reason of the fact that several of its members had had experience on Everest. It seemed that success was highly probable. My son John was again employed in the capacity of assistant naturalist and in the convoying of the expedition mails and money, as well as for interpreting work. The first misfortune of the party was the breakdown, owing to fever, of General Bruce, who had to return to India from a place called Dochen, only two marches out from Pharijong. The leadership was taken over by Colonel Norton.

In addition to the fact that my son was with the expedition, we were even more interested in their welfare and progress this year owing to the presence in Yatung of Mrs Noel, the wife of the official photographer to the party. I was able to accommodate her comfortably in a small cottage in the Yatung Bazaar. Mrs Noel was psychic, and her foreknowledge of

299

coming events was positively uncanny, as well as her knowledge of the past. The first indication I had of her powers in this direction was when she told me that someone had died a violent death in the house she was living in. She asserted that she was not in the least nervous, as the spirit that was present could not harm her in any way. What she told me was correct in every detail. Some years before, a transport agent had committed suicide in that very house, but I had not mentioned this for fear of alarming her, as no other house was available. I had also warned my family against saying anything, and as Mrs Noel spoke none of the Chumbi Valley dialects of Hindustani she could not have understood any of the local people, even had they wished to inform her of the occurrence.

We had another visitor in Yatung at this time, in the person of Mr Francis Helps, an artist, attached to the Everest Expedition, who was painting types of the hill peoples. He prepared a large collection of these, which he later exhibited in one of the London galleries. Among other models, he painted portraits of my two elder daughters in Nepalese and Tibetan dress.

One day Mrs Noel, who seemed very worried, asked me if I had any news of the expedition. I had received nothing later than her own letters from her husband. She insisted that some tragedy had occurred on the mountain, but at the same time was convinced that her husband was not involved. She said, however, that a dear friend was concerned. She was afterwards proved to be right in her fears, for several days later the news of the death of Mallory and Irvine, on the very day she had come to me, came through. Mr

Mallory was an intimate friend of the Noels: he and Mrs Noel had played together as children.

The deaths of these two climbers naturally cast a gloom over the whole expedition, and when we entertained them on their return to Yatung, Mallory and Irvine were sadly missed. Colonel Norton and the rest of the party gave my family a lunch "*à la* Everest," in the expedition's mess-tent, and under the same conditions, as far as was possible, as they had their meals while at the base camp at Everest, and with the same menu.

In connection with the Everest Expedition another small party, under the leadership of Lieutenant-Colonel Haddick, attempted to bring a Citroen-Degresse tractor through Sikkim to Tibet under its own power. Unfortunately, two of the four members of this party, Messrs Cundell and Fitzgerald, were taken ill with dysentery before they really got started, leaving Colonel Haddick and Mr C. F. Milwright, a one-time supply and transport officer in Gyantse, to carry on alone. They managed to get the tractor as far as Sedonchen, ten thousand feet above sea-level, and half-way up the great Himalayan "staircase" between Rongli and Gnatong, but there it stuck. For several months it lay in the Sedonchen dak-bungalow compound, and was finally taken back to Darjeeling by Mr Milwright. As a matter of fact, to anyone who has been over this road, the surprising thing about the affair is not that it stuck where it did, but that it had got so far. The road is one of the worst in the world, very narrow, and zigzagging every few yards. The surface consisted, where it was not just mud, of small boulders,

many of which were on end. This tractor was similar
to those which crossed the Sahara in 1922. Colonel
Haddick came up as far as Yatung, where he entertained us by reading the drafts of the lectures he was
preparing to deliver all over India on the Everest
Expedition, for which he was one of the officially
appointed lecturers. I heard afterwards that his lecture
tour was a great success.

In June 1924 two notable visitors, in the persons
of Captain Kingdon Ward, the well-known botanist
explorer, and Lord Cawdor, passed through Gyantse,
where I had the pleasure of entertaining them at the
Agency. They were bound for south-eastern Tibet,
where they hoped to explore the middle reaches of the
Brahmaputra river, where it cuts through the eastern
Himalaya. They did not go so far north as Lhasa, but
kept along the southern frontier. So far as I know,
they succeeded in their object. Once they had left
Gyantse, I did not see them again, for they left Tibet
by way of the Abor country.

News came from Lhasa, in July 1923, by telegram,
that a European was in that city. He turned out to
be Brigadier-General Pereira, a retired officer of the
British army, and a former military attaché of the
British Legation in Pekin. He had made his way
through Tibet overland from China. In due course
he arrived at Gyantse, where I happened to be at the
time, and I had the pleasure of entertaining him, and
of hearing an account of his adventures. The General,
an elderly man, had not enjoyed the best of health
during his march, and was certainly not at all fit at the
time of our meeting. He was limping, and appeared

very weary, yet one could not help being impressed by his air of quiet determination and by his powers of endurance. He told me he had walked practically the whole way from Lanchowfu to Lhasa, taking an occasional lift on some kind of pack-animal. The General was unable to take much in the form of solid food, and lived almost entirely on soups while he was with me. He said that the soup he got at my table was the first real soup he had tasted since leaving Lanchowfu. General Pereira was no novice in Asiatic travel, for he had been for years engaged in exploration and research work all over China and along the Sino-Tibetan frontier, which he knew from one end to the other.

Whether his last journey was inspired by motives other than exploration and the desire to be the first European to reach Lhasa from the Chinese side I do not know, nor did he tell me. Before leaving for India he drew for me a rough sketch-map, showing his route. Among other matters, General Pereira stated that he had passed a great mountain range, shown on his map as Amne Machin, the height of one of whose peaks he estimated to be as great as, if not greater than, Mount Everest. Having no instruments he was unable, unfortunately, to make any proper calculations of its elevation, but when it is remembered that he was an experienced observer, accustomed to estimating heights, it is not entirely without the bounds of possibility that a mountain of exceptional height does exist in eastern Tibet.

On reaching Calcutta, General Pereira was ordered into a nursing home, but before he was really fit his

restless spirit drove him off once more to the land he
loved, China. There, nearing Kantse, he died, without
a doubt owing to the effects of his previous journey
across Tibet. His notes on Tibet have since been
published by Sir Francis Younghusband. General
Pereira was an authority on China and the Chinese,
and was probably the most widely travelled European
in that country.

During the greater part of the time I was stationed
in Tibet we had few visitors, other than officials
inspecting various departments. Until recently, apart
from the annual visit of the Political Officer in Sikkim,
sometimes accompanied by his wife, only the State
Engineer of Sikkim and the Superintendent of Posts
and Telegraphs ever came near Gyantse or Yatung.
Among the wives of the various Political Officers
who have visited Tibet, Lady Bell was very popular
among the Tibetans, by reason of her deep sympathetic
interest in the people, especially the womenfolk.

In 1919 the experiment of purchasing mules in
Gyantse for the Transport Corps of the Indian army
was tried, and Major A. de C. Rennick and Captain
Bentham, the veterinary officer, remained there for
three months. The mules used in Tibet are almost
all Chinese-bred, coming from Sining Fu, being
marched half-way across Tibet. This long journey
weeds out all the weaklings, so that practically every
animal that came into the market at Gyantse could be
assumed to be hardy and in first-rate condition. Only
on this one occasion did the Government of India
purchase mules in Tibet itself, since that time the
mule-purchasing officers have made their headquarters

at Kalimpong, in British India, at the head of the Indo-Lhasa trade route.

I feel I cannot leave the subject of visitors to Tibet without mentioning the names of Mr and Mrs Percy Brown. Mr Brown, for many years the Director of the Indian Museum in Calcutta, and the Principal of the Art School attached to that institution, has been a very dear friend to me. To his advice is largely due the merit of my small collection of Tibetan and Chinese curios. He and his wife came up as far as Gyantse. He is an authority on Sikkim, and its arts and crafts. Another most interesting visitor to the Chumbi Valley was Princess Lieven, now Lady Studd. She was an artist, and my daughter still treasures a pen-and-ink sketch of a Russian scene that Princess Lieven drew for her in her autograph album. Widely travelled, she was full of interesting anecdotes concerning out-of-the-way places. We were all sorry she could not prolong her visit.

Tibet, right from the days of Warren Hastings, has always exercised an attraction on the Governors of Bengal, and of recent years several of them have visited the country. It doubtless affords a pleasant break in the hurly-burly of Bengal politics. While the present governor, Sir Stanley Jackson, has not been up to Tibet, Lady Jackson has made a tour as far as Yatung.

As mentioned elsewhere, one of the Tibetan boys sent to England after the Younghusband Mission was trained as an electrical engineer. When he returned to Tibet his Government decided to erect a hydro-electric plant in Lhasa. A very large plant was ordered, and the component parts were shipped out from

Britain. They were so heavy, however, that great trouble was experienced in transporting them from railhead to Lhasa. The parts should have been made much smaller. The machinery was taken as far as Gantok, the capital of Sikkim, up to which place there is a cart road, but after Gantok the real difficulties began. First of all, the Tibetan Government sent down their own conscripted coolies to carry the equipment across the Nathu Pass into the Chumbi Valley. After a few days of very arduous work most of these coolies, who received no payment, decamped, and the plant lay for several months rusting in Sikkim.

At last an arrangement was arrived at whereby the Sikkim Government undertook to have the parts carried as far as the pass, and placed on Tibetan territory. Once on their own ground, the Tibetan Government were able to see that their forced labour did not run away, but it was only after several more months of superhuman effort that the plant eventually arrived in Lhasa. Some of the pieces were so heavy and awkward that each took twenty men to carry it, their daily progress being less than four miles. At the Mint, near Dode, power is provided for lighting Norbu Lingka, the summer residence of the Dalai Lama. Beyond this nothing has been done, and all the schemes for lighting the city have been abandoned. The importation of this plant was a mistake, for the work it does could be performed by an ordinary country-house lighting plant, costing one-tenth the price. Ringang, the electrical engineer trained in Britain, is in charge. The Tibetans of the lower classes, who had to do the hard, unremunerative work of transporting the machinery, have named it the "Destroying Light" (Lak-Zhu). In Tibet all Government works must be performed by the peasantry free of payment, which constitutes a real burden on this class.

Captain (now Sir Frederick) O'Connor, C.S.I., C.I.E., C.V.O., the first British Trade Agent appointed to Gyantse, in 1904, was also the first to import a modern mechanical device into Tibet. This took the form of a motor-car. It was not entirely on account of his generosity that he was popular, but largely because of his own attractive personality. Moreover, he was able to converse with the Tibetans in their own language.

To return to the matter of motor-cars. The first to enter Tibet, if I remember rightly, was a two-seater Berliet, then the latest model in automobiles. It was carried in pieces from the plains of India, and assembled at Pharijong, in 1905. Captain O'Connor had done what he could to improve the track across the plateau from that town to Gyantse, and had strengthened all the bridges. After considerable trouble the car reached the latter place, having caused no little excitement along the road, those Tibetans who saw it regarding it as proof positive of the liaison between the British and the supernatural. It made a few trips between Gyantse and Pharijong, but it never ran in a really satisfactory manner. Due to the extreme rarity of the atmosphere, at fifteen thousand feet above sea-level, faulty carburettion seemed the main defect. The lowest part of the road over which it was required to travel was thirteen thousand feet. In those days, 1905, carburettors were not so efficient as to-day, and as every drop of petrol had to be imported from India on mules, motoring was a very expensive hobby in Tibet.

When the car did go out of Gyantse it was customary for riding-animals to be led behind it, so that its occupants always had some certain means of getting home again after the inevitable breakdown. It was used intermittently for a couple of years, and was then garaged in a shed. As far as I know, it lies rusting still in Gyantse.

Apart from the motor-cycle taken to Lhasa by Mendong Kusho in 1921, mention of which has already been made, no other motor-vehicle entered Tibet until 1926. Transport of mails and rations by motor-car and lorry had been under discussion for some time prior to this. While I was in Tibet I was against the introduction of such vehicles, as I knew that their use would lead to friction with the Tibetans. It was, however, decided that the experiment should be tried. Three Dodge cars were purchased, and taken to Pharijong.

These ran satisfactorily, but the cost of maintaining the postal service and of carrying the rations was far greater than by animal transport. Before long, Tibetans along the trade route found that they had lost their principal market for their grain and fodder, of which they had been supplying large amounts to feed transport animals.

Pony and mule owners found that they could no longer hire out their animals. The result was that these Tibetan peasants were unable to meet the taxation they had been paying to their Government. The latter also soon realised that, if the cultivators could not sell their produce, the whole revenue of that part of Tibet would shrink. Accordingly, representations were made to the Government of India, which, after looking into the matter, abolished the use of cars for this work. Everything is now carried as before, by animals. The cars were sent back to India and sold by auction, for what they would fetch. I was told recently by a high Tibetan official that his Government did not object to the cars because they were an innovation. He intimated that had they been handed over to the Tibetans to run on a contract basis, and hire paid by the Political Department, no resistance would have been raised, as the revenue would not have suffered to any great extent.

CHAPTER THIRTY-ONE

IN April 1924 Mr Williamson, I.C.S., was appointed to take over charge of the Gyantse Trade Agency. On his way up from India, however, he was unfortunately incapacitated from taking over from me by a severe attack of some form of neuritis, and was not able to resume duty for two months. Only careful attention and nursing on the part of Major Hyslop, I.M.S., then in medical charge of the Tibet Agencies, saved his life. I eventually handed over to Mr Williamson on 21st June 1924.

Before finally leaving Gyantse I was entertained by each of my Tibetan friends in that city and neighbourhood. All expressed their regrets, which I really believe were sincere, at my departure from their country. I feel that the Tibetans in Gyantse were as sorry to lose me as I was to bid them farewell. The Dalai Lama and the Tsarong Shap-pe talked to me by telephone from Lhasa, and expressed their intention of moving the Government of India to retain me at Gyantse for a few more years, but I persuaded them not to do this. My time for retirement was rapidly approaching, and as no extension of service would have been granted, as I had reached the age-limit, no useful purpose would have been served by His Holiness communicating with the Government of India. Major Hyslop and Captain Cobbett, then commanding the escort, rode out, with the mounted infantry, about six miles from the city, to see me off. The officer commanding the Tibetan troops in Gyantse also turned out all his men as a guard of honour, and paid me the highest compliments in his power. His buglers blew a fanfare, an honour usually reserved for the Dalai Lama and the chief ministers of Tibet. I proceeded direct to the Yatung Agency, where I remained in charge till my retirement.

In August 1924 I was permitted to sit for the Higher Proficiency Test in Tibetan, which, of course, I passed with ease, receiving a reward of two thousand rupees from Government. In a way, this test was a farce, for I had been appointed an examiner in the Degree of Honour test in that language as far back as 1906. This is a higher examination than that for which I was allowed to appear. However, the rules admitted of my appearing, and I did so. During my tour of duty in Tibet it was not an uncommon occurrence for high Tibetan officials to come to me to draft important letters for them to the Dalai Lama and the ministers, as I certainly knew more of the honorific dialect of their own language than they did themselves. My exceptional knowledge of Tibetan had undoubtedly a great deal to do with my influence among Tibetans of all classes, as it was never necessary for me to work through interpreters, whom the Tibetans distrust.

On returning to Yatung from Darjeeling, where I had sat for my examination, I applied for fourteen months' leave preparatory to retirement. Having taken no long leave during the whole of my thirty-two years' service under Government, this was granted without any delay, and on the 14th October 1924 I handed over charge of the Yatung Agency to Mr Williamson, the British Trade Agent at Gyantse, and a few days later I left Tibet for all time. My wife had preceded me to Kalimpong, to get my house there ready for occupation.

I was given a great send-off from the Chumbi Valley, all the people turning out to see me on my way. The headmen, with tears in their eyes, implored me to remain, saying that they would present such a strong petition to the Viceroy that he would extend my service for a few years. Not unaffected at this display of friendship, I felt as though I was being parted from my own family, for I had watched many of my Tibetan friends grow up from childhood, and they themselves looked on me almost as an institution in their country. I found out later that the Dalai Lama and the Kashak, or Council of State of Tibet, had approached the Political Officer in Sikkim in the matter of getting me an extension of service in Tibet, but without success. All the members of the Tibetan Government wrote me letters full of regret at my departure from their country, and they expressed the wish that, wherever I might be, the friendship existing between us would never grow less. To this day they correspond with me frequently, and I have been able to help them with advice on various matters from time to time.

Personally, I have found that once having gained the real confidence of the better-class Tibetans they will remain loyal and true to friendship. It is not easy, however, to do this.

In Kalimpong, practically on the Indo-Sikkim

frontier, whence on a clear day the jagged peaks of the Tibetan frontier can be seen, I am, though retired from the service, still in touch with the affairs of Tibet, and almost every Tibetan of any importance who is passing through comes to call on me, and we talk over the old days.

Printed in Great Britain
by The Riverside Press Limited
Edinburgh

INDEX

MORE TITLES ON TIBET
FROM PILGRIMS PUBLISHING

www.pilgrimsbooks.com

For Catalog and more Information Mail or Fax to:

PILGRIMS BOOK HOUSE

Mail Order, P. O. Box 3872, Kathmandu, Nepal
Tel: 977-1-4700919 Fax: 977-1-4700943
E-mail: mailorder@pilgrims.wlink.com.np